ROOKWOOD POTTERY

ROOKWOOD POTTERY
THE GLORIOUS GAMBLE

Anita J. Ellis

CINCINNATI ART MUSEUM

Published in conjunction with the exhibition:
ROOKWOOD POTTERY
The Glorious Gamble

Exhibition Schedule

The Nelson-Atkins Museum of Art
Kansas City, Missouri
December 20, 1992 to February 14, 1993
Made possible through the generosity of
Mr. and Mrs. Richard M. Levin
and Anonymous Donors

Cincinnati Art Museum
Cincinnati, Ohio
March 3, 1993 to June 6, 1993

Corporate support provided
by Scudder, Stevens, & Clark,
Private Investment Counsel

Sterling and Francine Clark Art Institute
Williamstown, Massachusetts
July 3, 1993 to September 12, 1993

First published in the
United States of America in 1992 by
RIZZOLI INTERNATIONAL PUBLICATIONS, INC.
300 Park Avenue South, New York, NY 10010

Copyright © 1992 by Rizzoli International Publications, Inc.,
and Cincinnati Art Museum

Library of Congress Cataloging-in-Publication Data
Ellis, Anita J.
Rookwood Pottery: the glorious gamble/ Anita Ellis.
Includes bibliographical references and index
ISBN 0-8478-1586-2; ISBN 0-8478-1603-6 (pbk.)
1. Rookwood pottery—Exhibitions.
2. Art pottery, American—Ohio—Cincinnati—Exhibitions.
I. Rookwood Pottery Company. II. Cincinnati Art Museum. III. Title.
NK4340. R7E44 1992   738.3'09771'78—dc20   92-10107   CIP

Designed by Steven Schoenfelder
Printed and bound in Singapore

Jacket illustration: Vase, 1900, Tiger Eye glaze line (plate 25)

CONTENTS

FOREWORD
Millard F. Rogers, Jr. 6

LENDERS TO THE EXHIBITION 7

ACKNOWLEDGMENTS 8

INTRODUCTION 9

ROOKWOOD POTTERY: THE GLORIOUS GAMBLE
Kenneth R. Trapp 10

EIGHT GLAZE LINES: THE HEART OF ROOKWOOD POTTERY
Anita J. Ellis 42

NOTES 58

PLATES 65

INDEX 163

FOREWORD

◆

Rookwood remains unrivaled as the preeminent art pottery of the United States of America. As the firm was located in Cincinnati, it is not surprising that the Cincinnati Art Museum, dubbed the "Art Palace of the West" when it opened its original building in 1886, should house the finest public collection of Rookwood pottery in the world.

Both the Cincinnati Art Museum and Rookwood Pottery were creations of the late nineteenth century. Their histories were often intertwined throughout Rookwood's eighty-seven–year life span. The Rookwood Pottery was founded in 1880, and the Museum just one year later in 1881. Rookwood's kilns, offices, and decorating studios were housed in a building not far from the Museum in Eden Park. Joseph H. Gest served both as the second Director of the Cincinnati Art Museum (1902–29) and as Director of The Rookwood Pottery Company (1902–34). As might be expected, the Cincinnati Art Museum's ceramic collections became influential with the addition of the work of Rookwood artists.

Since 1880, when Rookwood Pottery first produced and decorated its ceramic ware, the Museum has collected more than three hundred Rookwood objects. Rookwood was one of the Museum's first collection areas. The Women's Art Museum Association, initiators of the Cincinnati Art Museum, donated twenty-nine pieces in 1881.

Since then the Museum has added to its collection by gifts and purchases, always seeking unique and outstanding examples of Rookwood pottery.

This extensive, scholarly study of Rookwood pottery was first suggested by Curator of Decorative Arts Anita J. Ellis in 1984, but no exhibition was then connected with the project. By November 1985 an exhibition was envisioned, and the Cincinnati Art Museum began planning "Rookwood Pottery: The Glorious Gamble." The publication and the exhibition are the first in-depth studies of the aesthetic merits of Rookwood pottery.

The Cincinnati Art Museum is grateful to the Nelson-Atkins Museum of Art, Kansas City, Missouri, and the Sterling and Francine Clark Art Institute, Williamstown, Massachusetts, for joining us in the exhibition of the finest examples from America's greatest art pottery. My thanks for the support and interest of their Directors, Marc Wilson and David Brooke. We are also indebted to Anita J. Ellis, who initiated, developed, and wrote the publication, and to Kenneth R. Trapp, Curator of Crafts and Decorative Arts at the Oakland Museum in California, who contributed the title essay.

Millard F. Rogers, Jr.
Director

LENDERS TO THE EXHIBITION

◆

Jonathan Alk
George Edward Breen
Esta and Jim Brett
Nancy Daly
Charles E. Deye
Elizabeth Dooley-Warner
R. A. Ellison
Fer-Duc, Inc.
Margaret Pogue Fisk
Mr. and Mrs. W. Roger Fry
James J. Gardner
Dr. and Mrs. William E. Heil
Constance A. Hudson
Edwin J. Kircher III
Carole and Ray Kolb
Truett M. Lawson
Jay and Emma Lewis
Isak Lindenauer
Calvin and Karen Long
Helen Kohnen Lynch
Don F. Mahan
Milton Mazo, M.D.
Elizabeth and George
    Meredith
The Charles Hosmer Morse
    Museum of American Art

Judge and Mrs. Norman A.
    Murdock
Joseph David Nelson
The Newark Museum
Mrs. George Newman III
Dr. and Mrs. Herman J. Nimitz
Mr. and Mrs. Harold K. Omer
Max Palevsky
The Philadelphia Museum of Art
Daniel J. Ransohoff
Mr. and Mrs. Ivan R. Rudy
Mr. and Mrs. Randy Sandler
Marge Schott
Evelyn and Stanley Shapiro
Gloria Shapiro
Jerome and Patricia Shaw
Fern Simon
William A. Stout
Blumie Sway
Roz and Peter Thayer
Mr. and Mrs. Thomas W. Ulrich
David and Mary Verkamp
Mr. and Mrs. Ronald F. Walker
Private Collection in memory of
    Mr. and Mrs. E. N. Woistmann
Private Collectors (three)

ACKNOWLEDGMENTS

◆

Many people have contributed their support, advice, and expertise to the success of the exhibition and catalogue. I am indebted to the individuals who so generously gave me access to the four major sources of holographic material and artifacts related to The Rookwood Pottery Company: Library Director Laura Chace and her staff at the Cincinnati Historical Society Library; Manuscripts Librarian Mattie Sink and her staff in Special Collections at the Mitchell Memorial Library, Mississippi State University; Dr. Art and Rita Townley, owners of The Rookwood Pottery Company; and Joseph F. Rippe, General Partner of the Rookwood Pottery Restaurant, the former site of Rookwood Pottery. I express my utmost gratitude to Kenneth R. Trapp for his expertise and consultation throughout the project. Special gratitude is also due to Michele and Randy Sandler, Riley Humler, and Edwin J. "Jack" Kircher III for their unfailing encouragement and counsel. My wholehearted appreciation goes to all of the collectors and dealers who allowed me to visit and view their collections. And particular thanks goes to Don F. Mahan for his assistance.

Within the Cincinnati Art Museum I wish to thank Director Millard F. Rogers, Jr., for his commitment to the exhibition. Throughout the project I have been able to call upon the staffs of numerous departments for their counsel and skills: in the Operations Division, Assistant Director, George E. Snyder, Jr.; in the Finance Department, Manager of Accounting Services, Debbie Bowman, Assistant Manager of Accounting Services, Laura Gramman, Accounting Clerk, Patty Hafley, and Bookkeeper, Diane Landers; in the Buildings and Grounds Department, Superintendent, Mike Lotz, and his staff; in the Security Department, Chief of Security, John Edwards, and his staff; in the Development Division, Assistant Director, L. James Edgy, Jr., and former Development Officer, Pat Wallendjack; Grants Writer, Leslie Klahn; in the Public Affairs Division, Assistant Director, Gretchen A. Mehring, former Associate Coordinator of Media Relations, Jane Durrell; in the Education Department, Curator, Anne El-Omami; former Assistant Curator, Peggy Sambi, and Coordinator of Programs, Beverley Lamb; in the Mary R. Schiff Library, Head Librarian, Mona L. Chapin, Assistant Librarian, Cathy Shaffer, and Circulation Clerk/Book Processor, Yolanda Shelton; in the Membership Department, Coordinator, Cece Marshall; in the Volunteer Department, former Coordinator, Kristi Horner; in the Publication and Photographic Services Department, Coordinator of Publication and Photographic Services, Ann Cotter, Associate Coordinator of Photographic Services, Joy Payton, and Assistant Coordinator of Publications, Carol Schoellkopf; in the Collections Division, Assistant Director, Elisabeth Batchelor; in the Registration Department, former Registrar, Ellie Vuilleumier, Registrar, Mary Ellen Goeke, Associate Registrars, Mark Buten and Susan Currie; and Chief Preparator, Mark Rohling, and his crew. Within the Department of Decorative Arts, I offer sincere gratitude to clerk-typist Lynette Crosby and volunteer Fleurette Kitchens. To Associate Curator of Decorative Arts Cecelia S. Chewning, I owe special recognition for her selfless assistance throughout the project.

My most affectionate thanks goes to my sister, Linda, for her thoughtfulness and patience during this period.

And of course, more gratitude than can be expressed is owed to the lenders, noted on page 7, who have made it all possible.

INTRODUCTION

◆

*T*he purpose of this exhibition and catalogue is, quite simply, to demonstrate the superior product of The Rookwood Pottery Company. It is not meant to be a chronological survey, a decorator showcase, or a technical review.

In demonstrating Rookwood's quality, the extraordinary range of production also comes to the fore. The fact that the pottery's remarkable diversity can be sensed in a selection of only one hundred objects, not in any way meant to be a retrospective, is telling. Not to notice is not to look. No art pottery in the world could boast of a more sophisticated, wider range of production than Rookwood.

While the exhibition showcases one hundred objects, there are more than one hundred superlative examples of Rookwood. The exhibition could be done several times over and still have objects to spare. Preparation for the show and catalogue included extensive research, travel throughout the United States, and the viewing of more than eight thousand pieces of Rookwood. The choices were the curator's alone, drawn from what was available at the time.

No Rookwood catalogue would be complete without an essay from the noted Rookwood scholar, Kenneth R. Trapp. In light of the exhibition's purpose to demonstrate the artistic quality of Rookwood, Mr. Trapp was asked to write the title essay on the aesthetic history of the pottery. That is to say, he was asked to examine Rookwood's artistic evolution, chronicling changes in design philosophy, technique, and expression. This he has done superbly in "Rookwood Pottery: The Glorious Gamble," offering a focused context for the art. The second essay, "Eight Glaze Lines: The Heart of Rookwood Pottery," is included because it is important for a basic understanding of the identity of Rookwood.

Anita J. Ellis
Curator, Decorative Arts

Detail from a Rookwood advertisement.

ROOKWOOD POTTERY
THE GLORIOUS GAMBLE

◆

Kenneth R. Trapp

When Maria Longworth Nichols founded Rookwood in the summer of 1880, there was little reason to expect that her pottery would survive long, and no reason at all to imagine that its name would become synonymous with artistic excellence in ceramics. But slim chance against enormous odds did not dissuade her.

Awed by the ceramics and other arts Japan sent to the Centennial Exhibition in Philadelphia in 1876, Maria Longworth Nichols, a socially prominent young woman born to the wealthy Longworth family of Cincinnati, determined to have her own pottery. She even briefly contemplated the notion of importing a Japanese pottery complete with workmen. In the summer of 1880 Nichols began to fulfill her dream when she opened Rookwood, named after her childhood home, and founded in a converted Cincinnati schoolhouse above the banks of the Ohio River.

At this time Nichols had one year's experience decorating pottery seriously, as a guest in the granite ware manufactory of Frederick Dallas. She knew little about pottery production or about marketing wares profitably; she had no experience in running a business or in managing its employees. And yet Rookwood was established with distinct advantages. The first and most tangible blessing was Nichols's open and capacious purse. Although Longworth wealth alone could not buy success for Rookwood, it could pay for costly mistakes and buy the time that Rookwood needed to establish itself.

The pottery's Cincinnati birthplace offered noteworthy advantages that encouraged Nichols's venture and helped to explain why the "Queen City" became a major center of artistic ceramics in the nineteenth century. The ex-

1. Maria Longworth Nichols's studio at Rookwood, 1881.

isting commercial potteries provided a pool of experienced craftsmen from which Nichols could and did hire her technicians. The School of Design of the University of Cincinnati, later transferred to the Cincinnati Art Museum in 1884 and renamed the Art Academy of Cincinnati in 1887, supported the combination of art and industry through formal training in industrial, or decorative, art.

Rookwood enjoyed another important advantage. The pottery was founded as the logical culmination of a movement sweeping Cincinnati in the late 1870s, a movement that encompassed china painting and pottery decoration as primary art forms. Spearheaded by women and comprised of amateurs who used local potteries as training grounds, this trend provided Nichols with positive reinforcement. She was encouraged to continue with Rookwood, knowing that the pottery was more than the fulfillment of her own cherished dream.

To watchful eyes in Cincinnati's business community, Rookwood showed no spectacular results during its first year. In June 1881 Frederick Dallas died; shortly thereafter his pottery closed, freeing the superintendent, Joseph Bailey, Sr., to join Rookwood. Bailey had given

Nichols invaluable technical assistance with her first decoration attempts at the Dallas pottery, and he continued to do so at Rookwood. Bailey's many years of experience and his empirical knowledge of clay and pottery production were vital in transforming Rookwood from a fledgling, parochial enterprise into a pottery of international authority.

In its first two years, Rookwood produced primarily utilitarian household objects and tablewares of English shape and chaste form, with simple beading and engine-turned designs (fig.1). These wares were mass-produced in durable stoneware of cream or gray color. Although Rookwood was commended for making inexpensive ware pretty, these objects were a far cry from the art Nichols wished to create. She envisioned pieces decorated individually by artists, each piece an original. Her concept, of course, required artists and a division of labor that had only recently been entertained by potteries in Cincinnati. Without artists, however, Rookwood could not attain her dream.

In September 1881, almost a full year from Thanksgiving Day in 1880 when the kiln was first fired at Rookwood, Nichols hired nineteen-year-old Albert Robert

Valentien (originally spelled Valentine) as the pottery's first full-time decorator. During the following two years, Nichols employed seven other decorators. Like Valentien, they had received some formal instruction in art at the School of Design, and also like Valentien, they entered Rookwood as amateurs. Their inexperience was not necessarily detrimental, for each came to Rookwood unfettered by doctrine. Because Nichols imposed no artistic dogma upon her decorators and left each free to pursue an individual aesthetic, a variety of decorative styles and approaches resulted. A charming primitiveness distinguishes the earliest decorated wares of Rookwood, which is due more to the limitations of the raw materials, the number of kilns available, and the inexperience of the decorators than to a deliberate decorative approach. Exploration in decoration was encouraged, and rigorous experiments were conducted to perfect clays, coloring and glazing materials, and firing conditions.

DECORATION

From its beginning, Rookwood emphasized surface decoration. Because the artists received prefabricated forms, their challenge was to conceive decorative schemes that would harmonize with those forms. Although the earliest Rookwood shapes were thrown, rarely were they manipulated to change their form or silhouette. Freehand incised designs, intricate patterns impressed with cut nailheads, carved intaglio designs, and hammered surfaces, all worked on solid-colored bodies, were practiced for a short time. Carving, in particular, demanded a carefully conceived design and patient concentration.

The antithesis of carving is underglaze slip painting, which demands rapid execution. Slips, or liquefied clay, mixed with mineral oxides, which constituted the coloring agent, were used to paint blossoms and plants, birds, insects, reptiles, and marine life. Integration of the painted slip decoration in slight relief to a form was accomplished by painting thick slip grounds and by vigorous swirling brushwork. The very painterliness and colors of slip decoration were its greatest attraction. Underglaze slip painting suggested traditional oil painting on canvas, a fact not lost upon Rookwood artists. No doubt, another allure of slip painting was its level of difficulty for successful execution. The colors that appeared on a piece before it was submitted to the kiln were dramatically altered and transformed by the firing process. It took time to master palettes and to predict the final transformation.

As a workshop studio activity, decoration at Rookwood relied upon specific designs rather than memory or inspiration. Sketches, published graphics, and photographs were regularly copied. It was not uncommon for decorators to interpret English, French, German, and Japanese decorative designs upon shapes themselves copied from European or Asian prototypes. Such eclecticism and historicism, which characterized Rookwood in the pottery's infancy, reflect the aesthetic of the Victorian era.

In the 1880s Rookwood used earthenware and porcelaneous bodies that covered the full spectrum of color from light to dark, from cream and yellow to ginger, sage green, gray, and deep red. Clays from the Buena Vista iron district in Ohio and from Kentucky, Indiana, Tennessee, and Alabama were used. There was also much experimentation with clays from newly found deposits. Occasionally, a white body was tinted blue or green. While these different bodies offered wide possibilities for decoration, their individual properties dictated firing temperatures, which in turn determined the suitable decoration. With so many bodies available and so many decorative styles being entertained, the chances for establishing an artistic identity were increased while, at the same time, the search for this identity was complicated by the range of alternatives.

Rookwood's first glazes were limited to a colorless lead glaze that could be tinted yellow, green, or blue. Often vessels were glazed inside to make them impervious to liquids, while the exterior surface was covered with a smear glaze, barely discernable to the untrained eye (nos. 1, 3–10). Although not deposited in glassy form, the smear glaze is a light covering that creates a "dull" surface and closes the pores of the clay, forming a durable finish. A marked feature of Rookwood in the 1880s is the use of gilt, applied liberally by brush or sponge (no. 1), or carefully painted to outline designs (no. 8). Gilt and, to a lesser extent, platinum offered a surface richness also used to cover or disguise defects.

If any single impulse can be said to inform the aesthetic in Rookwood's infancy, it was a shared acceptance of Japonisme (nos. 1, 3–5, 13, 19–20).[1] Nichols's own work spawned Rookwood's disposition to Japanese art. Undisciplined exuberance, more than schooled talent, characterizes her grotesque, Japanese-inspired decoration. Unlike other amateur ceramic decorators in Cincinnati, who paid homage to the natural world, particularly floral subjects, Nichols established an idiosyncratic aesthetic in her first decorative designs of the 1870s. Upon her forms she sculpted dragons in relief and painted a variety of grotesque subjects: spiders in their webs, marching crickets, battling frogs, owls perched on limbs below full moons, flying bats, swimming fish, tortoises with flowing seaweed tails, and other sea creatures. The impressionable young decorators followed her lead. In some instances, it is almost impossible to distinguish the Japanese-inspired decoration of Matthew Andrew Daly, Laura Anne Fry, William Purcell McDonald, and especially Valentien from that of Nichols. As other decorators contributed to the repertory of subjects, more lyrical motifs such as flowering prunus sprays, chrysanthemum blossoms, flying swallows, and leafy bamboo painted calligraphically in black came to dominate Rookwood's decoration. Despite the wealth of decorative subjects that the arts of Japan offered, Rookwood's artists selected motifs and themes rather narrowly and never developed the richness that Japonisme attained in France and other countries in Europe.

For a brief time in 1881, Rookwood produced tablewares and other objects decorated by the transfer-print process in blue and brown, their designs taken directly from Japanese-illustrated books. The images of fish, crustaceans, and insects that appealed to Nichols, however, were less than popular among a public in the market for tablewares. Moreover, such slavish copying of designs presented no artistic challenge, and the costly effort was soon abandoned.

The Japanese influence at Rookwood did not always come directly from Japan. In August and September 1881 Nichols decorated four pieces in obvious imitation of the Nancy ware of Emile Gallé: shape 102, two French crushed vases of the same shape but in different sizes; 107, a vase; 110, a corrugated pitcher; and, 115, a French crushed pitcher. In an article in the *Cincinnati Daily Gazette* of October 7, 1880, Gallé's ceramics were mentioned among those recently arrived from Europe: "Less rare, but very pleasing, is the Nancy faience, unique in shape, and with exquisite decoration, by Gallé." [2]

The interest in Japonisme was not limited to decoration. Japanese forms in metal, ceramic, and bamboo—some in Nichols's personal collection—were copied. Except for the most obvious copies of prototypes, these forms do not announce their source. While Rookwood was searching for a distinctive mode, the company freely adopted many shapes that were copied unabashedly from a myriad of sources. In the 1880s harmonious proportions and geometry were often ignored, and the resulting forms now appear contrived and self-conscious.

THE BUSINESS OF ROOKWOOD

We have thus far considered the characteristics of early Rookwood productions as art, but we must remember that the pottery was a business. That Nichols was not a businesswoman had become all too apparent by 1883. Forced to balance the dictates of commerce with her dream of creating art, Nichols hired William Watts Taylor to manage the fledgling pottery in June 1883.[3] An experienced cotton broker, a gentleman of culture, and a personal friend, Taylor proved a brilliant choice. More than any other single person, Taylor guided Rookwood in its first generation to artistic and technical preeminence in American ceramics.

Upon discovery that Rookwood kept no records of the shapes in production or the types of decoration employed, Taylor instituted the recording of shapes in a two-hundred–page ledger. The first *Rookwood Shape Record Book*, now preserved by the Cincinnati Historical Society Library, is the most valuable single document for the study of Rookwood from 1883 to about 1900 (fig. 2). The first two hundred shapes were generally recorded with thumbnail photographs, a practice soon changed in favor of sketches. The earliest entries were typically very detailed, noting such valuable information as the source of the shape design; the method of fabrication (press, molded, thrown, cast, or jiggered); the decorator and method of decoration; the dimensions; the shape; the size (from "A," the largest, to "F," the smallest); and records of the number of pieces sold, when, and to whom.[4]

Taylor made no changes drastically disconsonant with Nichols's vision. Although a single-fire decorative process could have increased production and reduced cost significantly, such an option was never entertained seriously. Taylor maintained the division of labor already set in motion by Nichols. Furthermore, he followed the promotional and marketing practices that she had begun. Taylor sent Rookwood to regional and national expositions. And in September 1883 he sent a second lot of wares to agents on the East Coast for salability assessment, the first lot having been sent a year earlier.

Two unrelated events in 1884 were to have far-reaching impact in establishing Rookwood as a recognizable artistic entity. The first occurred when, unpredictably, a certain combination of body and glaze met particular kiln conditions to yield a resplendent crystalline effect. Pieces emerged with what appeared to be gold or metallic flecks suspended in the colorless glaze. Said to be the first such aventurine glaze produced,[5] Rookwood's crystalline glaze emerged in one of two forms or in a combination of both. When the crystals were randomly scattered and appeared as glitter, the effect was called Goldstone (nos. 22–23). When concentrated in a sheet resembling molten gold, the effect was called Tiger Eye (nos. 24–25), an obvious reference to the liquid-like gold of the stone. Even Rookwood was at a loss to explain how these effects appeared, but they convinced Taylor that Rookwood must standardize its clays and glazes, and control kiln conditions in order to predict such transformations by fire.

The second critical event occurred sometime between June and October 1884 when Laura Fry introduced

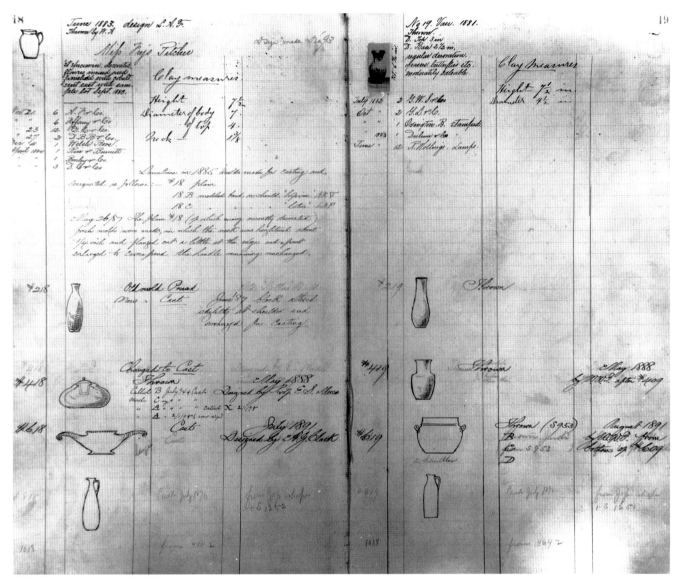

2. *Rookwood Shape Record Book*, 1883–ca. 1900. Pages 18 and 19.

the application of color in delicate gradations through the use of a mouth atomizer.[6] Operating on the same principle as the airbrush, a device later adopted, the atomizer permitted the integration of slip-painted decoration and background into a unified decorative scheme. Color could be sprayed on the form at any stage of decoration whether it be to the wet, leather-hard, or dry form, to the biscuit-fired piece, or even over the glaze.[7] The color could, in fact, be applied in any combination of these stages, and later colors were sprayed on between layers of glaze.

Of the first seven decorators that Nichols had hired, only Valentien and Laura Fry remained by 1884. And in two years Fry would leave. In 1884 Taylor hired Anna Marie Bookprinter (who married Valentien in 1887), Matthew Andrew Daly, and William Purcell McDonald,

all of whom were to become well-known decorators.[8]

After the death of her first husband, George Ward Nichols, in September 1885, Maria Nichols married the prominent Cincinnati attorney and aspiring politician Bellamy Storer, Jr., in March 1886. Thereafter, she used the name Maria Longworth Storer, though she is best known by the Nichols surname by Rookwood followers. With this change came Maria Storer's gradual detachment from the pottery as she devoted more of herself to her new husband's political career, but not before the culmination of her dream for Rookwood was realized.

In 1887 Rookwood hired Japanese artist Kataro Shirayamadani after several unsuccessful attempts to retain a Japanese decorator. In May of that year Kataro Shirayamadani arrived from Boston, where he had been employed by Fujiyama, an import retail and decorating shop operated by Louis Wertheimber.[9] Born in 1865 in Tokyo, Shirayamadani was a skilled porcelain painter whose talent proved most useful to Rookwood.

Shirayamadani had been in Cincinnati in 1886 as a member of the traveling Japanese Village, which appeared at the Thirteenth Cincinnati Industrial Exposition and caused a sensation.[10] Examples of his decoration at Rookwood were first shown at the Piedmont Exposition in Atlanta in October 1887.[11] But for an extended absence in Japan from 1911 to 1921, Shirayamadani worked at Rookwood until his death in 1948.[12] The extent of his influence on other Rookwood decorators is unknown, although such an imposing talent must have been an inspiration. More important, Shirayamadani brought an international stature to Rookwood. It was his art that helped the pottery to capture the gold medal at the Exposition Universelle in Paris in 1889.

STANDARD WARE

By the mid-1880s Rookwood had begun to create the distinctive wares that would establish its recognizable artistic identity. These included what would later become known as Standard ware (nos. 11–21), introduced in 1883. Standard ware involved underglaze slip painting applied to a white or yellow body with a glossy, yellow-tinted glaze combined with atomized grounds for warmth of effect.[13] Taylor himself referred to this distinctive line as "rich glazed ware" or "dark ware."[14] A variation of the dark ware is "Mahogany" (no. 22), which combines a red body with a high-gloss, yellow-tinted lead glaze to resemble polished mahogany. The Standard ware can be divided into categories based upon the predominant color: yellow, green, and brown.

Because of their slick smoothness and high-gloss sheen, the transparent glazes applied as a protective finish over the underglaze painted decoration of Rookwood's dark wares create a reflective, mirror-like surface that can be very distracting. Kiln burns and crazing, or cracks in the glaze, were so common in these glazes that Taylor considered them not defects but rather marked features of the dark wares. On the other hand, when the glazes fractured and began to peel and fall off, this characteristic became a distressing flaw. Not until the twentieth century were such crazing and glaze peel largely eliminated at Rookwood.

From her first decorative work at the Dallas pottery, Nichols was discouraged by the cold colors and hard effects that plagued her efforts. Kiln temperatures were so high as to burn the heart out of almost all colors. These same problems followed her to Rookwood. The need to control color soon became an imperative that drove Rookwood to produce a brighter and warmer palette and new glazes for its underglaze slip-painted decoration. Increasingly, too, the market demands were for lighter-colored pieces.

While Rookwood struggled to establish an artistic identity, it sought a mark that would identify the company. The earliest marks included the name "Rookwood" incised, impressed in block letters, or painted in black on the wares. On June 23, 1886, Rookwood adopted the reversed-R-connected-to-a-P logogram as its official mark.[15] Impressed into wet clay on the bottoms of pieces, this mark was soon altered to indicate the year. Beginning in 1887, the addition of a flame—or index, as Taylor referred to it—above the reversed-RP mark identified the year. Flames were added for each year from 1887 to 1900, after which a Roman numeral impressed below the monogram indicates the year.

By 1886, with the adoption of a corporate logogram, Rookwood's aristic identity was reinforced, expressed both in the high-glazed dark wares and in the lighter colored Cameo and Dull Finished wares. This identity was based upon underglaze slip painting on wet forms in decorative schemes deeply indebted to the Japanese treatment of flowers and marine life. Following the biscuit firing, pieces were glazed with a colorless or yellow-tinted high-gloss glaze or a slightly visible smear glaze, which is found only on Dull Finished wares. The naming of the Cameo ware marks an important marketing practice and the self-conscious awareness of the pottery's unique productions. Between 1886 and 1889 Rookwood solidified its artistic identity as the richly painted and colored wares with their high gloss glazes gained ascendancy.

Concurrent with its dark-colored Standard and Mahogany wares, Rookwood produced two variations of a pastel-colored ware from the early 1880s to the early 1890s. These two wares are soft in palette—shell pinks and corals, creams and yellows, greens and blues—and differ only in the finish applied to the dense, porcelaneous white body. The Cameo is covered with a colorless, high-gloss glaze, whereas the Dull Finish is covered with a smear glaze. Atomized grounds in pastels or in dark contrasting hues complete the color scheme and help to define the underglaze, slip-painted decoration. In some instances, the necks, feet, and handles of pieces are embellished with bands of intricately impressed patterns, which are gilded (no. 5) or finished with platinum.

By 1889 the Cameo and Dull Finished wares were being phased out of production, with Taylor requesting Rookwood's retailers to return unsold specimens. It is clear from Taylor's surviving letters that he did not care for the Dull Finished ware, perhaps because it was too suggestive of Worcester's porcelain. The Cameo ware was

3. Josephine Zettel, sketch of flowering prunus spray, 1895–1900.
Pencil, india ink, and watercolor on tissue paper.

"made entirely in useful pieces":[16] tablewares, tea and coffee services, plant holders, and vases. Taylor no doubt considered such utilitarian wares disconsonant with the pottery's higher ideals. He regarded Rookwood's dark wares as the most artistic since they were the most difficult to produce and demanded the greatest skill of the decorators and the technical staff.

Although the dark wares and the Cameo and Dull Finished wares have contrasting palettes, both follow the same mode of decoration. By the end of the 1880s underglaze slip painting had become the standard method of decoration at Rookwood. This was the same process developed between 1877 and 1878 by Cincinnatian M. Louise McLaughlin as a result of her visit to the Centennial, where she fell captive to the underglaze painted faience exhibited by Haviland and Company.[17] At Rookwood, however, McLaughlin's process was refined, perfected, and used to present a decorative repertory consisting primarily of floral subjects. (Birds, aquatic life, and, to some extent, human and animal figures, and conventional geometric designs were, however, not entirely ignored.)

Symmetry is presumed by the very nature of the forces required to create thrown clay shapes and the casts made from them. The floral decoration applied to Rookwood's shapes, however, was anything but symmetrical. The positioning and arrangement of burgeoning blossoms, branches, stems, leaves, and floral sprays appear to be as randomly casual as nature's own fine extravagance. But the impression of spontaneity and naturalness was intentional. It is a deliberate, highly crafted illusion. The best of the floral compositions on early Rookwood pieces evidence the high degree to which the decorators had assimilated the principle of asymmetric aesthetic equilibrium that so distinctively vitalizes Japanese art.

In choosing decorative subjects from the Japanese, Rookwood's decorators consulted the design vocabulary available in woodblock prints, screens, stencils, textiles, lacquer, metalwork, and pottery and porcelain. There are also similarities in color, in atomized grounds, and in the slight relief of the slip-painted decoration of Rookwood's yellow and orange-colored standard and Japanese lacquer and the Mahogany and Chinese cinnabar.

Taylor knew that Rookwood's aesthetic achievements mattered little without public exposure. He lent pieces to regional and national expositions, gave pieces to museums, and cooperated with serious writers for national publications. Far more importantly, however, Taylor developed a national network of retailers.

In less than a decade, Rookwood was represented by almost one hundred retailers throughout the midwest and the plains, along the eastern seaboard, in the south to Florida, and westward to California. Rookwood's "agents," as Taylor referred to them, were more than intermediaries retailing the pottery. Taylor saw these retailers, who were primarily prestigious department and jewelry store merchants, as proselytizers educating the public with an understanding and appreciation of Rookwood's unique artistic vision: "What we want are agents who are enthusiastic enough about Rookwood to push it. Merely to put it on their shelves helps us little."[18] They confirmed the fact that Rookwood was art. Moreover, these retailers were patronized by women of education and means, women who were arbiters of taste. Agents played an important role in advising Taylor what sold and what did not. In turn, Taylor used every major award bestowed upon Rookwood to promote the pottery's desirability.

Despite the constant aggravation of technical problems, Rookwood nonetheless made impressive gains in its quest to establish an artistic identity and a market for its wares. The pottery received special mention in London at the Twelfth Annual Exhibition of Paintings on China in 1887. The following year, Rookwood was awarded first prizes at the Pottery and Porcelain Exhibition in Philadelphia in the categories of modeled and decorated pottery and in underglaze painted pottery. And in 1889, the pottery showed successfully in national expositions throughout the United States and in Melbourne, Australia. Although these expositions and the awards and commendations were important for the pottery, none matched the validation the company was yet to receive.

Emboldened by recent accolades earned for both technical and artistic successes, Taylor decided to enter Rookwood wares in the Paris Exposition Universelle of 1889. As trying as the endeavor proved, Rookwood reaped a gold medal for its Tiger Eye and dark wares, the second highest honor after the Grand Prix. Considering the political maneuverings that surrounded the conferring of coveted awards at international expositions, it is something of a miracle that Rookwood was given the gold medal in its first international competition. Rookwood encountered stiff competition because it was a small enterprise with no established reputation in Europe and only a modest reputation in its native land. Even more of an obstacle, however, was the fact that Rookwood was an American pottery.

Taylor was pleased with the gold medal, "a most gratifying result for beginners,"[19] and he could be confident that Rookwood earned the award in Paris because of the pottery's technical and artistic excellence. This fact was evidenced by the French imitations of Rookwood already being produced before the exposition ended, in an attempt to exploit Rookwood's sudden acclaim.[20] Although poor, these imitations forecast what Rookwood would soon face as its reputation grew. With the gold medal came recognition that no amount of self-promotion could have achieved. Even the French government purchased pieces for the Musée des Arts Décoratifs. Although Rookwood had been moving steadily toward financial independence since the mid-1880s, the triumph in Paris ensured the pottery's profitability.

In 1890, Rookwood was incorporated with Taylor as president and treasurer. The new board of directors considered moving Rookwood to a new building at a more suitable site, one befitting a company of international stature. Convinced that Rookwood could prosper without her subsidies, Maria Longworth Storer presented the company to Taylor as a gift in 1891.[21]

Nine years after he took command of Rookwood, Taylor saw one of his own dreams realized. In 1892, Rookwood moved into its spacious, newly constructed plant. Within easy walking distance of the Cincinnati Art Museum and Art Academy and the verdant hills of Eden Park, the new facility perched on the crest of Mt. Adams, overlooking downtown Cincinnati. The Tudor-revival building deliberately alluded to the distant, romantic past when handicraft was an integral part of the daily rhythm of life.

The prominent location gave Rookwood better exposure and opportunity than it had formerly known. A close relationship soon developed with both the Cincinnati Art Museum and the Art Academy of Cincinnati. Taylor continued to hire decorators who were graduates of the school and encouraged Rookwood artists to use the collections of the Museum to inform and inspire their designs. In time Rookwood itself became a major tourist attraction. Its location, relationship with the other art institutions, and attractive architecture all heightened its popularity.

Designed to accommodate all operations of the pottery production to maximum advantage and efficiency, the new building was also equipped with three gas-fired kilns, which enabled Rookwood to fire hundreds of pieces of pottery simultaneously, though considerable damage and dead loss was still encountered. Not surprisingly, the 1890s witnessed intensified experimentation as Rookwood sought greater control over its technology and materials and as the company determined to introduce new decorative wares and treatments.

Throughout the 1890s the Standard ware prevailed as the principal artistic production of Rookwood. To enhance the Standard glaze line in preparation for the 1893 World's Columbian Exposition in Chicago, Taylor approached the Gorham Manufacturing Company in Providence, Rhode Island, with the idea of having silver overlay designs applied to Rookwood pieces. The first silver overlay pieces appeared in September 1892.[22]

Once Rookwood shipped its pieces to Gorham, the pottery relinquished all artistic control over the final re-

4. Decorator Matt Daly at the Rookwood Pottery Company.

sult. After the designs were applied, Gorham shipped the pieces to Rookwood's retailers. The application of reflective silver designs to pottery already covered with a mirror-like glaze gilded the lily. (Silver overlay designs, more often than not, are overly exuberant and dominate the ceramic forms they were intended to complement.) The collaboration lasted about two years, and at no other time did Rookwood send its wares outside the pottery to be embellished by another firm.

Pieces resulting from the Rookwood-Gorham venture were among those included in a large display at the 1893 World's Columbian Exposition. Here, Rookwood introduced plaques (nos. 15–16) and vessels (nos. 17–18) painted with portraits of Native Americans from the Great Plains and the pueblos of the Southwest. At this exposition, as at the triumphal one in Paris four years previously, Rookwood received encomia and high awards. Also in this year, Rookwood garnered considerable praise from Edwin Atlee Barber in his monumental treatise *The Pottery and Porcelain of the United States*: "It is safe to assert that no ceramic establishment which has existed in the United States has come nearer fulfilling the requirements of a distinctively American institution than the Rookwood Pottery of Cincinnati, Ohio."[23]

PORTRAIT DECORATION

The "distinctly American" nature of Rookwood carried over to the subjects the pottery had chosen for portraiture. Rookwood's introduction of Native-American portraiture occurred as this illustrative method was used increasingly to diversify the glaze line and challenge decorators to paint other than floral subjects. The use of Native-American portraiture coincided with the disappearance of the western frontier. But Rookwood's romantic renderings, painted after photographs, reveal little about the plight of their subjects. Haunting though some are, the portraits narrowly portray the First American as the noble savage unhumbled by crushing defeat and dispossession.[24] White Americans—including those who purchased from and worked at Rookwood—cherished the belief that Native Americans, and African-Americans as well, lived intuitively, were closer to nature, and were not subject to the refined sentiments of their "civilized" conquerors.

The fascination with Native-American people from the Great Plains and the Southwest was fed by western pulp novels, by the canvases of the Cincinnati painters Henry Francis Farny and Joseph Henry Sharp, both of whom traveled to the West to paint Native Americans, and of course by the Buffalo Bill Wild West shows that made periodic visits to the Queen City.

Some special circumstances contributed to the interest of Cincinnatians in Native Americans. In 1895 a group of Cree from Havre, Montana, were abandoned by a Wild West show across the river from Cincinnati in Bellevue, Kentucky. The Cincinnati Zoological Gardens allowed them to camp on its grounds as part of an ethnological village. Similarly, Sicangu Sioux from the Rosebud Reservation in South Dakota lived at the zoo for three months in 1896 and also presented Wild West shows.[25]

In addition to portraits of Native Americans, Rookwood introduced images of African-Americans and images after Old Master and contemporary German portraits. Even domesticated and wild animals were added to the decorative repertory. However, portraiture as a decorative theme was largely confined to the 1890s, to be abandoned shortly after the turn of the century as Standard ware declined in popularity.

Taylor believed the Columbian Exposition to be of such importance that he sent all of Rookwood's employees to Chicago to see firsthand the great profusion of art manufactures shown there. Two significant and positive developments occurred as a result of this experience. Rookwood was encouraged to introduce new decorative wares in marked contrast to Standard ware, and Taylor was convinced to continue sending senior decorators and technical staff abroad for further study.

In 1894 Rookwood introduced in quick succession three new decorative wares: the Aerial Blue (no. 30), the Iris (nos. 31–45), and the Sea Green (nos. 26–29). These three wares shared the same fundamental characteristics. Each was painted with colored slips on a pure white body while the clay was still moist. Following the first firing, the biscuit ware was covered with a high-gloss lead glaze.

Of these three new glaze lines, only the Aerial Blue failed to enter production. Described as "a delicate monochromatic ware with a quiet decoration in celestial blue on a cool, grayish white ground,"[26] the Aerial Blue is in fact a variant upon the earlier Cameo ware. The dense white porcelaneous body is painted in blues that range from a vivid royal blue to a soft powder blue. The Aerial Blue was no doubt Rookwood's attempt to capitalize upon the popularity of Royal Copenhagen's porcelain wares painted in blues, wares much admired by the crowds in Chicago.

We do not know why Rookwood abandoned the Aerial Blue soon after it was introduced. Perhaps the effect of the royal blue seemed too cold, while the softer powder blues were confusingly similar to the Iris. It may be that Taylor, who always took care to promote Rookwood as uniquely American, considered the Aerial Blue too like Royal Copenhagen and feared Rookwood might be faulted as a blatant imitator of a European manufactory.

The Sea Green and the Iris were produced regularly for more than a decade. Technically these two wares are alike. The major difference is that the Sea Green is covered with a transparent gloss glaze tinted a limpid green, so that the dominant color is green even when the underglaze slips are themselves colored. As its name suggests, the Sea Green emphasizes aquatic life in its decoration. The illusion of water in the finest specimens of the ware is created and reinforced by the play of light upon and within the liquid-like transparent glaze.

Practical reasons dictated the naming of decorative lines. Because Rookwood created an art for the home, lovely names that carried feminine associations were used. And just as the artists's ciphers and the company's official marks impressed in pieces helped Rookwood to monitor its large inventory, so the names given to decorative lines served the same purpose.

Of all the decorative lines that Rookwood introduced during its eighty years, none is lovelier or more elegant than the Iris: "The Iris has a real pottery quality, a softness quite other than that of porcelain, a mellowness in fact that marks it as 'Rookwood,' distinct from other makes of light ware."[27] The only ware named for a flower, the Iris is as soft and pastel in effect as the Standard is earthen and smoky. Creams, yellows, pinks, corals, lavenders, blues, greens, and grays fill the palette. Airbrushed atmospheric grounds that bleed from either top to bottom or from bottom to top, and that range in color from a charcoal gray to white or faintly tinted pinks or gray-greens, enhance the watercolor-like effect of the Iris.

Flowering plants prevail as the primary decorative subjects of the Iris. Carefully chosen for their extravagant blossoms and the decorative design of their leaves, stems, and tendrils, these plants comprise a varied catalogue: irises (nos. 35, 40), water lilies and other varieties of lilies, orchids, sweetpeas, roses (no. 43), wisteria (no. 39), poppies (nos. 34, 36, 45), dahlias, peonies, oleander, dogwoods, clover, milkweeds (no. 32), grapes, and wild carrots. Nonfloral subjects include flying geese, herons (nos. 38, 41), dragons, dragonflies, fish (no. 33), mushrooms (no. 37), and human figures.

In the 1890s, Rookwood underwent significant

changes. As the pottery grew from a small, fledgling enterprise into a sizable art industry, its operations were modified to increase production. Processes of production were largely standardized to reduce costs, to maximize efficiency, and to control quality at all stages. Standardization of production was imposed upon shapes, bodies, glazes, and decoration. Shapes became more refined and were reduced to several basic forms. With the emphasis on harmonious proportions, geometric balance, and elegant silhouettes, contrived and eccentric shapes were abandoned. To facilitate and control the mass production of shapes, Rookwood turned to mold casting with greater frequency. Using *The Rookwood Shape Record Book* as a guide, we discover that in the early 1890s forms were usually thrown and sometimes were later used to create molds for castings. By the turn of the century Rookwood used cast forms almost exclusively. To be sure, the throwing of forms on the wheel had not been totally abandoned, but as a method for creating shapes for high-volume production, throwing was too labor-intensive and occasioned too many errors and inconsistencies.

By the 1890s Rookwood could no longer produce wares in several bodies and glazes using widely different decorative treatments and, at the same time, increase profits. By adopting a white body and limiting glazes to a transparent lead glaze that received tints well, the pottery could better exercise control over what emerged from the kiln, although dead loss from flaws and damage remained high.

Throughout the 1890s, Rookwood continued to emphasize surface embellishment. By mid-decade, however, the placement of the decoration was no longer the only consideration. Decoration became integral to the form, becoming a compositional element that complemented the line, size, and volume of the overall object. With the standardization of shapes, body, and glaze, Rookwood also moved to a formulaic decorative process: asymmetrical arrangements of floral subjects were painted in slips under the glaze on simple forms to suggest informality. Such formulaic decoration manifested most clearly the mature assimilation of Japonisme at Rookwood. The lessons to be learned from Japanese art were indeed learned well at Rookwood.

As is often the case, success can become its own burden. And so it was with Rookwood's underglaze slip-painted floral decoration. The insatiable taste of Rookwood's patrons for flowers became, in fact, oppressively dictatorial. By the early 1890s more than two hundred cultivated and wild plants were being painted at Rookwood. And this number continued to increase. Of course, other decorative subjects were painted, but none so dominated the decorative repertory as did blossoms and floral

subjects.[28] The constant repetition of floral subjects could not help but result in some mediocre pieces, though Rookwood's decorators strived to paint these subjects with inventiveness.

Before a decorator was hired, Taylor determined that the artist could paint floral subjects in watercolors and oils in a convincingly naturalistic manner. Prospective decorators were required to submit paintings and sketches for evaluation. Underglaze painting demands concentration, patience, a steady hand, and rapid execution. And yet the painted underglaze slip decoration must always appear entirely spontaneous. It was important that the decoration not appear stiff, contrived, or labored if the illusion of spontaneity were to be convincing.

DECORATIVE DESIGNS

The manner in which decorators chose, conceived, and then applied decorative designs to forms is helpful in explicating the formulaic approach to decoration at Rookwood. Because floral subjects dominated Rookwood's sales, Taylor required the decorators to keep sketchbooks in which designs were drawn from nature and traced from secondary sources. To aid the decorators in choosing their subject matter, Taylor maintained an extensive library of books, periodicals, folios (fig. 3), sketches, and photographs, and held Saturday morning classes in nature studies at the pottery.[29] Live floral specimens were provided both by Rookwood's own garden and the plants that covered the surrounding hills. Noteworthy specimens of Rookwood's own productions were kept as references, and Rookwood collected ceramics from other potteries and objects from other cultures for the same purpose.

After studying the form, the artist could design the decorative scheme. Sketches on tissue paper lightly wrapped around a form could suggest how a particular design might look. Before a decorator began to paint with and to model the slips, the design was incised lightly with a stylus or drawn on the moist form in graphite pencil or India ink, of which the latter two would burn out in the fire. These outlines gave the decorator a guide to follow. Decoration proceeded in stages, but the exact sequence cannot always be determined. The decoration and airbrushed grounds might have been painted and applied separately or in unison. Once the decorated piece was thoroughly dried, it was submitted to the first of two firings. Following the biscuit firing, the piece was glazed and then fired again.

When rendered in slips, interpretations of designs from the decorator's own sketches or from secondary sources underwent changes that distanced the final decoration from the prototype. Colors changed, especially in

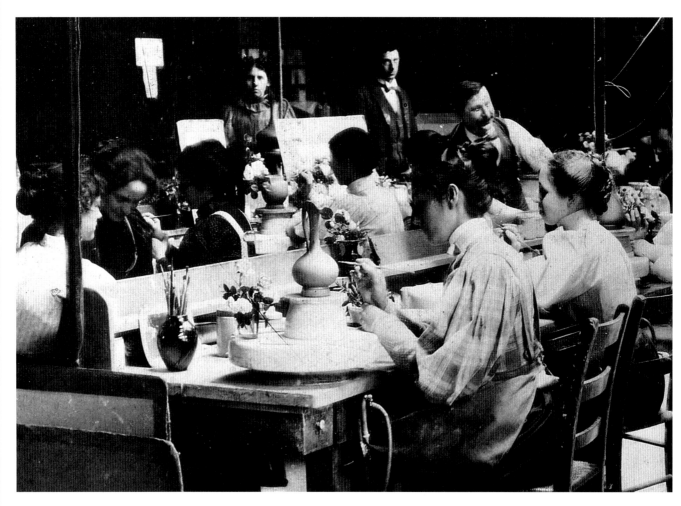

5. Rookwood's decorating department sometime between 1892 and 1899, at the new location in Mt. Adams.

the Standard and Sea Green wares in which the tinted high-gloss glaze also acts as a color and alters underglaze colors. Because slip-painted decoration is slightly modeled in relief and is painted on surfaces that often are curved, differences between the decoration and the inspiration are apparent.

The romantic naturalism celebrated by Rookwood gloried in botanical detail and exactitude. Indeed, some of Rookwood's decorators were accomplished botanical artists, in particular Anna and Albert Valentien. Between 1890 and 1910 at the height of Rookwood's use of floral decoration, artists depicted the life cycle of flowering plants, from root or bulb to bud and full flower; sometimes the changes are so subtle as to escape immediate notice.

The successful interpretation of the natural world, however, was more than the accurate recording of observable facts. Rookwood's decorators faced the same challenge that nature writers confronted: to reveal the natural facts scientifically and at the same time to respond to those facts subjectively. Rookwood's decorators captured

the botanical details scientifically and accurately, but they also revealed their feelings toward the decorative subjects, conveying poetic allusion and the significance of the human experience with nature.

Floral decoration at Rookwood in the 1880s and 1890s emphasized blossoms and, to a lesser extent, roots, buds, stems, leaves, and tendrils. Although some wildflowers were painted, most subjects were cultivated plants known to the buyer. Rookwood's floral decoration is painted much like botanical illustration. There is no reference to sky, field, insects, birds, or other flowers and plants. The flowers are removed from their natural environment and rendered in isolation.

Rookwood's artists did not interpret nature's floral bounty with any general iconographical intent, though there are exceptions. A rare vase of 1900 by Matthew Daly (no. 21) is decorated with luna moths and poppy pods, both traditional symbols of sleep and death. In 1899, Harriet Elizabeth Wilcox decorated a vase, "Dawn Awakening" (no. 10), in which a sensuous young woman draped in a diaphanous garment greets the new day in a languorous pose; poppies complete the decorative scheme. Such symbolism in Rookwood decoration is, however, unusual.

As mentioned earlier, the attendance by Rookwood's staff at the 1893 World's Columbian Exposition was a successful managerial experiment. Aware that Rookwood's financial independence rested upon the company's artistic excellence and technical authority, hence upon the decorators and technicians, Taylor determined to send selected personnel abroad for further study. In the fall of 1893, Shirayamadani left for his native Japan to study techniques that might be helpful to Rookwood's productions. He returned to Rookwood early in the following year, accompanied by the metalworker E. H. Asano.[30]

Soon after Shirayamadani's return, Rookwood instituted its own metal department. Interestingly, that same year Maria Longworth Storer first began her metalwork.[31] When her husband was appointed American minister to Belgium in 1897, Storer invited Asano to Brussels to guide and assist her in metalworking.[32] No doubt Asano agreed to go to Europe because Rookwood was about to discontinue its metalworking department due to the expense of such experimentation. The extent to which Storer's interest in metalwork relates to the experiments with metal overlay designs at Rookwood has yet to be detailed. There is no doubt, however, that such a connection exists.

The talent and creativity of the decorators depended upon Rookwood's ability to predict and to control the transformations in the fire with some accuracy. To this end, the young Stanley Gano Burt, whose studies at Yale University concentrated in chemistry, joined Rookwood in July 1892. In 1894, he was sent to Berlin, where he studied ceramic chemistry and technology at the Königliche Hochschule. Also in 1894, Artus Van Briggle was sent to Paris, where he remained, until June 1896. In July 1894, Albert Valentien left for Europe for three months of study in what was described as the "Pottery's Artistic Interest." Matthew Andrew Daly was sent to Europe for three months in 1895.[33]

The year 1896 stands out as a most important experimental time for Rookwood. Burt and Van Briggle returned from their studies in Germany and Paris respectively. Burt brought back the ceramic-based Seger cone for measuring kiln temperatures,[34] and Van Briggle began his glaze experiments.

Van Briggle must have been familiar with the senior Bailey's experiments of 1894 to replicate the classic Chinese *sang de boeuf* (oxblood) glaze before he left for Paris.[35] Soon after Van Briggle returned, he embarked upon a venture to produce a "dead," or mat, glaze similar to ones he saw on Chinese ceramics in Paris. Whether Van Briggle had indeed studied Chinese and Japanese ceramics or had

examined the work of French potters influenced by Asian tradition is a question that has been raised recently.[36]

With Joseph Bailey, Sr., and Burt paving the way technically and Van Briggle adding the weight of his artistic experience, Rookwood began to experiment with mat glazes in 1896. Two early experimental mat glaze pieces, decorated with landscapes and dated 1896, are now in the Hermitage State Museum in St. Petersburg.[37] Also in 1896, Storer created, or had created, copper lustre-glazed vessels at Rookwood that were then mounted to bronze supports cast to her designs. Storer, who was Van Briggle's patron, turned to the young man for artistic and technical advice in creating these ceramic vessels.

The last of the decorators to be sent to Europe to study were William P. McDonald and John Hamilton Delaney Wareham, each of whom left in 1898 for a seventeen-week absence.[38] At no other time did Rookwood subsidize its employees' studies abroad. One might question the extravagance of a small company in sending seven of its employees to travel and study abroad, but by doing this, Taylor both rewarded and expressed his confidence in them. Taylor was motivated, however, by more than altruism: he knew that the trips abroad for the pottery's senior artists and youthful technical supervisor would benefit Rookwood and help to keep the company in the forefront of increasing competition. Once Rookwood had earned admission into the select circle of international art manufactures, Taylor knew that the pottery required direct contact with European and Japanese decorative art in order to maintain its position.

The senior decorators who studied in Europe were not sent by the company without a specific destination. Although travel elsewhere was no doubt encouraged, Taylor had determined that they were to study in Paris because, by the end of the nineteenth century, Paris had indeed superseded all other European cities as an art center, even in the decorative arts. But there well may be an even more specific reason for Rookwood's affinity with Paris. It seems likely that Siegfried Bing, who opened L'Art Nouveau Gallery in Paris in 1895, thus giving a name to the new art, had visited Rookwood when he came to the United States in 1894.[39] It may have been that Bing encouraged Taylor to send the pottery's decorators to Paris. Bing would certainly have known Rookwood from the pottery's success in Paris at the 1889 Exposition Universelle and from the awards in Chicago in 1893. Indeed, it was this exposition that encouraged Bing to sail the Atlantic to assess what America was contributing to the decorative arts. Nor was Bing unknown to Rookwood, for the pottery subscribed to Bing's *Artistic Japan*.

Although it has yet to be documented that Bing traveled to Cincinnati to visit Rookwood, such a visit would have been easy and logical. Indeed, the director of the Royal Copenhagen porcelain manufactory visited Rookwood in 1889. Little at Rookwood happened accidentally. Moreover, the timing in sending Rookwood's senior decorators to Paris coincides too closely with Bing's visit to the United States to be mere happenstance.

Measured in human terms, Rookwood's financial success in the 1890s is evidenced by the growth of the company's decorating department. From 1890 to 1899 thirty-seven new decorators were hired, an expansion never before realized in such a short time. Nine of these artists were to remain at Rookwood thirty years or more, among them Lenore Asbury, Edward Timothy Hurley, Sara Sax, Carl Schmidt, and John Wareham. It is important to remember that these decorators were in addition to the thirteen decorators hired in the 1880s who continued with Rookwood through the 1890s.

In promoting Rookwood, Taylor was careful to make a distinction of some importance: the pottery was a workshop art industry and not a factory. A factory employed workers to tend machines and maximize production at the lowest cost for the greatest yield of profits. In contrast, Rookwood treated its employees like family members and adhered to a system of production that limited output and operated with marginal profits. Taylor knew well that Rookwood's most valuable resource was its workers. He took care to promote the staff's welfare and to increase their knowledge through lectures, exhibitions, and travel. Social events were more than a chance to have fun: costume parties, hayrides, picnics, and riverboat cruises reinforced the familial atmosphere at the pottery.

Taylor's enlightened administration had direct bearing on the fact that Oscar Lovell Triggs, the Chicago intellectual and Arts and Crafts advocate, targeted Rookwood as the ideal workshop. Triggs noted that Rookwood was begun with "the desire to produce a perfect product." And subsumed within that desire was "the intention to perform a social service . . . ." Triggs understood that Rookwood was more than a pottery workshop: ". . . it is in a sense a school of handicraft, an industrial art museum, and a social center."[40]

Rookwood did indeed perform a social service. The pottery offered reliable employment for decorative artists who lived in a culture that traditionally devalued their work and their contributions to society. As a patron of the arts, Storer recognized this fact when she wrote, "It is . . . more philanthropic in the end to give sure and steady employment to people of talent and skill than to indulge only in spasmodic and intermittent fits of generosity."[41]

At the turn of the century, Rookwood's promotional literature proudly declared that a single piece might pass through as many as twenty-one hands before it left the pottery, a fact no doubt meant to impress the prospective buyer.[42] Such a complicated division of labor increased the chances for mistakes and damage or dead loss, as well as increasing production costs (then passed on to the buyer), therefore compromising artistic ideals. But Rookwood placed communal cooperation and the company's vision above any one individual's artistic expression.

As Rookwood's spokesman and principal promoter, Taylor proclaimed that the pottery's wares were art because each piece was one-of-a-kind. This claim, true to the extent that all handwork is unique, is misleading. Many shapes were mass-produced and their decoration followed an artistic formula. But to maintain the artistic integrity of the pottery, Rookwood had to emphasize that each buyer's purchase was an original work of art by a known artist.

By 1899, perhaps sooner, Rookwood had begun considerable preparations for the Paris Exposition Universelle to open in 1900. To prepare an exhibition of hundreds of pieces for such a prestigious world's fair, Rookwood gave the senior decorators time to create "exposition" pieces. Whereas most decorators painted two or three pieces in a day, these virtuoso pieces required many days, or even weeks, from conception to completion.

It is evident that participation in international expositions pushed Rookwood toward experimentation so that the pottery could premier spectacular new wares. The years between the world's fairs in Chicago in 1893 and in St. Louis in 1904 witnessed an intensified program of systematic experimentation. In these eleven years Rookwood installed more fuel-efficient and cleaner-burning gas-fired kilns in its new plant and adapted the cone and the pyrometer, both devices for temperature testing. Despite such improvements, however, Rookwood was still plagued with a high percentage of damage and dead loss. Experiments were carried out to control both raw materials and firing conditions more accurately and with greater predictability. Such experimentation was also necessary in order to introduce new glazes and decorative treatments that, in turn, helped Rookwood to maintain its artistic and technical supremacy over encroaching competition.

There is one decorative treatment that Rookwood perfected to an astonishing degree and yet never put into full production. In a brief period from about 1897 to 1903, Shirayamadani and a few other artists decorated some magnificent vases embellished with electro-plated copper and silver-plated copper designs of fish, crabs, octopi, seahorses, frogs, water lily blossoms, leaves and pods, cattails, and rocks (nos. 19–21, 24, 41). Such images complement similar decorative motifs on the ceramic pieces. Shirayamadani developed the electro-plating process at Rookwood for show, especially for international expositions—Paris (1900), St. Petersburg, Russia, Buffalo, New York (1901), and Turin (1902). However, these electroplated designs were labor-intensive and cost-prohibitive.

Ever open to artistic possibilities, Rookwood experimented with a red and a green body for a few special pieces in 1899.[43] Also apparent at this time is a reemergence of the emphasis upon Japonisme in which Japanese-inspired subjects, such as swimming sea tortoises and waves, are painted with a lyricism previously unseen. Japanese subjects permitted Rookwood to bow to the Art Nouveau movement in a manner consonant with its own conservative decorative philosophy.

But even as Art Nouveau swept across Paris and the Continent from the mid-1890s to World War I, Rookwood never fully embraced the sensual nature of this movement. The pottery shied away from its aesthetic of flowing lines and ripe organic forms, no doubt uneasy with the charged eroticism and openly emotional character of the style. Of the Rookwood designers in Paris at the time—Van Briggle, Daly, McDonald, the Valentiens, and Wareham—it was Van Briggle and Anna Valentien who most willingly succumbed to the charms of the Art Nouveau style. These two decorated pieces with modeled female nudes, their hair flowing loosely in streams, "swim-

ming" languidly around vessel openings, or "growing" out of the forms they adorn. Although Anna Valentien, who studied briefly at the academies of Colorossi and Rodin in 1899–1900, was unsuccessful in persuading Rookwood to introduce the human figure as a featured decorative subject, she did create some exquisite pieces that are rare uses of the figure (no. 54).[44]

Because he was aware of the tremendous importance of the 1900 Paris exposition and had been dissatisfied with the manner in which Rookwood's exhibitions previously had been handled, and because he recalled the political intrigue surrounding the Paris exposition of 1889, Taylor himself went to France for five months to supervise Rookwood's exhibit and to await the conferring of official awards. He was not disappointed. Rookwood was honored with the coveted Grand Prix. Individual awards went to Albert R. Valentien and to Stanley Gano Burt. Taylor himself was decorated with the Chevalier of the Legion of Honor.[45]

Although it is impossible to reconstruct piece by piece the exhibition that Rookwood sent to Paris, we can document in several ways which pieces were shown: Rookwood's specially printed paper labels affixed to pieces; photographs the company had taken for publicity

6. Two loving cups and vase shown by Rookwood at the Paris Exposition Universelle in 1900. From left: William Purcell McDonald, decorator, Iris glaze with silver-plated mount; John Hamilton Delaney Wareham, Iris glaze; and Harriet Elizabeth Wilcox, decorator, Standard glaze with silver-plated mount.

and for official records; published illustrations (fig. 6); pieces that European museums purchased; and, lastly, pieces in the Cincinnati Art Museum as of 1916 recorded by Stanley Burt in his holograph of Rookwood pieces on loan to the Museum. The wares exhibited in Paris represented its three principal glaze lines—Standard, Iris, and Sea Greens—and variations upon these, including pieces with metal mounts.

Rookwood had been a singular presence in American art pottery at the 1889 Paris exposition, but in 1900 the company had to share the spotlight with other American potteries. Both the Grueby pottery of Boston and the Newcomb pottery of New Orleans received awards, and the Roblin pottery of San Francisco, founded in 1898, received an honorable mention. One can imagine that Taylor must have looked upon these upstarts with some astonishment because none had been in operation for more than three years. Although neither Grueby nor Newcomb displaced Rookwood as the nation's preeminent art pottery, nonetheless notice was served that Rookwood had to share a burgeoning field.

The proliferation of art pottery ventures in the United States in the first two decades of the twentieth century heralded an art pottery movement. By 1900 Rookwood had begun to encounter stiff competition from imitators of its underglaze slip painting. The Lonhuda, J. B. Owens, Roseville, and Weller potteries in Zanesville, Ohio, in particular, and competitors as far west as the Stockton Art Pottery Company in Stockton, California, were blatant imitators of Rookwood's Standard ware. Nor was imitation of Rookwood's underglaze slip painting limited to the United States. Within several years, imitations of the Standard were in production in Britain and in scattered places across Europe. While the extent of Rookwood's influence upon art potteries in the United States is widely recognized, as yet its influence upon European ceramics has been little noted.

Even with the competition, Rookwood welcomed the twentieth century with confidence, its artistic and technical authority affirmed by the honors bestowed in Paris in 1900. In the decade between 1900 and 1910 Rookwood sent exhibits to expositions in the United States and in Europe in rapid succession: the Pan-American Exposition in Buffalo and the Exposition International de Céramiques et de Verrerie (International Exposition of Ceramics and Glass) in St. Petersburg, Russia (1901); the Prima Esposizione Internazionale d'Arte Decorativa Moderna (First International Exposition of Modern Decorative Art) in Turin, Italy (1902); the South Carolina Interstate and the West Indian Exposition in Charleston (1902); the Louisiana Purchase Exposition in St. Louis (1904); the Tricentennial Exposition in Jamestown, Virginia (1907); and the Alaska-Yukon-Pacific Exposition in Seattle, Washington (1909). Of these expositions, the world's fair in St. Louis was the most important, as Rookwood officially introduced its supreme achievement, the Vellum glaze, and instituted its first mail-order catalogue.

At no other time in its history did Rookwood exhibit in so many expositions with such frequency and at such far distances as it did in the first decade of the twentieth century. While Rookwood's participation in European expositions produced little direct monetary gain when weighed against the cost, the exposure affirmed the pottery's standing as an honored member among international art manufactures.

And as Rookwood entered the twentieth century, a second generation of artists began to emerge in the pottery. In the first decade of the new century, Rookwood bid farewell to some of the pottery's longstanding and most accomplished artists. Artus Van Briggle left in 1899 because of ill health and moved to Colorado Springs, Colorado, where he established a pottery in 1901. Matthew Daly, Olga Geneva Reed, and Amelia Sprague left in 1903, followed by Grace Young and Josephine Zettle in 1904. The architectural faience department, opened in 1902, claimed William McDonald in 1904 and Sara Alice Toohey in 1908, thereby removing the talents of two more seasoned decorators from the department. In 1905 Anna and Albert Valentien left Rookwood and, in 1908, settled in San Diego, California, where they opened a pottery in 1911.

Despite the departure of so many veteran decorators, Rookwood's general artistic and technical excellence did not weaken. Sara Elizabeth Coyne, Edward T. Hurley, Frederick Henry Daniel Rothenbusch, Sara Sax, Carl Schmidt, Shirayamadani, and John H. D. Wareham remained. Lorinda Epply and William Hentschel, who joined Rookwood between 1900 and 1910, were the only decorators to remain at the pottery long enough for their talent to mature and their artistic potential to be realized.

Just as Rookwood experimented with the Standard ware to diversify its artistic possibilities, so the company developed hybrids of the Iris ware to increase its decorative potential. From about 1898 to 1912, two rare variations upon the Iris ware were produced—the relief style Iris and the Dark or Black Iris (nos. 40–45). As its name suggests, the relief style Iris has decoration built up in slip to create a sculptural effect. The decoration never becomes fully three-dimensional and remains an application to the form that it decorates.

The Black Iris is so named because the ground of the ware is an intense cobalt blue that looks black. Against this ground, the decoration is painted thinly in a watercolor-like effect in vivid and contrasting blues, violets, pinks, grays, creams, and whites. The Japanese iris predominates as a decorative subject, although water lilies, poppies, cattails, flying geese, herons, fish, and human figures also appear. Black Iris is one of the most stunningly beautiful wares ever produced at Rookwood, its crisply executed painting suggestive of a jeweler's precision and sensitivity. Because they are rare and peculiar to a particular time period, the relief style and the Black Iris appear to have been created expressly for expositions.

The palette of the Black Iris has counterparts in European ceramics—Royal Copenhagen, Meissen, Sèvres, Rorstrand, and Bing & Grøndahl—as well as in porcelains imported from Japan. Rookwood's decorative wares of the 1890s and early 1900s evidence an affinity with the etched glass of Emile Gallé and Daum brothers in France and other studios on the Continent, especially in use of floral and landscape subjects and in colors. The relationship between the art potteries being produced on both sides of the Atlantic and art glass has yet to be investigated.

By the turn of the century, arbiters of taste had begun to fault Rookwood's high-glazed wares for their conspicuous refinement, excessive attention to detail, and overly precious sensibility. Ironically, some critics faulted Rookwood's high-glazed wares for their feminine character. Highly reflective glazes and painstakingly detailed naturalism fell out of favor at the turn of the century as mat finishes gained ascendancy in popular taste.

Of all the changes to occur at Rookwood in the first decade of the twentieth century, none was more decisive than the shift from high-gloss glazes to mat finishes (nos. 46–59). This change involved more than the replacement of one type of glaze with another. Mat glazes heralded a fundamental change at Rookwood in which decoration was subordinated to glaze. Previous to the mat glazes at Rookwood, the glaze had been treated as a protective covering. With the mats, however, the glaze did not protect a decoration beneath it, but rather became the decoration. Mat glazes were part of a cultural value that glorified honesty, sincerity, harmony, and, above all, simplicity, as virtues to be practiced and honored.

Contrivance and conspicuousness were inimical to the cult of simplicity, itself the central precept of the Craftsman period from 1900 to 1915, so named for Gustav Stickley's periodical *The Craftsman*. Artistically, adherents of simplicity demanded modest forms, clean planes and lines, subdued flat colors, stylized conventional designs, and unassuming finishes. Such an aesthetic naturally placed a high premium on mat glazes.

Although Rookwood had produced mat glazes since 1900, designating the mat glaze with a stamped "Z" among the marks, the company did not officially intro-

duce them until 1902. That year Rookwood published a forty-seven–page promotional pamphlet, *Rookwood Pottery*, which, unlike *The Rookwood Book* published in 1904, was not a mail-order catalogue. Illustrated with twenty black-and-white photographic reproductions, *Rookwood Pottery* pictures forty-four individual pieces and describes nine categories of Rookwood: Standard Rookwood, Tiger Eye, Sea Green, Iris, Flowing glaze, Mat glazes, Metals Applied, Lamps and Electroliers, and Architectural Faience.

Interestingly, Rookwood separated the Tiger Eye from the Standard in *Rookwood Pottery*, suggesting that the aventurine glaze was produced on a systematic basis. (In truth, Rookwood never mastered the Tiger Eye to the extent that it could be produced with predictable consistency.) Mat glazes are presented as a generic finish, with no differentiation made between types of decorations or uniqueness of finish within the category. Architectural Faience is included in the catalogue because the department had just been instituted. In future publications, however, Rookwood devoted special catalogues to its architectural faience and garden pottery.

An intriguing variety of categories described in *Rookwood Pottery* is unfortunately not illustrated. The Flowing Glaze is described only in vague terms. "This deep and heavy glaze has a quality resembling in many respects some of the old Chinese. It has a similar luminosity, and at the same time a peculiar richness of texture. The decoration is painted upon the piece in slight relief, in forms and colors so simple that the glaze may flow pleasantly over them."[46]

To date, no example of Rookwood's Flowing glaze has appeared that can be unquestionably identified. Nor is there an illustration to help define the Flowing glaze. Guided by Rookwood's description of the Flowing glaze, we may assume, with some hesitation, that the glaze was translucent, refractive, and reflective. That the Flowing glaze had a similar "luminosity" to some glazes on early Chinese ceramics suggests revealing synonyms such as "brilliance," "shininess," "lucency," and "resplendence." These are not descriptive adjectives of mat glazes. Whether "a peculiar richness of texture" was a tactile or visual attribute remains open to question. Finally, it seems safe to assume that the decoration painted in slight relief under the glaze—whether upon the wet or upon the biscuit-fired form is unclear—was not greatly obscured by the flow of the glaze.

Why did Rookwood announce the Flowing glaze so prominently in its 1902 catalogue and then discontinue the ware? Perhaps the Flowing glaze was never sufficiently developed to be placed into systematic production. Or it may simply be that the Flowing glaze was announced prematurely in an excess of hope at a time when mat finishes were gaining ascendancy on both sides of the Atlantic. In the end, whether or not the Flowing glaze is a high-gloss covering, an opaque mat glaze, or a hybrid finish with some qualities of both is a moot point.

Similar questions arise concerning some of Rookwood's later wares produced in the 1920s and 1930s. Rookwood took little effort to make certain that particular names of wares could be easily identified with actual pieces. Indeed, Rookwood seems to have made a deliberate effort not to identify fully every named glaze and decorative effect, perhaps to avoid the problems of replicating a particular finish or decoration.

Rookwood Pottery fails to explain whether the metal fittings in the category "Metals Applied" were specially created for individual pieces or were mounts purchased in advance and imported to be fitted to such pieces as seemed appropriate. It seems the term applies to the latter because Rookwood had discontinued its own metal department in 1903, and the only metal fitting pictured in *Rookwood Pottery* is a lamp base imported from Japan. Taylor himself insisted that metal should be fitted to pottery and not pottery to metal, although the creating of pottery to mount on imported metal bases would have presented no great problems.

Two portraits are illustrated in *Rookwood Pottery*: one, a vase on which is painted an elderly man with a white beard who wears a cap and dark clothing in the manner of an Old Master painting, and the other, a framed plaque of an American Plains chieftain in ceremonial feathered headdress. These images suggest that portraits were still being painted when, in fact, this mode of decoration was practically at its end. The plaque, however, is a form that Rookwood would soon use frequently in conjunction with the Vellum glaze.

Not until Rookwood published its mail-order catalogue in 1904 did the company distinguish among its various types of mat glazes. In describing the mat glazes in 1902, Rookwood announced a fact of some importance:

> . . . as the applied decoration now becomes subordinate, the heavy enamel, or glaze, with which these pieces are invested is no longer designed merely to protect the colors beneath, nor to reveal them as though swimming in a lustrous depth. The glaze is now itself the chief and highest interest.[47]

Did this pronouncement—that the applied decoration had become subordinate to the glaze—mean that the role of the decorator at Rookwood had become less important? Such does not seem to have been the case. What is important is that Rookwood's traditional separation of processes—creation of forms, decoration, and glazing—

was synthesized into a more coherent aesthetic statement. Importantly, glazes became an integral part of the total artistic presentation rather than a protective or enhancing covering.

Rookwood's tentative experiments with mat glazes, begun in 1896, led to spectacular results by 1904. That year Rookwood unveiled its newest mat glazes and decorative treatments to large audiences at the Louisiana Purchase Exposition in St. Louis. In conjunction with that world's fair, Rookwood published *The Rookwood Book*, a thirty-six page mail-order catalogue with 116 illustrations, of which fourteen are shown in full color.

The Rookwood Book describes and illustrates eight types of Rookwood that could be ordered: Standard, Sea Green, Iris, and five new types, Mat Glaze Painting, Conventional Mat Glaze, Incised Mat Glaze, Modeled Mat Glaze, and Vellum Ware. A number of each type were offered, including twenty-three Vellum, twenty Standard, eighteen Iris, twelve Modeled and Incised Mat, nine lamps and electroliers in mat glaze, and five each Sea Green, Mat Glaze Painting, Mat Glaze with Conventional Decoration, and Incised and Modeled Mat with Geometric Designs. The catalogue presented forty-three high-glazed wares and seventy-three mat-glazed wares. The prospective buyer could order a piece by number, glaze type, and decorative subject. Forty-two floral subjects were available; seven non-floral subjects comprising of birds, insects, sea creatures, dragons, and scenic marine views were offered; and five incised geometric designs were advertised. Prices ranged from one dollar for an Incised Mat-glazed bowl, to two hundred dollars for an Iris vase painted with flying storks.

There are similarities and differences between Rookwood's two catalogues of 1902 and 1904. Each includes the Standard, Sea Green, and Iris wares as distinct varieties. Illustrations 35, 37 (no. 34), 38, and 63 in the 1902 catalogue were repeated in the 1904 catalogue. Both catalogues include lamps and electroliers, although the 1904 publication grouped these lighting devices under-mat glazes. Whereas the earlier catalogue simply referred to the new dull finishes as Mat Glazes, the 1904 publication distinguished five named types. Omitted from the 1904 catalogue are Tiger Eye, Flowing Glaze, Metals Applied, and Architectural Faience. Nor does the 1904 catalogue illustrate portraits, an indication that these were no longer available.

The Rookwood Book was part of an ambitious marketing campaign that included advertisements in magazines for women. That the mail-order catalogue trade was a dismal failure is not difficult to explain. The catalogue was intended primarily to serve those living in small towns or in rural areas. But those citizens were generally among the least educated and sophisticated segment of the population, and they were also the least able to afford Rookwood. Even a piece priced at one dollar represented about one-fifth of the wages earned by a rural laborer for a six-day workweek.

Rookwood itself contributed to the failure of its first mail-order catalogue. Instructions headed "How to Order Rookwood" included this disclaimer: "The pieces illustrated in this book were in the pottery studios at the time The Rookwood Book was issued, but possibly when you receive this copy there may not remain unsold a single one of these pieces."[48] Even the most enthusiastic prospective buyer would have been put off by such a caveat.

Rookwood's attempt to democratize its product must have seemed a step down from its high ideals. In declaring that its product was art, however, Rookwood also established that it was a luxury, and for many, Rookwood remained unaffordable and unattainable. Although Rookwood operated at a marginal profit in order to create its art, the pottery nonetheless had to succeed in a competitive market. In the inflationary years of the early twentieth century, Rookwood experienced increasing tension between its own artistic ideals and economic survival. The dilemma would eventually be resolved in favor of economic survival.

It takes no careful scrutiny to see that *The Rookwood Book* represents a major shift in Rookwood's aesthetic from high-glazed wares with underglaze slip-painted decoration to mat finishes and broadly painted or stylized decoration. This shift was in fact part of a national movement that placed the highest value on simplicity in design and the way people lived. By 1904, Rookwood's high-glazed wares were passé and were being phased out of production. No doubt the Standard, Sea Green, and Iris wares were included in *The Rookwood Book* with the hope that surplus stock could be sold. Then, too, the inclusion of these high-glazed wares evidenced an artistic continuity. Through the dynamics of the market, Rookwood changed its wares to meet popular taste even as popular taste was molded by the changes the pottery made.

The Rookwood Book describes in sensory detail its new line of five mat glazes, available in a wide array of colors and textures to suit all tastes:

> Rookwood Mat possesses hitherto unknown range of color in glazes of astonishing variety of texture. Now it seems solid as quartz, and partaking of its crystalline structure; again one sees a more mellow surface, suggesting that of firm, ripe fruit; or again, it suggests the quality of old ivory, or of stained parchment; but always showing a slight translucency, a sense of depth, and a pleasure in the feel of it which makes it delightful to the touch.[49]

The first of the five mat glazes presented in *The Rookwood Book* is Mat Glaze Painting (nos. 49–53). Without explaining why the process of decoration was "of the greatest difficulty," the catalogue compares Mat Glaze Painting with "flowing enamels." The rarest of Rookwood's mat glazes, the Mat glaze painting is known by a few specimens decorated chiefly with floral subjects. Most of the Mat glaze painting specimens known were painted by Harriet Elizabeth Wilcox. With but a few examples and one predominate designer, some questions naturally arise. Were Rookwood's decorators assigned to a particular glaze line or decoration because they were adept in handling its peculiarities, or did some decorators ask to decorate in a specific mode and with a particular glaze? With some eight glazes and decorative lines being produced simultaneously by Rookwood, how did the company determine how many wares of a particular type would be created in a given time? Were pieces created to fill orders as they came in, or were some wares stocked in advance of orders? Unfortunately, company records that might have answered these questions have been lost.

Described as "a mat glaze with flat, conventional decoration in colors," the Conventional Mat glaze (nos. 47–48), the second of *The Rookwood Book's* five mat glazes, was promoted as a type that "appeals to a taste for simple, flat decorations rather than naturalistic treatment, and reflects an important movement in modern art."[50] Taylor no doubt expected that the reader would know that an "important movement in modern art" alluded to the international poster style in which designs were rendered in strong, black outlines and colors were applied flatly with little or no modeling. The black outlines on the Conventional Mat glaze were fired in the biscuit state and emerged as slightly raised ridges. The color was then applied within these outlines, comparable to the metal technique of cloisonné in which enamels filled in those areas defined by raised outlines. In some instances the colors of the Conventional Mat glaze overflowed their delineated area to create a painterly effect.

Of the five types of new wares that Rookwood unveiled in St. Louis in 1904, the Incised Mat glaze (no. 46) is the simplest, the least ambitious technically and artistically, and a radical departure from Rookwood's own pictorial tradition. The ware is characterized by simple shapes with incised geometric designs, inspired by Native-American pottery and the textile traditions of the Southwest. The ware was covered with plain mat glazes in dark reds, purples, blues, greens, deep yellows, browns, and in a black that served also as their decorative effect.

In 1905 Rookwood published a second mail-order promotional piece, *Rookwood Mat Glazes*, an unpaginated pamphlet of sixteen pages, illustrating forty-one mat-glazed pieces. Although not identified as Incised Mat glaze, it is clear that the pieces pictured are of this type. To support this conclusion, the pamphlet declares that "the Mat Glaze is the only one of the eight types made at the Rookwood Pottery in which the various designs are repeated with some similarity." And Number 942 is described, "This handsome Vase, like many of the others of American Indian design, is made in six different sizes."[51]

A newspaper article from about 1900, found in the McDonald family archive, reported decorator William McDonald's departure for a week's trip to New York and Washington, D. C. He was to study the Indian relics on view at the Smithsonian Institution. While in Washington he was to "pay a visit to a photographer there famous for his pictures of Indians."[52]

Rookwood's appropriation of the arts of the Navajo and Hopi reflected a national fascination with the ancient cultures indigenous to the Southwest. In the early years of the twentieth century, the Clifton Art Pottery in Newark, New Jersey, the Niloak Pottery in Benton, Arkansas, and Tiffany & Company in New York were among American firms that drew upon designs from the vocabulary of the Southwest. In addition, architects such as Irving John Gill in San Diego and company architects who designed railway stations for the Santa Fe and the Southern Pacific railroads were inspired by pueblo adobe architecture.

At the St. Louis world's fair, the introduction of the Incised Mat glaze coincided with the first major showing in the United States of recent developments in German and Austro-Hungarian decorative arts. Those familiar with trends in contemporary decorative arts would have recognized the affinities between Rookwood's geometric designs and the geometric designs prevalent in secessionist art circles in Germany and Austria-Hungary.

Although the Incised Mat glaze was the least innovative of Rookwood's newest lines, the ware nonetheless represented a radical departure from Rookwood's well-established artistic tradition and fundamental commitment to create art. Rookwood could sell the Incised Mat glaze wares as cheaply as it did because pieces were incised by ordinary workers in the casting room. To reduce labor even further and speed production, Rookwood had the option of creating molds from incised prototypes. This meant that the intaglio designs were an integral part of the mold, although some further work on the decoration might have been necessary and desirable. Such pieces were not, of course, signed by an artist. Only when Rookwood systematically mass-produced cast pieces with in-mold designs did the pottery succumb to the needs of commerce. The surrender did not happen until the 1920s, and became more pronounced in the 1930s.

As its name suggests, the Modeled Mat glaze (nos. 54–56), the fourth in Rookwood's 1904 line of mat glazes, is decorated with sculpted subjects. Manipulation of the clay ranges from incised lines to carved decoration in low to moderately high relief. From the illustrations in *The Rookwood Book*, it is clear that the decoration of the Modeled Mat glaze was a conservative bow to the Art Nouveau. Decoration ranges from stylized applications in an asymmetrical pattern to conventionalized floral motifs applied as repeating units that encircle a form. In some instances a piece has pierced openings on the shoulder and neck; in others, the modeled decoration rises above the lip.

The sculpted decoration of the Modeled Mat glaze is in higher relief than that in the underglaze slip-painted decoration, and it remains so much a separate element that forms often appear to have been slipped into their decoration or that the decoration has been created and then wrapped around the shape it embellishes. The Modeled Mat glaze seems especially suited to lamps, electroliers, and candlesticks.

In both its 1902 and 1904 catalogues, Rookwood showed some vases elevated by wood stands, no doubt purchased from an importer of Chinese and Japanese wares. Much like the easels on which framed canvases were displayed for effect, these stands presented Rookwood vases as works of art.

The Vellum glaze (nos. 60–76) is the last of the five new mat glazes that Rookwood introduced in 1904. Developed by Burt, the Vellum is Rookwood's supreme technical achievement. A hybrid cross between a transparent gloss glaze and a mat finish, the Vellum differs greatly from Rookwood's other mat glazes, "Devoid of lustre, without dryness, it partakes both to the touch and to the eye of the qualities of old parchment." This description matches the name of the Vellum, for the finish does suggest the soft translucency of fine parchment. Whereas the other mat glazes permitted "little decoration other than modeling or very flat and broad painting," because of their opacity and thickness, the Vellum retained "for the artist all those qualities possible hitherto under brilliant glaze alone."[53]

Often referred to as a transparent mat glaze, the Vellum is in fact a translucent covering. Although the glaze permits the transmission of light, the light is diffused in refraction and the colors of the underglaze slip painting are softened. The thickness of the application of the Vellum glaze determines the ethereal quality of the underglaze decoration.

It is no accident that the painted decoration of the Vellum appears softly focused as in Pictorialist photographs or Tonalist paintings of the period. Both Shirayamadani and Hurley were accomplished photographers. Hurley's photographs of local landscapes were used later as models for Vellum decoration. Furthermore, Hurley painted scenes of Cincinnati and the surrounding landscape in a Tonalist manner, choosing a muted palette to paint subjects softly, as if not fully in focus.

Because the Vellum glaze was neither fully transparent nor fully opaque, the finish proved especially versatile and permitted the company to continue the tradition of underglaze slip painting while making concessions to the new aesthetic of dull glazes. Today the Vellum is most closely associated with vases and plaques painted with landscapes and scenes of the Venetian lagoon. Now commonly called Scenic Vellums (nos. 64–65), these subjects were never so designated by Rookwood.

Subjects in the Vellum decorative repertory are varied: landscapes, blossoms and plants, fish, and birds. In some instances decoration is rendered in a poster-style manner, the colors applied flatly within outlines, or the designs airbrushed with stencils. Highly stylized designs of natural subjects appear as repeated discrete units; for example, daffodils, fuchsia blossoms, rose balls, or peacock feathers become patterns that encircle the forms they decorate. To reinforce the poster-style aesthetic, motifs might be separated from the ground in bands of contrasting colors.

The Vellum glaze could be applied to modeled (no. 60) and incised decoration without obscuring it. Another important property of the Vellum glaze was its ability to accept tints, as in Green Vellum (nos. 74–76) and Yellow Vellum, named for their predominant color. The Green Vellum, along with other green mat glazes, was popularized as its color became the one most associated with the Arts and Crafts movement.[54]

The landscape pictorials were used on both vases and plaques with varying results. Vases present a challenge in the use of landscapes as a decorative subject. The volume and curvature of the forms make it impossible to establish a single vanishing point to suggest space. The subject is revealed in stages as the vase is turned or as the viewer walks around it. To compensate for this formal limitation, Rookwood's decorators devised a simple solution. Landscapes were reduced to a formula in which contrasting vertical and horizontal elements comprise the composition. In these landscapes, trees are the dominant vertical element; they are used to establish grounds and spatial relationships within the composition; they add visual interest; and they reinforce the upward thrust of the vase. In contrast to the dominant verticals, courses of water, distant clumps of trees and woods, hills, clouds, and streaks of color in the sky encircle vases in irregular bands and establish the horizon line. Spatial depth is suggested in two ways: by diminution of decorative forms and by tonal variations to suggest atmospheric space.

Rookwood's artists made regular use of flat wall plaques for their Vellum glaze creations. An extension of the architectural tile, the wall plaque was introduced at Rookwood soon after the company instituted its architectural department. Although plaques offered painters the luxury of flat surfaces, Rookwood could not fire large ones lest they warp, split or crack. Even if it had been possible to fire a plaque the size of a large canvas, the piece would have been prohibitively heavy and unwieldy. Had Rookwood wished to create large wall pieces, it could have used multiple tiles or plaques. But the weight alone would have presented problems. Moreover, the appealing intimacy of the Scenic Vellum landscapes would have been lost. For these reasons, Rookwood's plaques are small; most are no more than several inches in height or width and are usually less than an inch thick.

The decorators at Rookwood approached their work on the Scenic Vellum plaques (nos. 65, 68, 70, 72) fully conscious of the oil-on-canvas convention. The flat clay tile became their canvas as they followed the time-honored easel tradition, even initialing their plaques on the painted surface. And the Vellum glaze, with its fine cracklature, does indeed have the mellow look of varnishes that have aged and cracked over canvases. Before plaques left Rookwood, they were suitably framed at the pottery in oak. Unvarnished, but stained or rubbed with color, these frames have a dull finish that does not compete with the plaque itself. Often plaques were titled with small, typed paper labels applied to the back of the frame. Titles rarely identify a landscape, but are poetic allusions to nature: "Sunset on the River," "Early Blossoms in the Spring Sun," "Winter Enchantment," and "Hushed Twilight."

Rookwood's Scenic Vellum landscapes fall into three categories: landscapes drawn from the meadows, wooded fields, and hills of the Ohio river valley (nos. 66–71, 73); snowcapped mountains from the American West (no. 72); and scenes of the Venetian lagoon (nos. 64–65).

The landscapes inspired by scenes of the Ohio river valley present slices of nature touched by human presence but without people. The absence of people is so obvious as to appear to be a conscious elimination. While these landscapes were certainly painted with the aid of sketches and photographs, their abstraction suggests that memory also served as a guide. Rookwood's Scenic Vellum landscapes evoke shared experiences from a collective memory.

More specific, but still a type, are scenes of snowcapped mountains. These scenes appealed to Americans who had traveled to the West or who were familiar with the West from their reading of novels and travel literature. The mountain scenes almost never appear on vases, for the obvious reason that they present problems in composition and spatial relationships between grounds. Of all the types of landscape Rookwood's artists painted, western mountain scenes presented perhaps the greatest challenge, the grandeur of the majestic peaks discouraging their reduction to the scale demanded by small plaques.

Marine scenes with *bragozze*, two-masted fishing boats, in the foreground, and distant views of Venice with familiar landmarks on the horizon—Santa Maria della Salute, Campanile, San Giorgio Maggiore, and San Marco—are the most specific Scenic Vellum locales. In turning to Venetian scenes, Rookwood continued the tradition used by many American artists from the mid–nineteenth century through the first two decades of the twentieth century.[55] Rookwood's Venetian Scenic Vellums, however, relate to Venice only loosely. They do not celebrate the architectural patrimony of the city, but are softly mellow paeans to a romantic past. It is unlikely that Carl Schmidt, who painted most of the Venetian Scenic Vellums, had ever visited the city. Nor had he need to do so, for hundreds of romantic pictures of Venice were readily available for him to consult.

Scenic Vellum landscapes and Venetian scenes capture the haunting, ethereal qualities of natural light in its myriad seasonal and daily transmutations: in the first rays of daybreak; in the lingering colors of twilight before darkness falls; in the glow of a full moon; and in the play of light reflected in water or on freshly fallen snow. So versatile is the palette of light in the Vellums that it defies easy description. Whether in silvery whites and grays, in yellows and blues, in the soft pinks and corals of early morning and of enveloping dusk, or in the muted reds and purples of a winter sky, Rookwood's landscapes universalize the hushed, tranquil moments in which solitude and reflection are paramount pleasures. Rookwood's Scenic Vellum landscapes are elegiac evocations of perfect serenity; they are lyrical scenes inviting introspection and surrender to a nostalgic past. A deep sense of longing haunts the finest of Rookwood's Scenic Vellums.

The last of the mat glazes produced at Rookwood was the Ombroso (no. 59), introduced in 1910 to celebrate the pottery's thirtieth anniversary. For this reason, Rookwood printed two small promotional brochures, each illustrated with the same color cover of a simple vase finished with a brown, mottled glaze. In the smaller, undated brochure, Rookwood described the Ombroso in detail:

> The chemical structure of the glaze is crystalline and its surface tends to gloss slightly more than the other Mat Glazes of Rookwood. The result is a texture which makes immediate appeal to the sense of touch even before the eye penetrates beyond the surface into the quiet beauty of the underlying colors. The colors of Ombroso are generally in tones of gray and brown, but they often show delightful accents of blue, green or yellow. Ornamentation, if any there be, is brought about not by painting, but by incised work or modeling in relief.[56]

An Italian adjective, *ombroso* translates variously as shadowy, shady, touchy, and susceptible. Rookwood may have adopted the name because of the muted tones of the glaze. Rookwood may have logically named its wares after inherent properties in a glaze or color, or because a decorative effect suggested an immediate and natural appellation.

The Ombroso is a transmutation glaze that separates as it matures into what appears to be different colors. Sometimes softly streaked in color and suggestive of fur, and at other times showing a subtle crystalline surface, the Ombroso is one of Rookwood's most understated glazes. The Ombroso evolved from two influences at Rookwood "The one was a tendency towards a ceramic medium with non-reflecting surfaces and the other the demand for an architectural material embodying color in permanent form."[57] Although the decorating and the architectural faience departments were separate entities, there was a cooperative relationship between the two, especially in glaze research and application.

From their introduction in 1902 as a category, mat glazes were always produced in some form at Rookwood until the company closed in Cincinnati in 1960. In fact, mat glazes in varying colors were applied to unsigned mass-produced items—vases, bowls, ashtrays, candlesticks, lamps, small figurines, and bookends.

William Watts Taylor's death on November 12, 1913, ended his enlightened reign of three decades. Joseph Henry Gest, then vice president of Rookwood, was appointed the company's director in January 1914. Concurrent with Gest's position as Rookwood's chief administrator was his role as director of the Cincinnati Art Museum, an office he had held since 1902. Gest permitted the Rookwood Pottery Company to house many hundreds of pieces of its pottery at the Museum on extended loan.

Soon after 1913, Rookwood amended its promotional literature in a significant way. "Absolutely no printing patterns are used nor any duplicates made" was changed to read that no duplicates "of signed, decorated pieces" were made at Rookwood.[58] A practice that had been fact for some years was now acknowledged after Taylor's death. Whereas Rookwood had not mass produced unsigned duplicates previously, this alteration to the company's promotional literature suggested this future possibility.

Having set in motion the celebration of an anniversary by introducing new glazes and decorative treatments in 1910, Rookwood introduced the Soft Porcelain in observance of its thirty-fifth anniversary. Officially identified with an impressed "P" among other company marks, Soft Porcelain refers to the body of the new ware. A simple promotional leaflet, *Soft Porcelain*, announces that "the making of porcelain at Rookwood marks an interesting departure in the development of a new body and new glazes."[59] Inspired by and developed from the study of old Chinese ceramics of "the soft-paste type," Soft Porcelain had received "years of chemical research and kiln trials to perfect," according to the leaflet. Such painstaking development was a particular point of pride for Rookwood in maintaining its reputation for excellence.

Soft Porcelain also drew comparison between the new ware and Chinese varieties of the soft-paste type, noting that "the new Rookwood is a soft porcelain with a rich glaze flowing over forms perfectly plain or enriched with subtle low-relief modeling, or sometimes a dark border design flatly painted on the clay body." (Interestingly, the description of the Soft Porcelain recalls that of the Flowing glaze, announced thirteen years earlier.)

The extent to which Chinese porcelains were studied is unclear. Superintendent and technical expert Stanley Gano Burt may have studied Chinese Far Eastern pottery and porcelain when he was in Europe between 1894 and 1896. Chinese ceramics were also available for study in the United States; locally, the Taft Museum in Cincinnati provided ample opportunity to study the Chinese porcelains in its collections.[60]

In *Soft Porcelain*, Rookwood furthermore promoted the Soft Porcelain as the perfect accompaniment for large, colorful floral bouquets, evidence that such displays were in new vogue.

> The colors of the glazes are refined and quiet, as well as brilliant, with the intention that the pieces shall be suited for the arrangement of flowers; and the colors as well as the shapes have been carefully studied with reference to their value in the display of flowers in a new and beautiful setting.

With its high-gloss glazes, brilliant colors, and highly refined body, the Soft Porcelain style (nos. 77–79, 87–94, 96) is the antithesis of the style of the Arts and Crafts movement. The new ware heralded a joyous release from austere simplicity. And the reappearance of elaborate floral bouquets, so jarringly out of place in Craftsman interiors, announced a new era in home decoration.

Despite the return to a high-gloss glaze and brilliant colors, Rookwood declared in *Soft Porcelain* that "there is no effort at elaborate painted decoration in any way resembling that on other types of Rookwood." Indeed, Soft Porcelain ware was used to produce unsigned duplicate wares. Contrary to Rookwood's own claim that the Soft Porcelain attempted no elaborate painted decoration, there soon appeared pieces as elaborately embellished as any that Rookwood ever did. Arthur Conant—who joined Rookwood about 1915 and who is reputed to have worked at Herter Looms in New York, where he studied the rugs and textiles of the Metropolitan Museum of Art—painted pieces with fanciful designs of leaping ibexes and flowers, designs distinctly indebted to the motifs of textiles from Western Asia.[61]

With the Soft Porcelain, Rookwood achieved the consistency and brilliance of color that the pottery had long sought. In the more elaborate pieces of Soft Porcelain, color itself becomes an emphatic decorative feature, with sharply contrasting colors juxtaposed. Furthermore, colors are rarely primary or secondary, but are hybrids. For example, a turquoise might be contrasted with a plum or crimson, or a deep blue with an apple green. Brilliant and rich color is a pronounced feature of the Soft Porcelain, and the considerable artfulness made in the selection of vivid hues complements the artifice of the decoration.

Rookwood's introduction of a new glaze, body, or decorative treatment did not result in the immediate discontinuation of other glazes or wares. But a census of Rookwood objects in collections indicates that by 1915, the Conventional Mat glaze (nos. 47–48), Mat glaze painting (nos. 49–53), and the Incised Mat glaze with geometric Native-American designs (no. 46) had essentially ended.

Although Rookwood suffered no interruption in production during World War I, the ascendancy of modernism and the machine age in the aftermath of that conflict brought new social and cultural developments that were to affect the pottery adversely. As the Arts and Crafts movement waned, the intensive labor of handicraft and one-of-a-kind production fundamental to an art industry such as Rookwood became a romantic anachronism.

In 1920, Rookwood observed its fortieth year and embarked upon its fifth decade,[62] the last extended period of prosperity and artistic continuity that the pottery would enjoy, even though the company would manage to survive for almost another five decades, closing its doors for the last time in Starkville, Mississippi, in 1967.

From 1920 to 1930 Rookwood hired only ten decorators, none of whom were to remain for an appreciable length of time. Of these new decorators, Louise Abel, Catherine Pissoreff Covalenco, and Jens Jacob Herring Krog Jensen were born and educated in Europe.[63] Interestingly, at a time when the United States chose to follow isolationism as a foreign policy and when Rookwood itself had ceased to exhibit in foreign expositions, the company

7. Interior of the Rookwood salesroom in the early 1920s. Table and bench in foreground have legs molded of Rookwood faience.

quietly abandoned its previous practice of hiring only American-born decorators (with, of course, the notable exception of Shirayamadani). Boastful nationalism had become, in the 1920s, a parochial contradiction to the international reputation of Rookwood.

It would be misleading to conclude that because so few decorators were hired in the 1920s, the size of the decorating department at Rookwood was stable, or that the company was in decline. In the 1890s, the decade when Rookwood hired the most decorators, the company produced solely artist-signed wares. By the late 1910s and 1920s, however, Rookwood had become, in effect, several potteries sharing the same name and coexisting under the same roof. This fact was noted in a Rookwood promotional flyer that declared, ". . . Rookwood is really the house of half a dozen potteries, each of which might well have a separate existence."[64] These "potteries" produced a wealth of wares: signed artistic wares; unsigned duplicates or industrial wares; architectural terra-cotta and tiles; and garden pottery. The architectural faience department, itself a sizable industry, generated considerable income. Despite the diversification of Rookwood's productions, the company did not displace its artistic wares as the primary focus.

Although the artistic wares that Rookwood produced in the 1920s are some of the pottery's finest—both aesthetically and technically—and are exceptionally diverse, they remain undervalued by collectors and have not received the scholarly attention they deserve. Such a lack of scholarly investigation is understandable in part because Rookwood's artistic wares of the 1920s are not easily categorized. In some instances decoration appears to be merely a revival of an earlier style; at other times it is in step with modern style. That Rookwood could create art pieces of consummate grace and beauty, and at the same time produce cheap industrial wares is, to some scholars, more than an embarrassment: it seems treason against the higher ideals of art. What has not been sufficiently understood and should be reiterated is that by 1920 Rookwood was not one pottery but several potteries that managed very effectively to operate as a company with multiple identities.

Much to our exasperation today, Rookwood failed to identify its artistic wares in the 1920s in any conclusive manner, either by copyrighted names, by distinguishing marks or labels, by color photographs in promotional literature, or by accurate descriptions. And when Rookwood did describe its wares, the words chosen are often so vague and ambiguous as to be meaningless. It may be that Rookwood chose not to name each of its many artistic wares because such a practice seemed unnecessary: the buyer purchased "Rookwood," itself the most important name. And perhaps, too, particular glazes and decorative treatments were not produced in sufficient numbers to warrant naming them.

Even though Rookwood did not consistently name its artistic wares, ten types of decorative ware produced in the 1920s were named, or have been named, based upon the body or characteristics of the glaze or decoration: Empire Green and Gold-Chartreuse Tiger Eye (nos. 84–86), Flambé, Oxblood (no. 94), Jewel Porcelain, Wax Mat, Mat Moderne (nos. 95, 97), French Red (nos. 81–83), Butterfat, Coromandel, and Black Opal (no. 90). (These names do not cover the full range of decoration produced by the pottery.)[65]

To celebrate its fortieth anniversary, Rookwood revived the Tiger Eye, though this aventurine glaze differs markedly from its predecessor in that the high-gloss covering is a rich golden color with a decidedly greenish cast, and might rightfully be called Golden or Green Tiger Eye to distinguish it from its predecessor. What we now call Flambé is described as "a deep magenta or purplish maroon base color, obscured by patches of luminescent white haze" and the glaze known as Oxblood, "a crimson glaze with touches of white at rims."[66] The high-glazed Coromandel, Flambé, and Oxblood evidence inspiration from the antique lacquer and ceramics of China, a culture that repeatedly inspired Rookwood in the 1920s and 1930s. Whether Rookwood itself ever used the names Flambé and Oxblood for wares is unclear.

Rookwood's marketing strategy for names could mislead or confuse readers in introducing a glaze or decoration as new. For example, Jewel Porcelain is nothing more than Soft Porcelain marketed under another name. Soft Paste Porcelain was first established around the turn of the century in order to retain the colors in underglaze slip decoration because the high temperatures required for the Hard Paste Porcelain fired out the colors. During this period of innovation, "Soft Paste Porcelain," or as Rookwood called it, "Soft Porcelain," were fashionable terms in ceramics. Later, when the original reason for the term was forgotten by the buying public, this term connoted an inferior body. So, as a marketing strategy, Rookwood changed the name of "Soft Porcelain" to "Jewel Porcelain." The marketing of the ware by its body rather than its decoration or glaze represented a fundamental shift in the promotion of Rookwood.

Among the mat glaze types produced at Rookwood in the 1920s were the Wax Mat and a type that I call Mat Moderne. The Wax Mat lent itself to decoration painted freely and boldly, a quality further enhanced by a slight separation of colors, which suggests faint curdling, even a watercolor effect. The Wax Mat is described by Mary L. Alexander in a *Cincinnati Enquirer* article as "an unctuous rich glaze that suggests the texture of fruits and vegetables. The soft, satiny texture of this glaze undoubtedly suggested the name of 'wax mat' to the experts."[67] From this description it is clear that Rookwood's glazes are tactilely inviting and sometimes more easily understood by touch than by sight. The Wax Mat is not dry to the touch, dense, or dull in appearance, although it is an opaque glaze. So the allusion of the "unctuous" quality of the glaze to wax is quite apt.

In the late 1920s Elizabeth Barrett and William Hentschel, two of Rookwood's most prominent artists, decorated a distinctive line of wares in elegantly stylized modern designs. The wares were finished with dry, opaque mat glazes in hybrid hues of blues, greens, and purples. Because the decoration of gazelles, fish, blossoms, leaves, fruits, and geometric designs is built up in pastes in irregular lines and forms, and because the finish is dull and flows unevenly over the decoration, the appearance of the Mat Moderne (nos. 95, 97) is not mechanically perfect or slick. Rather, the effect is solid and strong. The Mat Moderne is, in fact, an updated version of Rookwood's earlier carved and incised mat wares.

Had the United States accepted the invitation to exhibit at the 1925 Exposition Universelle of modern decorative and industrial arts in Paris, the world would have seen that Rookwood was in step with the modern style. Of all the decorative wares produced by Rookwood in the 1920s, none is more closely aligned with the so-called Art Deco in its highest style than the French Red, a term I introduced in 1983.[68] Called French Red (nos. 81–83) because "the unusual rich red slip background was created from a color imported from France,"[69] the ware achieves an intensity and vibrancy of red that eluded Rookwood for decades. The few known specimens juxtapose the vivid red with other rich colors—most spectacularly against a dense black with either a glossy sheen or a mat finish. The decoration of floral motifs and birds is often stylized and treated graphically in colors applied flatly within black outlines. Both high-gloss and mat glaze may appear on the same piece (no. 81). The consciously poster-like, static quality of the decoration is reinforced by the enclosure of the designs in panels or by the stylization of a decorative motif such as the rose ball suspended against a ground of contrasting color.

One of the most easily identified glazes that Rookwood unveiled in the 1920s is Butterfat, a thick covering in white, cream, or pale yellow with an uneven surface suggestive of butter. Because of the thickness and opacity of Butterfat, the glaze is most effective when applied to large forms with expansive surfaces. Although the Butterfat does not preclude decoration, its qualities determine that the design be broadly painted and reduced to basic forms. The oil-like surface and the bumpy, glob-like texture of Butterfat characterize one of Rookwood's most distinctive but least appreciated glazes.

One unnamed decorative effect exclusive to the 1920s deserves mention. Upon simple, strong forms with soft swells and gentle curves, a thick opaque glaze flows heavily and freely. Patches of vivid reds, blues, and greens appear irregularly in the darkly unctuous covering. The uneven glaze is intentionally flawed and pitted, components of the overall effect. Glaze and decoration are inseparable in the painterly surface. In fact, the decoration is often so submerged that it becomes recognizable only when the piece is viewed for some time. These extraordinary and rare pieces are almost always signed by Edward T. Hurley.

Brief descriptions of decorative lines and glazes cannot convey the richness and diversity of Rookwood's artistic wares in the 1920s, about which generalization must allow for many exceptions. Nonetheless, the wares of this decade display a marked turn to pictorial decoration in the international modern style, the use of lively colors from a wide-ranging palette, and the adoption of classically proportioned Asian vase forms. The attention given to new shapes demonstrates how important forms were in Rookwood's response to modernism. At no other time in Rookwood's history were the sympathies of the decorators and technical staff so closely united.

The pictorial decoration at Rookwood in the 1920s differs markedly from the pictorial naturalism so prevalent at the pottery from the 1880s to the 1910s. Most apparent is the deliberate decorativeness and artifice that informs Rookwood's designs in the modern period. Derived mostly from the study of secondary sources and not from the direct study of nature, Rookwood's pictorialism of the 1920s is art about art.

In searching for subjects and motifs, decorators had a wealth of resources in Rookwood's extensive reference library of books, folios, periodicals, photographs, sketches, prints, clippings, and textile swatches, as well as the company's own collection of ceramics and other objects. If Rookwood's library failed to satisfy a decorator's quest, the artist could search the collection and library of the Cincinnati Art Museum, the Public Library of Cincinnati and Hamilton County, and the collection of paintings and Chinese porcelains at the Taft Museum.

That Rookwood's decorators consulted published secondary sources for designs was nothing new. What is

unusual about such a practice in the 1920s, however, is its eclecticism. A renewed interest in Japonisme led Rookwood's decorators to several much-used publications—*Artistic Japan, Céramique orientale, La Céramique dans l'art d'Extrême-Orient,* and *Étoffes japonaises.*[70] Interestingly, each of these publications came from France, a country that left an indelible mark upon Rookwood in the 1920s. In addition to examining impressive portfolios imported from France, Rookwood's artists could study fine pieces of contemporary French ceramics in the Cincinnati Art Museum.

Textile and other patterns from the folk traditions of Europe, Western Asia, Persia, and ancient Peru were among the cultural sources incorporated into Rookwood's decorations. Lorinda Epply, a weaver as well as a ceramic decorator, responded to such patterns in a way that only one knowledgeable about fiber and pattern could fully understand.

Soon after Howard Carter and the Earl of Carnarvon opened the tomb of Tutankhamen in 1922, Egyptomania swept through Europe and the United States much as the Japanese-mania had done in the 1880s. Rookwood promptly incorporated this latest rage into its decorative designs.

Always fascinated with color and experimenting to achieve a full range of hues, Rookwood had developed a palette of unparalleled brilliance and complexity by the 1920s. Vivid primaries and secondaries and hybrid mixtures in reds, purples, blues, greens, oranges, yellows, and pastels of these colors fill Rookwood's palette. One of the most compelling "colors" is black. In a dull, metallic finish or high sheen suggestive of hematite or obsidian, these jet blacks contribute a signal elegance to their forms. There is a delightful abandon in the way color is used at Rookwood in the 1920s. Juxtaposed colors create dramatic effects and intensify the visual impact of the individual hues: soft white offset with a deep magenta, turquoise placed next to plum, cadmium red contrasted by black. In some pieces stunning effects are achieved by multicolored designs applied thickly in high gloss, and emphasized by grounds in a dull black or in another dark color.

Just as Rookwood's decorators had drawn freely upon Japanese imagery since 1880, the pottery turned eagerly to the ceramic traditions of China for glazes and shapes. Beginning in 1896 with the search to develop a mat glaze, and continuing with the introduction of the Soft Porcelain in 1915, Rookwood found increasing inspiration in the pottery of ancient China. In 1920 Rookwood introduced several new shapes based upon antique Chinese and Persian prototypes.[71] In other instances Rookwood appropriated specific Chinese forms to serve its purpose.

The classic Shang-Yin dynasty ritual bronze Ku was interpreted as an elegant tall vase with a banded waist and flared, trumpet mouth.[72] Pear-shaped bottles; jars with globular bodies and short, cylindrical collar necks; tall vases with high, broad-rounded shoulders and short or tall necks; and squared vases with upward, flared openings all reveal their indebtedness to Chinese shapes. The rises, swells, sinuous curves, elegant silhouettes, and correct proportions of these shapes were perfect complements to the glazes and decorative treatments applied to them.

Because Rookwood is usually studied primarily as an artistic enterprise and only secondarily as a business, we tend to forget that the company was an experimental center for ceramics. Although the company's first experiments were conducted for artistic ends, there can be no doubt that as the company diversified its productions, experimentation became a major pursuit. A comprehensive history of Rookwood would necessarily chronicle the pottery's constant experiments to perfect clay bodies, glazes, colors, decorative treatments, and kiln firings. But whatever record might have been kept for the future of American ceramics, Rookwood's extensive technical library has been lost for the most part.

As noted previously, at no time in Rookwood's history were the decorators and technical staff more productively allied than in the 1920s. Two circumstances in particular account for this happy collaboration. First, the company had amassed a huge reference collection of clay bodies, glazes, and color trials and formulas. Second, and most important, in the 1920s Rookwood's decorators were skilled artists of diverse experience, special talents, and exuberant creativity that found expression in an uncommon variety of styles.

Writing in 1930 as he reviewed the past decade, Arthur Van Vlissingen, Jr., noted: "Rookwood has for many years employed laboratory control and research. The artistic development which has taken place would not have been possible . . . without the technical proficiency and chemical control." He added an important point: "When an artist visualizes an effect he wishes to obtain, reference to the library [of recorded and fired bodies, glazes, and colors] may show him how to get it."[73]

In the mid-1930s, Rookwood had on hand "nearly a quarter million mixtures of glaze ingredients, colors, and bodies, . . . about forty thousand of which are usable, desirable, and different in color, tint, and texture," according to Harold Bopp.[74] Most of that inventory had been accumulated prior to 1930. Furthermore, the company kept in stock over five hundred glazes, hundreds of decorating colors, and clays from which several different bodies could be composed.

By 1920, Rookwood operated fifteen kilns and employed some two hundred people. The company was as sophisticated in its technology as any ceramic manufactory in the world. Never content to settle for the ordinary, Rookwood constantly pushed the limits of its raw materials and technology. Nowhere was this effort greater than in the company's development of glazes. Harold Bopp observed in 1936 that "most of the glazes used at Rookwood are of freakish composition and on line between the development of widely different glazes."[75] Such precariousness occurred especially with "the crystalline type such as the transmutation mats" in which a few degrees in the firing either too low or too high left the glaze undeveloped or totally ruined.[76]

To its credit, Rookwood maintained its traditionally rigorous standards throughout the 1920s. The company could face no competition more challenging than its own achievements and aspirations. The unceasing search for new glazes and colors meant that every triumph imposed even higher expectations.

But Rookwood's last decade of good fortune drew to an ominous close with the collapse of the stock market in October 1929. Doubtless seeing her days at the pottery numbered, Harriet E. Wilcox left in 1930. William P. McDonald died the following year, having worked uninterruptedly at Rookwood for forty-seven years. Faced with plummeting sales and burdened with a large inventory, Rookwood had to take drastic action if the pottery was to avoid bankruptcy. Rookwood closed in October 1931 for a brief time to take an accounting of its situation and to balance its budget. Reluctantly Wareham was forced to retire or dismiss eight decorators. We can imagine how terrible this blow was, for seven of the decorators had been with Rookwood since the 1880s and 1890s.

Although Rookwood survived the stock market failure and the subsequent global economic collapse that lengthened into the Depression, the company never totally recovered. While Rookwood produced some exquisite pieces of technical magnificence in the 1930s, it is clear that the jubilee kiln of 1930—a special kiln that drew 1,200 pieces bearing a commemorative mark of "50" enclosed in a black outline of a kiln and representing twenty-three artists—marked more than one event: it drew the curtain on Rookwood's golden age.[77] But to assume that the Depression had incapacitated Rookwood to such a degree that all artistic standards and aspirations were abandoned is to fail to understand the strength and tenacity of the company. Even with a severely reduced decorative department, Rookwood still had one magnificent resource—its storehouse of knowledge recorded in fired body, glaze, and color trials and in its technical library.

Descriptions of wares drawn from the golden jubilee kiln are noteworthy: "Outstanding . . . were several pieces in a rich red, other than ox-blood, as well as a number embodying new glaze qualities in wax mat, crystalline and aventurine, all of which have been perfected during the pottery's fiftieth year," declared the *Cincinnati Enquirer* on November 27, 1930.[78] As newspaper reportage is often inaccurate, such sources must be read with caution. The "rich red [ware], other than ox-blood" may well have been an oxblood type or variation. Whatever the case, Rookwood had mastered the one color that had eluded its quest for so many years. The jubilee kiln, which culminated many years of research and experimentation, established that Rookwood's palette was complete.

In the 1920s and 1930s Rookwood's wares were commonly described as modern. The jubilee wares of 1930 expressed "a fresh, modern spirit, different entirely from the classical European or the traditional Chinese or Persian types."[79] But what was fresh and modern in spirit about these wares? Are we to conclude that Rookwood abandoned its fascination with the ceramic traditions of Europe and China? The wares of the 1930s tell us differently.

> The "modern" style of decoration is distinctly noticeable in the product of late—but never in radical style. So considerable a proportion of the ware has been flowing in this direction, however, that one "stockroom"—in a purely commercial business it would be a showroom—has recently been furnished in the modern flavor to show these modern products to best advantage.[80]

Although the word "modern" is used three times in this quotation, there is no clear understanding of what it meant to Rookwood. No doubt Rookwood expected that the reader would understand it simply as a synonym for "new" or "up-to-date." For Rookwood, the concept of modernity threatened a distancing from, even a repudiation of, its former decorative styles.

In 1933, Wareham selected thirty-five pieces of Rookwood's latest wares to travel to Dallas, Fort Worth, Oklahoma City, Kansas City, Omaha, Minneapolis, and Milwaukee as a promotional tour. The choice of these cities is revealing, for Rookwood had not developed a strong market in the Great Plains. Along with decorative painting by Epply, Hentschel, and Shirayamadani were figural sculptures by Abel that were finished in soft monochromatic glazes with a waxy, satin surface. Rookwood had introduced figural sculpted works in the 1920s in such forms as bookends, flower vases, and bowls. In the 1930s and 1940s figurative subjects included small animals, birds, and fish, as well as human beings.

Included in the 1933 pieces sent to the Great Plains were "several pieces of oxblood red that vie in splendor with the tiger eye, but the piece de resistance is a bowl in the new iron red glaze which actually defies description except to state that it is a brilliant, deep mahogany red."[81] Once again, a contemporary description of Rookwood's glazes and decorative lines raises more questions than it answers.

It is striking that in a brief time Rookwood developed not one, but several varieties of red—Aventurine, Coromandel, Flambé, Oxblood, and the French Red. In more than name, the Coromandel, Flambé, and Oxblood were inspired by antique Chinese lacquer and ceramics. Except for the French Red, most, if not all, of these red glazes had some glitter, and it is impossible to differentiate them with any exactness today. No doubt differences resided in the intensity and tone of the red and in the properties of the crystalline glitter, which could appear within the glassy covering or be deposited directly on the glaze surface.

Unable to cope with the downward spiral of Rookwood, Joseph Henry Gest resigned in 1934, to be replaced by John "Dee" Wareham. Then sixty-three, Wareham was conservative in his views and management and no more capable of turning the tide of events than anyone else. His helplessness was the nation's helplessness. And as soup lines lengthened, art pottery more and more became a luxury that few could afford. As it became obvious that the United States would not recover from the the deepening depression in the foreseeable future, Wareham further limited the production of artist-signed wares. Although Epply, Hentschel, Hurley, Jensen, Margaret McDonald, and Shirayamadani remained with Rookwood, they decorated only intermittently.

That Rookwood managed to produce exquisite wares in the midst of economic adversity is clear from contemporary descriptions of the pottery. Bertha Joseph commented upon Rookwood's wares in a newspaper article in 1935, noting the splendor of the Tiger Eye, Iris, Black Opal, Butterfat, Sung Plum, Coromandel, and Aventurine.[82] Joseph observes that "these rare developments are exclusive to Rookwood and are costly to produce."[83] Unwilling to abandon Rookwood's commitment to artistic wares totally, Wareham must have known that these "rare developments" were little more than a gesture, an attempt to keep Rookwood's former grandeur alive. In another article from 1938, the Sung Plum is described at some length:

> Sung Plum is like oxblood or peach bloom, a triumph in technique and takes the peculiar type of fir-

ing to bring out its peculiar mingling of color. It is not just a plain plum color but rather has overtones of blue and red that give it its singular plum color and orange peel texture as well as its deep surface of glaze.[84]

Asserting that there was "no finer glaze . . . produced in America," the article further described the Sung Plum as "an irregular clotted glaze that flows and curtains down over the body form like thick skin that is rich and unctious [sic]." It also noted that "the forms of these pieces, squatty pots, gali pots [sic], and vases are very simple and like all primitive art have the ruggedness and hand-wrought quality."[85]

A careful analysis of the literature of Rookwood's wares in the 1930s reveals a fact of some importance: rarely is decoration mentioned. The silence is hardly surprising, for Rookwood had dismissed most of its decorators, and the few who were retained worked only sporadically. Accordingly, promotional releases emphasized glazes and colors. There is, however, one decorator whose work deserves note because of its inventiveness.

In the 1930s Jens Jensen created a body of work that is easily identifiable. Boldly and freely painted female nudes, obviously indebted to the neo-primitivism and expressionistic vigor of early twentieth-century European masters, announce Jensen's hand (no. 91). Even when painting flowers, animals, or fish, Jensen enlivened common subjects with an assertive brush and a dramatic command of form and color never before seen at Rookwood. Jensen painted in the idiom of his day with such authority and brio that his ceramic decoration announces a remarkable artistic talent.

As the Depression dragged on into the late 1930s, Rookwood's directors made several unsuccessful attempts to sell the pottery to a buyer who would refinance and reorganize the languishing firm. But no buyer was to be found for a luxury company in the midst of economic calamity. Finally, the inevitable came on April 16, 1941: Rookwood filed for bankruptcy.

The closed company was purchased at auction on September 30, 1941, by the automobile dealer, Walter E. Schott, and his wife, Margaret, his brother, Harold, and two other partners, Charles M. Williams and Lawrence H. Kyte. Retaining Wareham as business and artistic manager, the new owners of Rookwood planned to reopen the pottery as soon as possible and to recall former decorators. The hope of the new owners was to make pottery that was attractive and yet affordable by the many—the very goal that Rookwood's founder had envisioned in 1880. Rookwood reopened on November 19, 1941, as its sixty-first anniversary approached.

The optimism that cheered Rookwood's reopening was short-lived. Nineteen days after the pottery reopened, the United States was at war. Within weeks after the attack on Pearl Harbor, Rookwood was declared a non-essential industry. The necessary raw materials for the production of pottery, in particular the mineral oxides used in glazes and as coloring agents, were diverted to the war effort.

Despite the deprivations caused by the war, Rookwood managed to continue production, although on a greatly reduced scale. Featured in the exhibition "Art in Industry" at the Cincinnati Art Museum in January 1942, Rookwood unveiled the Tiger Eye in the colors of empire green, gold-chartreuse, and a "very new color" Rookwood called marine.[86] That Rookwood referred to the marine as "very new" suggests that the other two were not entirely new. Again, it is noteworthy that Rookwood received attention for new colors and glaze treatments rather than for any revelations in decoration or shapes.

When Rookwood was sold at auction, the purchase price included the 2,292 pieces of Rookwood dating from 1880 that were on loan to the Cincinnati Art Museum. Unaware of the historical value of this treasure, Rookwood's new owners recalled the vast loan from the Museum in February 1942 and sent the collection to B. Altman and Company in New York—which had been a Rookwood agent for ten years—to be sold. On March 22, 1942 the Sunday New York Times ran a half-page advertisement (fig. 8) offering three thousand pieces of artist-signed Rookwood and other ceramics for sale. Prices ranged from as low as five dollars to as high as seventy-five dollars. The sale included three lots: the Rookwood collection recalled from the Cincinnati Art Museum, Rookwood's own historical collection of art, and "Rookwood's collection of inspirational material from all over the world."[87]

Late in 1942, no doubt regarding Rookwood's days as numbered because of the war, the Schott group transferred Rookwood as a gift to the Institutum Divi Thomae (St. Thomas Institute), a scientific, educational, and research foundation under the jurisdiction of the Roman Catholic Archdiocese of Cincinnati. Because the Institutum was a non-profit foundation prohibited from operating a business, the foundation sold the commercial rights of the company to Sperti, Inc., in Cincinnati. Once more Rookwood was refinanced and reorganized. Wareham continued to direct the art and production activities of Rookwood, although the company's financial affairs were managed by Sperti, Inc.

By 1943 a greatly diminished Rookwood seemed stable. The reestablished decorating department included

8. B. Altman & Co., New York, advertisement for sale of Rookwood pottery. *New York Times*, March 22, 1942.

Lorinda Epply, Edward Timothy Hurley, Elizabeth Barrett Jensen, Jens Jensen, Margaret Helen McDonald, Wilhelmine Rhem, and Kataro Shirayamadani. Of these decorators, Rhem was the youngest at forty-four and the least experienced. Shirayamadani was the most experienced decorator and the oldest at seventy-eight. Rookwood was a company aging in more ways than one. And the prospect of infusing the company with fresh blood and new life in the midst of a world war was dim.

In March 1943 Rookwood introduced three new colors: wine madder, lagoon green, and aurora orange. Five months later, in August, the pottery unveiled a new decorative ware. Later named Designed Crystal because of its glass cover, the ware was described as

> . . . transparent, clear like spring water, a lambent and flowing glaze that has many ingratiating qualities. Its finest quality perhaps is its brilliance, for it glows like the brilliant skin of Chinese porcelain. With the new glaze has come a fine form of decoration that is more modern than anything Rookwood has yet brought forth. It is semiformalized in style with the glaze flowing at times over colored clay, with the decorative features cut out so the glaze over the body color gives it a beautiful cream white that glows like crystal. . . .[88]

From this description we can surmise that the Designed Crystal is covered with a transparent, colorless glaze, that the body is white possibly with a cream cast, and that the color is applied underglaze, either to the wet form or to the biscuit-fired form. It is unclear whether "colored clay" refers to slip painting or to an actual colored body. These considerations aside, we are left to determine how the Designed Crystal differed from the earlier Iris or the Jewel Porcelain. The Designed Crystal (sometimes called Crystal Glaze) seems to be little more than a variation upon earlier wares, and the decoration seems no more "modern" than some produced from the late 1910s through the 1930s.

When the war ended in 1945, Rookwood began to prepare for the future. John W. Milet, general manager of the pottery for Sperti, Inc., organized a "junior decorating department," with Lois Furukawa, who had been with Rookwood since 1942, in charge of ten to twelve young women.[89] Peck writes that "Those who demonstrated the requisite skills of slip decoration and painting on biscuit were promoted to full-fledged decorators."[90] Once disdained at Rookwood, painting on the biscuit ware had become more and more acceptable as the pottery succumbed to the exigencies of economics.

Despite efforts to revive artistic production after the Depression and World War II, it is evident that Rookwood had outlived its time. In 1948 Shirayamadani, then eighty-three, died from injuries sustained in a fall at the pottery. And that same year, Hurley painted a lovely Scenic Vellum vase with an autumnal landscape, perhaps as an elegy upon his time at Rookwood and on earth. Also in 1948 Rookwood discontinued its decorating department.

9. The decorating staff in 1943 at the Rookwood Pottery Company. Left to right: Loretta Holtcamp, Wilhelmine Rehm, Edward T. Hurley, Lorinda Epply, John D. Wareham, Kataro Shirayamadani, Margaret Helen McDonald, Jens Jensen, Elizabeth Barrett Jensen.

The decline and death of the Rookwood Pottery Company is sad only to the degree that we appreciate the happy inspiration of its birth and the extraordinary achievements of its high artistic eminence. The founding of Rookwood was a gamble—a glorious gamble that left a legacy of ceramics unparalleled in artistic and technical brilliance.

I am grateful to Anita J. Ellis, Curator of Decorative Arts at the Cincinnati Art Museum, for inviting me to write this introductory essay. Don F. Mahan kindly edited the manuscript. (Over the years I have learned to bow graciously to his pen.) Kim Cooper and Lisa L. Lock assisted with research. I am especially indebted to Kathy L. Borgogno who patiently reentered into the computer texts that I had "lost" in one way or another. M. Lee Fatherree and Linda Bailey, the Cincinnati Historical Society Library, and the New York Public Library all assisted with photography.

Glazing at the Rookwood Pottery Company.

EIGHT GLAZE LINES: THE HEART OF ROOKWOOD POTTERY

◆

Anita J. Ellis

Of the many glaze lines produced by The Rookwood Pottery Company[1] during its eighty-seven–year history, eight are of undisputable significance: Cameo, Dull Finish, Standard, Aerial Blue, Sea Green, Iris, Mat, and Vellum. These eight glaze lines gave Rookwood its identity and stature nationally as well as internationally, and together they composed the greatest part of the pottery's artistic output. Happily, we have sufficient documentation to support an informed discussion of these important lines.

Rookwood had more than five hundred glazes.[2] It is important to distinguish between a glaze and a glaze line. A glaze is the glassy skin, sometimes translucent, sometimes opaque, that covers a ceramic object.[3] A glaze line is defined not only by this skin, but also by the type of body and decoration used and a given parameter of dates for its use. For example, objects in the Cameo glaze line are covered with a clear, translucent glaze. Objects in the Aerial Blue glaze line are also covered with a clear, translucent glaze. Even though the glaze is perhaps the same, the two glaze lines are very different in dating, decoration, and possibly clay bodies. While glazes were important, it was the more broadly defined glaze line that gave the product its identity, and was used as the marketing device in advertising.

Noting that the clay body is an essential part of a Rookwood glaze line, a brief discussion of the bodies used is warranted. Rookwood's clay bodies are extremely difficult to define because they are very complex and do not fit neatly into such generally accepted categories as earthenware, stoneware, and porcelain. Today Rookwood is usually catalogued as earthenware, but more often than not, this is incorrect. In 1893, ceramic art historian Edwin Atlee Barber stated that "The chief body now in use [at Rookwood] partakes of some of the qualities of stoneware and some of the properties of semi-porcelain."[4] Barber received his information from William Watts Taylor, the illustrious manager and later president of The Rookwood Pottery Company. Even Taylor had problems resolving the question of Rookwood bodies:

> I have been much puzzled how to answer the questions about classification of Rookwood body. . . . The point has come up before and I could never settle it. . . . We have more than one body in use. One can be distinctly described as earthenware, but that is a very small part of our present production. Our chief body used to be a cross between White Granite and Cream Colored Ware, but this has been radically changed of late years. We have found by costly experiment that the point of complete or nearly complete vitrification [i.e. true porcelain] injures the colors but we go as near that as we dare. A piece of well-fired Rookwood biscuit will practically hold water without any glaze, but of course would absorb more or less of it. It partakes of some of the qualities of stoneware and some of those of porcelain—I am speaking of the body—but does not correspond with the formulas of either and still less with regular earthenware which it far surpasses in vitreous "ring." If you will excuse the simile I should say it was a semi-porcelain rather aristocratic young woman married into a solid high class, bourgeois stoneware family with Rookwood as the offspring! This is fanciful but hits pretty near the truth. I don't see how you can classify it under any of the ordinary heads.[5]

It is no wonder that Rookwood categorized its clay bodies by color, namely ginger, red, sage green, white, and yellow. At Rookwood it was important that the ceramic engineer know clay formulas, but for business purposes one needed only refer to clay colors. Bearing in mind that most Rookwood bodies range somewhere between stoneware and semi-porcelain, the distinctions made when describing a glaze line will be by color. This is the way Rookwood distinguished its bodies, and the only way to offer a popular understanding of a highly technical subject.

CAMEO, DULL FINISH, AND STANDARD GLAZE LINES

The earliest period at Rookwood—from 1880 to about 1884—was one of germination. Various glazes and clay bodies were used, and decorations were carved, printed, or painted underglaze. Gold was used profusely over the glaze. In the spring of 1883 William Watts Taylor was hired to be Rookwood's first business manager.[6] As a result, the pottery began to take on a distinctive style. For marketing purposes, Taylor organized the product into three glaze lines developed out of the 1880–84 period—Cameo, Dull Finish, and Standard.

The Cameo glaze line was first referred to as Ivory ware because of the color of the clay body. Taylor defined the body as "a sort of half china";[7] that is to say, not quite a porcelain. Most, if not all, of the pieces were slip cast or press molded and made for table use, such as plates, teacups, and saucers. By November 1887 meat sets, tea sets, and salad dishes had been added to the line.[8] Decoration was painted on the wet clay, biscuit fired and then covered with a colorless, translucent glaze for the final firing. It generally consisted of delicate white flowers over ground colors of pale blues, pinks, or browns, fading to white. Toward the end of the 1880s Rookwood was relying heavily on this product for financial stability. The Standard line was expensive to produce because of the high-loss ratio in firing, so Ivory ware, the useful ware as it was called to distinguish it from the ware variously called ornamental, decorative, or artistic, was pushed in the market. In a letter of October 24, 1887, William Watts Taylor wrote:

> We have by no means abandoned the rich tones in glazes [i.e., Standard ware], but are making less, as I write you, owing to the extreme risk of them. The gap is being filled with dull finish and the ivory ware, which later is much better adapted for table uses and suits our drift to more useful things.[9]

By the end of 1887, Taylor changed the name of Ivory ware to Cameo ware.[10] This was purely a marketing ploy "for the sake of a name, though often most inappropriate."[11] By February 1888 it was being advertised as "the new type of Rookwood ware."[12] Novel egg-shaped forms for holding bonbons and flowers were made for the Easter trade. Another form, a trembleuse cup and plate (fig. 1), was designed for invalid service and crowded receptions "as it can be held in one hand."[13] Unlike the artistic wares, Rookwood's useful ware was less susceptible to crazing or cracks. This is probably because it came so close to being true porcelain. Any piece that was found to be crazed could be returned to the pottery.[14]

By the late 1880s, there were two elements at work that signaled the end of the Cameo line: national and international recognition of Rookwood's artistic wares, and a demand for the Standard ware in lighter colors. At the Twelfth Annual Exhibition of Paintings on China held in London in 1887, the judges expressed their highest admi-

1. Cup and Plate, 1888, Anna Marie Valentien, decorator. An example of Rookwood's Cameo ware.

ration for artistic works from the Rookwood Pottery.[15] At the Pottery and Porcelain exhibition of the Pennsylvania Museum in Philadelphia held in November 1888, Rookwood was awarded first prize for "Pottery Modeled and Decorated" and "Painting Underglaze." In the following year at the Exhibition of the American Art Industry, also in Philadelphia, Rookwood received a "First Prize Gold Medal for Faience." But the greatest recognition achieved during this period came in the form of a Gold Medal award at the 1889 Exposition Universelle in Paris. All of these awards were granted for Rookwood's artistic wares, particularly the Standard ware. The Cameo ware, thought to be more useful than artistic, was never entered in these competitions.[16] With all of the recognition came greater sales of the Standard product and less dependence on Cameo ware to supplement income. To eliminate Cameo ware altogether in favor of the exclusive production of decorative wares was a dream taking shape at Rookwood. The heightened popularity of the Standard glaze line with its dark, rich tones prompted the buying public to

also request the same richness in lighter tints. Bowing to public taste, Rookwood looked to its lighter-tinted Cameo ware. However, though the colorless translucent glaze on the Cameo line was a good one, it did not exhibit the superior depth found in the refraction of the Standard line. Moreover, the colors used were pale. To achieve rich colors in the lighter range under a sumptuously refractive glaze was no easy matter. Nevertheless, Rookwood began experimenting in that direction.

In May 1889, Taylor wrote, "We might say, too, that our recent make of Cameo is richer in color. . . ."[17] By February 1890 he wrote that the Pottery had begun experimenting on decorative pieces in lighter colors, and presented the goal "to get at something as original in that way as our present effects [in the Standard ware] are in theirs," explaining that the "new trials are on that [Cameo] line but in far richer grounds and decoration. . . ."[18] A year later Rookwood's T. C. Van Houten wrote to the New York agent, ". . . [we] hope to show in a few months some new departures to startle you, and if they do not sell we had better quit on 'Cameo.'"[19] True to his word, late that May the "new departures" arrived in New York, "in this lot we wish to call your special attention to some new 'Cameo,' as you can see the treatment is entirely different to the old, and done in this way it will cost as much as in dark [i.e., Standard] glazes. . . ."[20] As the experiments continued in this line, more decorative and fewer useful objects were made. Different colored bodies, such as blue, were tried, and tints, such as green, were added from time to time to the increasingly refractive glaze. The ultimate result of all this experimentation came in 1894 with the announcement of three new glaze lines, namely Iris, Sea Green, and Aerial Blue. Useful ware was no longer necessary for financial stability, and the quality of the old Cameo had been so far surpassed that the line had evolved out of existence. What began in 1884 or 1885 came to a quiet end in 1892.[21] Between 1892 and 1894 experiments in the three new glaze lines continued until they were ready for the market.

The second of three glaze lines to emerge from Rookwood's earliest period was called Dull Finish (nos. 3, 5–9). Unlike Cameo, Dull Finish was suitable for the highest artistic achievement and thus considered decorative instead of useful. This time the name is descriptive, if not terribly appealing. The glaze used for this line is a smear glaze, a colorless, translucent glaze applied so thinly as to disappear. Often decorators incised an "S" on the bottom of such pieces as a signal to the glazer to use the smear glaze. Because the glass is not readily visible, objects covered by it, which are mostly thrown vases, are often erroneously referred to as unglazed. The appearance given is a dull finish, totally without gloss. Taylor wrote that the glaze "fills the exterior pores and is on the surface in a skin so thin as to give smoothness without lustre. It can be used and washed as well as any ware."[22] There were many who refused to believe that this line was glazed at all, and Taylor was quick to correct them:

> We have brought this process to such perfection that the result has puzzled others besides yourself, but if you were to see how decidedly some of our colors are modified in the glaze firing you would appreciate that the glazing is as thorough and complete by this as by our other method.[23]

The smear glaze was used for many of Rookwood's earliest products. It is seen on various bodies such as gray and red, but in the mature glaze line it is mostly on a yellow body. There are examples of Standard ware pieces (no. 6), and Iris ware pieces (no. 9), mistakenly in some instances and purposefully in others, being fired with a Dull Finish instead of the Standard or Iris glazes. Decoration is applied to the wet clay body, biscuit fired, and then glazed for the final firing. It is characteristically in the lighter tints of blues, whites, and pinks, although it can be in the darker colors used for Standard ware. Some of the finest natural flower (nos. 6, 8–9), fish (no. 5), and bird subjects ever produced by Rookwood can be seen in this line. Because of the nature of the smear glaze, there is extremely sharp definition to the decoration, which enhances the florid beauty. The Dull Finish carried on the earlier tradition of gold embellishment. More often than not, it accompanies the ornamentation in bands around the neck or base, and is always fired on over the glaze (no. 5). Because of the small-loss ratio in the glaze firing, this line produced more large vases of twenty inches or higher than any other. It had great sales appeal and by April 1887 it was the most popular style offered by Rookwood.[24]

Curiously, the Dull Finish was not Taylor's favorite glaze line and he often eschewed it. "We ourselves are much more proud of our [rich] glazed work than the dull finish,"[25] he said. "If you want very light tints we could give you something in the dull finish which is popular but not recommended by us. . . ."[26] His attitude was possibly related to the fact that the Dull Finish ware was often likened to England's Royal Worcester ware. Taylor was very sensitive about being accused of imitating other products, especially Worcester's. "We have not been copyists, but developed so far as we could an original style. We wish to emphasize this point because the little artistic ware made in this country so far (by factories) has been careful copies of the Royal Worcester and Belleek and we stand practically alone in working in lines essentially different."[27]

Another reason Taylor shunned the Dull Finish was because he thought the style had been carried to excess. "It is evident that your public is educated in the Worcester school of color and decoration and naturally take to the dull finish first, but we think that style has been overdone and though we still continue to make it we touch it cautiously."[28] At times he simply could not hide his contempt for the line: "We send a few more pieces [of Dull Finish] because we always find some people—not usually the most artistic—want it."[29] Prior to 1894, Dull Finish was Rookwood's only artistic offering in the lighter colors. Taylor knew of the developing success in turning the lighter-tinted Cameo line of useful wares into the three artistic lines of Iris, Sea Green, and Aerial Blue. He was eager to eliminate Dull Finish in favor of the promising three, thus squelching accusations of imitation once and for all. In September 1890 very little Dull Finish was being produced.[30] By 1891 it no longer seems to have been made as a serious profit line; Taylor writes, "We have no dull finish in stock. . . ."[31]

The third glaze line to evolve from Rookwood's earliest period of 1880–84 was called Standard ware, and it was by far the most celebrated. Not only did it give Rookwood national acclaim, it brought international fame as well. In fact, this glaze line became so synonymous with the Pottery that a record in the corporate minutes regarding the 1901 Pan-American Exposition in Buffalo points out that "probably ninety percent of the visitors did not know Rookwood in any but the Standard type. . . . "[32] Even today the popular concept of Rookwood Pottery rests with the Standard glaze line.

The name itself is telling. "Standard" suggests something regularly and widely used. At what date the name came into use is not known. Records suggest that Taylor rarely, if ever, used the "Standard" nomenclature. He generally referred to the line as "the rich glazed ware," or "the dark glazed ware."[33] Even in his detailed discussion of Rookwood Pottery for the September 1910 edition of *The Forensic Quarterly*, Taylor never used the "Standard" designation. Within the company's records the term is often used, though not necessarily as a proper noun. For example, one notation dated October 1887 discusses the base formula for the Standard glaze, suggesting that "the latter mix for Dark was adopted as the standard after successive trials. . . . "[34] And, in the corporate minutes for April 1895, Taylor offers one of his rare uses of the word when he submits, "they [the three new glaze lines] add freshness to the standard production. . . . "[35]

It was not until the corporate minutes of March 1902 that we see Taylor using the "Standard type" as a proper designation.[36] Published accounts do not seem to use the Standard appellation until about 1900. A flyer written in French, apparently used at the 1900 Paris Exposition, translates "Le Type Rookwood" as "Standard Rookwood."[37] In 1901, Rookwood decorator W. P. McDonald emphatically refers to "the Standard ware, as it is called."[38]

By 1902 the name is branded in history when Rookwood publishes a booklet in which "Standard" is designated as one of the varieties of Rookwood.[39] And so, when coined, the term referred to an already well-established glaze line. Because the "rich glazed ware" took time to become the standard product, such a name could only have come later in the line's history.

The Standard line (nos. 11–25) exhibits figural and floral underglaze slip decorations on various ground colors in the darker tones of yellow, brown, and green. One color often gently fades into another on a given piece. All decoration is applied to the wet clay, fired, glazed, and fired again. Today, depending on the predominant ground color, an example might be referred to as Yellow Standard (or Golden Standard), Brown Standard, or Green Standard. The Green Standard seems to be the least abundant

of the three. Pieces dating between 1899 and 1903 (nos. 19–21, 24) might incorporate electro-deposited metal mounts.[40] Also, pieces dated 1892–93 sometimes display a silver overlay by the Gorham Manufacturing Company of Providence, Rhode Island. Later objects dating roughly between 1900 and 1904 display an open silver overlay, but these are not by Gorham, and, unlike the 1892–93 examples, there is no indication in the corporate minutes that these were commissioned by Rookwood.

Articles in the Standard glaze line generally consist of thrown vases and ewers. Some, but not many, are slip cast. All are covered with a yellow-tinted, translucent glaze. Sometimes the tint is dark yellow and sometimes light yellow. Often there is a "DY" or "D", or an "LY" or "L" incised by the decorator on the bottom of a piece as a signal to the glazer indicating which one to use. A yellow-tinted glaze was first used in 1883.[41] The first slip-decorated piece in this glaze is thought by Taylor to date 1884.[42] The clay body is generally yellow, but ginger, sage green, white, and red can also be seen. Very rare examples exist with an experimental, artificially-colored dark green body. When the Standard glaze is on a red body it is called Mahogany (no. 22). The Mahogany line, as a subdivision of the Standard line, offers rich, warm red tones in its ground colors, so that whenever red is mentioned in the Standard line, it is a reference to Mahagony. Mahagony examples can be cast, but are generally thrown.

The Standard glaze line was much more expensive to produce than Cameo or Dull Finish. The difficulties of creating work in the rich colors with a fair degree of perfection were great. A certain proportion of the product came out darker than intended.[43] Others exhibited pinholes, crazing, cratering, peeling, or blistering. Nevertheless, it was the line with the greatest artistic merit and so Rookwood persisted in resolving the technical problems.

TIGER EYE

In October 1884 several pieces of Mahogany exhibited unexpected effects in the glaze.[44] The yellow-tinted, translucent glass displayed a crystalline structure that produced a gold, shimmering sheen, almost as if a sheet of gold foil were deep within. This uniqueness was not lost to Taylor, who immediately dubbed this new mistake "Tiger Eye" after the stone it resembled. Rookwood constantly tried to repeat this effect at will, but even as late as 1936, it could not.[45] The best that the Pottery could do was repeat the conditions under which the accident happened. Even then it was hit or miss. Taylor bemoaned, "We prepare for it but cannot count upon one piece in a hundred."[46] Moreover, the successful pieces were wideranging in quality. With some, the chatoyant Tiger Eye

2. The decorating department of the Rookwood Pottery Company in 1892 when it opened in its new building in Mt. Adams.

was barely visible, whereas with others the shimmer was radiant. Unfortunately, radiant examples were extremely rare. The exquisitely fine showpiece sent to the 1889 Paris Exposition was the only one of such quality to emerge in a four-year period.[47]

GOLDSTONE

"Goldstone" (nos. 22–23) is a second serendipitous effect that occurred on Mahogany examples in 1884, again named after the stone it resembles. Millions of little gold flecks seem captured deep within the glaze. As with Tiger Eye, Goldstone could not be produced at will and had a high-loss ratio. When not successful, it was practically unsalable.[48]

Whereas Tiger Eye shimmers, Goldstone glitters. There is often confusion whether a piece represents Tiger Eye or Goldstone because usually both effects occur and mingle in the same piece. This is also the reason Tiger Eye and Goldstone are almost always mentioned in the same breath. Taylor writes as if one evolves into the other during firing, "The red ware you refer to is what we call 'Goldstone' which passes in a few of the finest examples

into 'Tiger Eye.'"[49] Only the best pieces of both were offered for sale. Because of this, and because of the high loss ratio, as well as the fact that they were unique to Rookwood, the cost of these pieces was usually three to four times greater than the cost of a comparable specimen in Mahogany or Standard.[50] Since it was important to minimize risk, and since larger objects offer greater risks in firing, most of the Tiger Eye and Goldstone pieces are usually small, perhaps five or six inches high. Some can be found on a white body instead of the red, but these are rare. Early decorations were in underglaze slip reflecting the Standard output. These decorations usually ran in the firing, and in later examples, decorations, often of fishes, appear to be simply incised with no slip used. Sometimes the glaze itself is the only decoration. The luminous golden quality of Tiger Eye and the limpid glistening quality of Goldstone sent Rookwood to new heights of achievement within the world of ceramics. No other pottery was able to duplicate it, which comes as no surprise since even Rookwood had problems producing it at will.

Stanley Gano Burt, a chemist and later superintendent at Rookwood, mentions "false Goldstone," which he describes as the result of an overly pure color, usually red, that peels in the biscuit stage and then is glazed, creating unintentional white sparkles.[51] This is found on Standard pieces, generally Mahogany. The sparkles are not as small or as multitudinous as Goldstone, nor do they resemble gold flecks. False Goldstone is simply a firing flaw, not a glaze line. Later glaze lines produced in the 1920s, called Coromandel and Aventurine, also have sparkling effects but are not Goldstone. The easiest way to distinguish these is by date. Anything later than 1909 is not Goldstone. The same is true for a yellow or green Tiger Eye, also produced in the 1920s.[52] While it bears a resemblance to the original, it is not the same glaze line.

The Standard line, which includes Yellow, Green, and Brown Standard, Mahogany, Tiger Eye and Goldstone, was always considered the most artistic of the three early glaze lines. Because of its exceptional merit, it was the product the pottery emphasized in national and international competitions. From 1887 to 1893, Standard ware, especially Tiger Eye, and Goldstone, received numerous first prizes and gold medals in national and international arenas. Taylor noted that "when shown at Paris in 1889 it roused a ceramic world which had been practically asleep for many decades. It was echoed in imitations all over the world, especially after the Chicago Exposition in 1893,

when its fuller development had been shown."[53]

By 1900 Standard ware was giving way to the lighter tints and mat glazes. It was beginning to look old-fashioned after sixteen years. Pieces were still being made, but in greatly reduced quantities. The line is rarely seen after 1905, though Burt records a piece as late as 1909.[54] (In the 1920s Rookwood produced vases that mimicked the Standard style with floral decorations on a brown to yellow ground, all covered with a yellow-tinted glaze. Just as was often done on the older ware, decorators incised "LY" on the bottom of the later pieces to designate a light yellow glaze. The body used for the 1920s examples was a soft porcelain demanding a higher fire than the former white body, and the glass was not as refractive as the true Standard glaze.) What began in 1884 had spent its course after twenty-five years. But it was a glorious twenty-five years that had established Rookwood as the superior art pottery of the United States and ranked it among the finest potteries in the world.

AERIAL BLUE, SEA GREEN, AND IRIS

As noted in the discussion of Cameo ware, by February 1890 Rookwood was busy experimenting in lighter-col-

3. The decorating staff in 1889 at the Rookwood Pottery Company at its first location on Eastern Avenue. Standing, left to right: Matt Daly, Albert Valentien, Anna Valentien, Emma Foertmeyer, Artus Van Briggle, Amelia B. Sprague. Sitting, left to right: Grace Young, Harriet E. Wilcox, Sallie Toohey, Carrie Steinle, Louella Perkins, Mary Shannahan (in charge of the sales room).

ored artistic products. As a result, during the three-month period ending January 31, 1895, three new styles of ware, namely Aerial Blue, Sea Green, and Iris, were officially introduced to the public.[55] The shortest lived of the three was Aerial Blue. In 1894 the first piece of Aerial Blue produced incorporated a blue-colored clay body.[56] Later, the line also used a white body (no. 30). The objects mostly consisted of vases, creamers, and plaques that were thrown, slip cast, or press molded. In an undated circular, probably from 1895, Rookwood describes Aerial Blue as "a delicate mono-chromatic ware with a quiet decoration in celestial blue on a cool, grayish white ground."[57] It is indeed monochromatic, but the ground color is mostly a pale blue with delicate floral decorations picked out in white. Also common to the decorations are cows, wolves, ships, farms, Dutch scenes, and landscapes. The decorations were applied to the wet clay, fired, and then glazed before the final firing. The glass is always glossy, colorless, and translucent.

The inspiration for this glaze line was perhaps Royal Copenhagen. By 1892 the Royal Danish firm was taking the market by storm with a porcelain ware decorated with natural flora and fauna on a pale blue ground. Indeed, over the next ten years Rookwood was most often likened to Royal Copenhagen. For example, an article in *The House Beautiful* of September 1898 states, "The Royal Danish porcelain, made at Copenhagen, is the only Occidental product which can be at all compared with Rookwood in its management of high light colors."[58] And *Keramic Studio* November 1901 points out a contrast: "Rookwood achieves its results with faience while Copenhagen relies on the natural texture of porcelain. . . ."[59] We know that Philip Schou, director of Royal Copenhagen, visited Rookwood in 1888 and purchased several pieces.[60] In 1892, Rookwood returned the compliment by purchasing a Royal Copenhagen plaque for its corporate collection.[61] Keenly aware of Royal Copenhagen, Taylor wrote to Edwin Atlee Barber urging, "Don't fail to look at the Copenhagen ware when you are next in New York."[62] That Royal Copenhagen had any direct or indirect influence on Rookwood's Aerial Blue line is only speculation, but the coincidental similarity is hard to dismiss.

Aerial Blue is probably the shortest-lived glaze line in Rookwood's repertory. The corporate minutes for the fiscal year ending January 31, 1895, note the three new glaze lines of Iris, Sea Green, and Aerial Blue, and then curiously state, "The commercial success of some of these seems quite certain from the reports of dealers. . . ."[63] The fact that Iris and Sea Green went on to become successful, whereas Aerial Blue did not, suggests that the failure indicated in this remark was Aerial Blue. Looking at examples of Aerial Blue, it becomes obvious that Rookwood was never able to perfect the line. The monochromatic colors are often uneven, and the painting appears heavy and unfinished compared to the other lines. In the Receipt Book, which describes different clays used, a May 1895 notation comments that in the Aerial Blue line, "thrown pieces develop darker color than cast—partly perhaps because longer kept as well as more dense."[64] This problem, which was never resolved, appears to hold true. Thrown examples are generally much darker than the cast ones. If Aerial Blue appeared unrefined compared with Rookwood's other lines, it appeared downright crude next to the soft blue, delicate decorations of Royal Copenhagen. Unable to be controlled, and unable to compete in the market, the Aerial Blue line was discontinued soon after it began. Only two years, 1894 and 1895, are impressed on the pieces, and today it is a relatively rare commodity.

The second most accomplished of the three glaze lines that were introduced in 1894 was Sea Green (nos. 26–29). Testing of the glaze was first successful in 1893.[65] It proved to be a rich, green-tinted, translucent, high-gloss glaze. The earliest example from the Sea Green line was a vase produced in the fall of 1894.[66] Underglaze slip decorations compatible with the green tint of the glaze were utilized. Generally, this meant marine life including fishes and water fowl that could be painted in slips of greens, blues, or whites. The decoration was applied to the wet clay, biscuit fired, and then glazed for the final firing. The color as well as the subject matter made the name descriptive and appropriate. Sea Green examples with floral decorations do occur, but they tend to be rare. Between the years 1899 and 1903, pieces can be found with metal mounts. The most common body of this glaze line is white, however, blue, and, to a much lesser extent, an experimental green can also be found. The objects, mostly vases, are thrown or cast. Rookwood described the glaze line as an "opalescent sea green relieved by a few flowing warm touches, to a cooler green with bluish accents."[67]

As with all the richly glazed lines, which in our discussion includes Standard, Aerial Blue, Sea Green, and Iris, Sea Green had its share of technical problems. Sometimes the tin in the glaze would affect the copper in the clay and turn a painted decoration shell pink.[68] At other times pieces in the line could exhibit peeling, pinholes, cratering, blistering, or crazing. Peeling, pinholes, cratering, and blistering are definitely defects. Crazing is another story. A piece is said to be crazed when fine cracks appear in the glaze but do not penetrate the body. If the body is underfired, the crazing may not appear at once, but worsens with age. Burt often makes comments such as "could be heard crazing when examined," or, "This pc [piece] tho 30 yrs old shows no crz [crazing]."[69] If a body is overfired, the crazing stops shortly after taken from the kiln. Crazing, caused by expansion disagreement between the body and the glaze, was a major problem in art pottery throughout the world, including all of Rookwood's richly glazed wares. Taylor's letters are replete with its defense: "In regard to the crazing we count it as nothing . . . as no Pottery in the world can prevent it and obtain such colors," and, somewhat more emphatically, "The slight 'cracking' on the glaze you speak of is no defect. . . ."[70] In one letter he even goes so far to say that crazing "frequently adds to their beauty."[71] As for price, he insisted, "We do not regard 'crazing' on our richer colored ware as detracting from price. . . ."[72]

While in his public posture he negated the problem, behind the scenes at the pottery he was always striving to eliminate it. In the corporate minutes for the year ending January 31, 1898, he rejoices in the fact that "there seems a prospect of ultimately producing a non-crazing ware."[73] This still took many years to occur as technology eventually caught up with desire. Unfortunately, it was not in time to eliminate the problem in the richly glazed lines, including Sea Green. Today, the buying public still considers crazing a defect, so that non-crazed pieces are generally more expensive.

It is difficult to determine when the Sea Green glaze line came to an end. Burt does not list it beyond 1904.[74] The St. Louis Exposition for that year heightened the vogue for Arts and Crafts mat glazes. There was no longer the demand for the shiny Sea Green, which had begun fading into history after the 1900 Paris Exposition. The green glaze, with its limiting subject matter and color range, simply could not hold its popularity very long. What began in 1894 seems to have only lasted a decade.

The Iris glaze line (nos. 31–45) was the most celebrated of the three lines to make their debut in 1894. Not only was it the finest of the three, but one of the finest ever produced at The Rookwood Pottery Company. This glaze line evolved directly from the Cameo ware. Burt describes an 1889 pitcher that incorporated a white clay body, a clear glaze, and a blue blown decoration as "a forerunner of Iris."[75] He refers to an 1890 vase as a "very fair early sample of Iris—viz. same as Cameo but not the pink ground and clay completely covered [with ground color]."[76]

And so, the initial suggestion of Iris can be seen as early as 1889, and it was clearly developing into its full identity in the early 1890s. Burt lists genuine Iris examples for 1893.[77] The fact that Taylor notes its debut in the fall of 1894 suggests that this is when it was finally given a name.[78] The name itself is derived from the Iris plant, which was a common motif used for the line. The petals of the Iris flower and the glaze were thought to evince a similar delicate luminosity and opalescence.[79]

The Iris glaze line is noted for a white body, but there are also some with blue-gray or green bodies. The clay can be thrown or cast, and vases constitute most examples. The glass used is an incredibly limpid, highly refractive, colorless, translucent one. At Rookwood it was referred to as the "white glaze," and pieces can be found where the decorator has incised a "W" on the bottom to indicate the Iris glaze to the glazer.[80] Decoration in this line offers a considerably wider range of colors than the Sea Green. Pinks, blues, purples, greens, creamy whites, yellows, grays, blacks, and browns can all be seen in the Iris line. Generally the ground color fades almost imperceptibly from a dark to a light color. The subject matter consists mostly of flowers (nos. 31–32, 34–36, 39–40, 43, 45), but birds (nos. 38, 41–42) and fishes (no. 33) are also common. Somewhat rarer are pieces displaying figures, mushrooms (no. 37), frogs, etc. Decorator William P. McDonald offers a good description: "The decorations, whether of flowers, fish, birds, or whatnot are simply drawn and sparingly used, giving a feeling of rest and satisfaction. . . ."[81] Iris examples from the years 1899 through 1903 can also be found with Rookwood's metal mounts (no. 41).

The Iris line was renowned for the brilliance and clarity of its glaze and the delicacy of its decoration. The ware competed most successfully in the international arena that included Sèvres, Meissen, and Royal Copenhagen, among others. Its greatest triumph came at the 1900 Exposition Universelle in Paris, where it received international acclaim. Taylor modestly wrote that "upon the whole the Iris type was most favorably regarded."[82] And indeed it was. With the Iris glaze line in the competition, Rookwood was awarded the Grand Prix at the Paris Exposition.[83] Moreover, decorator Albert Robert Valentien received a first-place gold medal, and ceramic engineer Stanley Gano Burt received a second-place silver medal (the highest award that someone from the non-artistic section of the industry could receive). And if that were not enough, Taylor was decorated as Chevalier of the Legion of Honor by French President Emile-François Loubet. Commenting more openly, Taylor wrote, "We have thus received at the greatest Exposition ever held the utmost honors which it could confer and it is no exaggeration to speak of Rookwood as being now classed among those potteries which hold the highest rank in the world."[84]

There are several subdivisions in the Iris line, namely Relief Iris, Dark Iris, and Black Iris. The Relief Iris exhibits pale ground colors with floral decorations modeled in relief.[85] The only known specimens are vases by M. A. Daly dating to or around 1900, and the only published record of this subdivision is in 1901 by McDonald who referred to it as "Iris. Relief Style."[86] McDonald also gives us the only reference to Dark Iris, stating that it "is similar in general treatment [to the regular Iris] but the colors are much darker, the ground sometimes . . . a rich luminous black."[87] The darker colors he refers to are probably black, brown, and deep blue. For example, a Dark Iris vase might have ground colors shading from black to brown. The Dark Iris is so rare that generalizations are difficult to make, but known pieces date from around the turn of the century and are all vases. The "rich luminous black" to which Burt refers is without question what has come to be known as Black Iris (nos. 40–45). While it may have been considered Dark Iris in 1901 when McDonald was writing about it, by 1916 Black Iris was a subdivision all its own. It is the Iris glaze line with a rich black ground. The earliest recorded date for a Black Iris example is listed by Burt for an 1895 cup. He describes it as "wh. [white] clay iris gl [glaze] and color trial blk [black] underglaze."[88] From this it is at least known that in 1895, Rookwood was experimenting with the black color, which, in actuality, is a thick application of cobalt. Whether the cup had a solid black ground or one that faded to a lighter shade is not known. If it were solid, then it was a Black Iris example. The only other written record also comes to us from Burt's 1916 inventory. He lists fifteen Black Iris examples.[89] For a vase from 1900, he gives us the only recorded definition of Black Iris, namely, "clear gl [glaze] and black ground."[90] Currently the dates of the known Black Iris examples range between 1899 and 1912, with most dating around 1900, when high-gloss, floral decorations on black grounds were in vogue for the Paris Exposition.[91] Of the fifteen listed by Burt, nine are dated 1900. Virtually all Black Iris specimens are vases. One is known to be modeled (no. 44), and another to be metal mounted (no. 41). The beauty and rarity of the subdivisions known as Dark Iris and Black Iris make them among the most highly prized of Rookwood's products.

Like the Standard, Aerial Blue, and Sea Green lines, Iris had its fair share of technical problems including peeling, pinholes, cratering, blistering, and especially crazing. Burt rarely notes an Iris example without also noting whether or not it is crazed, and if so, how badly. Crazing could greatly diminish the lyrical compositions of the Iris ware, and so was always a noteworthy matter. Curiously, the one thing that contributes most to the beauty of Iris is also what was often regarded as its primary weakness, the highly refractive quality of the glaze. Even in the experimental stage in 1890 it drew disapproval. Typically, Taylor was quick to respond: "In regard to your artist friend's criticism of the high polish we can appreciate what he means, but we could not produce Rookwood and please

him. The ware like everything else has the defects of its qualities and the quality depends in great measure upon the high refractive character of the glaze."[92] The same criticism is echoed later at the 1900 Paris Exposition when Alexandre Sandier likens the glass to polished agate and states that it is "too brilliant."[93] His statement is repeated by Maurice Pillard Verneuil at the 1902 Turin Exposition, "the material is too brilliant and presents an unpleasant glossy aspect."[94]

This criticism could only have worsened as the mat glazes of the Arts and Crafts period soon took the market by storm. If the Iris glaze was too shiny in 1902, by 1912, when mats had been in vogue for at least a decade, it must have looked absolutely anachronistic. The last listing Burt records for an Iris example is for 1912.[95] Although it is impossible to determine with certainty, the Iris glaze line probably ended around this date.

Another factor contributing to the quiet disappearance of the Iris glaze line had nothing to do with fashion. It was the lead content in the glaze. Of all of Rookwood's lines, Iris was the most refractive, suggesting a very high lead content. By 1912, the risk of lead poisoning in the workplace was an international issue. At the International Exposition of Safety and Sanitation held that year in the New Grand Central Palace, New York, models showing the symptoms and effects of lead poisoning caused by inhalation formed part of the display of occupational diseases.[96] Included was an exhibition of English pottery produced without any form of lead. No serious study of the recognition of health hazards in the pottery industry or how the ensuing regulations affected the look of the products has ever been addressed. It is hard to believe that the push to eliminate lead and the concurrent disappearance of the highly-leaded Iris glaze line were coincidental. Whatever the case, the Iris glaze line had a long history, lasting for about twenty years, from 1893 to around 1912. During this time it competed successfully with the finest of its kind in the world. The Iris glaze line, including Relief Iris, Dark Iris, and Black Iris, can easily be considered one of Rookwood's great contributions to ceramic history.

MAT GLAZES

In 1896 Rookwood began experimenting with mat glazes.[97] Unfortunately, research into Rookwood's mats tends to pose more questions than it resolves. Nomenclature, as we have seen, was never an exact science at Rookwood. In the mat category some of the nomenclatural confusion at first appears virtually impossible to untangle. Published records refer to the categories of Incised Mat, Painted Mat, Conventional Mat, Modeled Mat, and Vellum.[98] Burt, writing after the publication of these names refers to "Incised Matt," "painted matt," "Modeled matt," and "Vellum."[99] Those match up easily enough with published records. However, he never refers to the Conventional Mat by name and makes reference to additional types such as "inlaid matt," "colored matt inlay," "inlay matt painted," "painted matt inlay," "Decorated Matt," "Plain matt," and "transmutation matt."[100] This trail of terms poses many questions. Is there a distinction between "painted mat" and "inlaid mat"? What is meant by Decorated Mat? And, where is the Conventional Mat in all of this? Let us begin with what is known and then tread cautiously into the quagmire of the undetermined.

As was noted, Rookwood began working in mat glazes as early as 1896, "largely with a view to its use for decorative tile."[101] However, late in 1900 the first mat-glazed holloware production of note came off the line.[102] It consisted of objects, usually vases, in either solid or variegated colors. The variegated look was caused by transmutation mat. A transmutation mat, even though a single glaze, affects many different colors in a given piece.[103] Of the solid and transmutation pieces, a proportion had incised designs done by the clayworkers under the supervision of decorator William P. McDonald. The incised decorations were taken mainly from Native-American designs.

Credit for the creation of the mat glazes was given to Stanley Gano Burt, who was the superintendent at Rookwood by 1900.[104] Decorator Albert Valentien, however, remarked that it was Artus Van Briggle who was the first to introduce mats to the pottery.[105] This is probably true. The earliest examples of mat glazed objects in Burt's inventory are dated 1896, and these are by Artus Van Briggle.[106] As Herbert Peck notes, Van Briggle left in 1899 for health reasons after he had spent almost three years of study in Paris at Rookwood's expense. He then moved to Colorado Springs, Colorado, where he started his own pottery. Rookwood probably resented this and thus did not give him credit for the mat glazes.

The clay body used throughout the Mat glaze line is a faience body that is very light buff to white in color and somewhat more granular, or coarse, than that used in the other lines. Burt mentions use of a yellow clay, but this seems a rare occurrence.[107] Pieces can be thrown or cast.

Unlike all the other lines, there is no decoration under the glaze in the Mat line; the glaze is the decoration. Mat glazes are opaque and do not allow for the necessary translucency to see a painted decoration underneath. Also, unlike the other glaze lines, the decoration (which is the glaze) is applied very thickly to the biscuit ware.[108] It is not applied to the unfired clay body. Because they are virtually non-refractive, mats produce a soft, lusterless ap-

pearance. The colors are wide-ranging and include reds, pinks, yellows, blues, greens, whites, blacks and browns, among others. Pieces made before January 31, 1903, might incorporate electro-deposited metal mounts.

It is impossible to distinguish a terminus date for the Plain, Transmutation and Incised Mats (no. 46). Because these products never passed though the decorating department (and are therefore unsigned by artists), they were cheaper and faster to produce. This made their continued existence favorable. The incised decorations after Native-American designs were probably discontinued sometime before 1915 when the vogue for all things Indian faded. The other products most likely evolved into Rookwood's line of commercial ware that continued throughout the life of the company.

Besides incised decorations, the Mat glaze line offers ornamentation modeled in low relief (nos. 56–58) and high relief (nos. 54–55). Motifs include human figures (nos. 54–55), dragons, reptiles, and flowers (nos. 56, 58). The first modeled pieces in Burt's listing were done in 1898 by Artus Van Briggle.[109] Many of the so-called Modeled Mats were mounted at Rookwood as "lamps or electroliers."[110] Unique pieces hand modeled by decorators are seldom seen beyond 1905. Many of these pieces were used to make molds and so are also seen as cast pieces, barely distinguishable from the hand-modeled examples. Modeled Mat pieces where the decoration is cast continued throughout the remaining history of Rookwood.

Plain and Transmutation Mats with their use of color, as well as Incised and Modeled Mats with their use of plastic embellishments, tend to be fairly uncomplicated categories. The categories of Conventional Mat, Decorated Mat, Painted Mat, and Painted Mat Inlay, however, invite pause. Important to the discussion of these mats is the fact that one of the biggest technical problems Rookwood had with the Mat glaze line was crawling.

The glass had a tendency to flow downward in the firing, causing any painted decorations to distort and run together. Burt's inventory for mats is replete with the notation for crawling.[111] Today it is not difficult to find a mat piece with this problem. For example, many have ground bottoms. The pottery often ground away any flow that pooled at the base of an object. Grinding, of course, did not help with painted decorations such as floral depictions. Because of crawling, such compositions often melted together in an undistinguished mess. Rookwood had to devise a solution to the problem of crawling as it affected its mat painted decorations. It devised several, some more effective than others.

The first for discussion is Conventional Mat (nos. 47–48), which displays conventional, or stylized, decorations in flat colors outlined in black. The compositions are

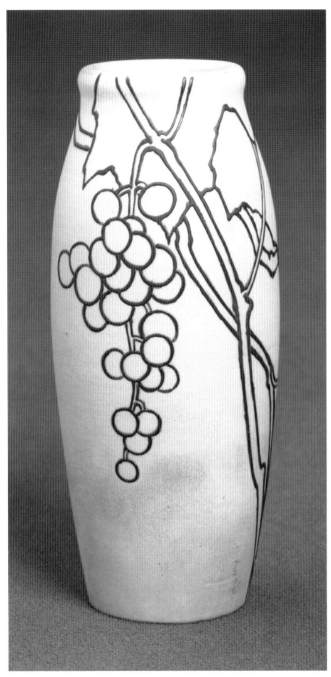

4. Vase, 1900, Albert Valentien, decorator. Conventional Mat example after biscuit firing.

trailed, or line-drawn, with a pastry-squeeze type of utensil, onto the wet clay, which was then biscuit fired. After the firing, decorator Albert Valentien intended to fill in the cloisonné-like spaces with mat glaze colors. Had this happened and had it been glaze fired, the vase would have been an example of Conventional Mat.

Rookwood said that the Conventional type of Mat reflected an "important movement in modern art."[112] Perhaps this is a reference to the Arts and Crafts movement. However, Conventional Mat more clearly reflects the end-of-the-century rage for the poster style spawned by line drawings made famous by the printing and publishing industries.

Burt never uses the prescribed term "Conventional Mat." Instead he uses "inlay matt" (sometimes "inlaid matt" or "matt inlay"), retaining a technical reference to the fact that the mat glaze was inlaid between the black cordons of the trailed slip. Burt's terminology no doubt predates the official name of the subdivision, which was published for the first time in the 1904 mail-order catalogue. His earliest listed example is in 1900, with others listed as late as 1916.[113] However, most examples, primarily vases, date between 1901 and 1905.

Painted Mat (nos. 49–53) is probably the rarest type of the Mat glaze line and also the most enigmatic. By all accounts it was a very difficult technique to master and required a great deal of time to produce. Rookwood defined it as "a process of the greatest difficulty, suggestive of flowing enamels, but with mat texture."[114] The first piece to represent this subdivision was decorated by Albert Valentien in 1900 according to Burt, who writes, "first pc [piece] of painted matt—dec [decoration] inlaid—slt [slight] crawl of gl [glaze]."[115] With this account, Burt defined Painted Mat as an inlaid decoration. The only surviving technical description of the process was provided in 1936 by H. F. Bopp: ". . . a tedious process of glazing the wet clay piece, then cutting the design through to the clay, and inlaying a glaze of another color."[116]

There are, however, problems with this definition, the first being the reference to the glazing on the wet clay. Taylor states that "the painting [in the Mat glaze line] is done on the biscuit pieces. . ."[117] Also, decorator signatures on these pieces are always painted, not incised, indicating that these vases were decorated in the biscuit state. The rest of the definition is considerably more cogent. Cutting a design into a ground color of glaze and removing the positive space to inlay another glaze color accords with what is known. Burt did define Painted Mat as an inlay technique. Moreover, the cutting out of a decoration could only be done to a layer of ground color that has been dried. Looking carefully at Painted Mat specimens ridges or shorelines, can be seen where the inlay meets

often of flowers or fruits. The black outline is meant to keep the colors from running together. A vase (fig. 4) in the collection of the Cincinnati Art Museum provides information about the technique used for Conventional Mat. The vase, which is dated 1900, is an unfinished piece in the biscuit state. On the bottom is an impressed "Z" designating that it was to be mat glazed before the final firing. On the body is a heavy black outline of a grapevine. The outline of the decoration had been slip-the ground color, suggesting that a wet glaze was in contact with a dry glaze. Currently this is as much as can be determined about the Painted Mat glaze process. If nothing else, we can safely assume that it is an inlay technique devised to keep ground colors from mixing with the decorations. Most of the decorations in this subdivision tend to be floral (nos. 49–53), but fishes were also used. All known examples are vases dating from the first five years of this century.

If Burt's references to "painted matt" are in fact Painted Mat, and if his references to "inlay matt" are in fact Conventional Mat, what does he mean by "painted matt inlay"? He offers no clear definition for what sounds like a hybridization of "painted matt" and "inlay matt," or Painted Mat and Conventional Mat. Does a crossbreed of Painted Mat and Conventional Mat exist that could shed light on this seemingly confusing mix of terms? A vase (no. 53) in the Cincinnati Art Museum exhibits both Conventional Mat and Painted Mat techniques. That is to say, in this vase the floral mat decoration of hanging wisteria displays the painted technique and is outlined, or separated, from the ground color, with the black slip-trailing of Conventional Mats. Both techniques are in one piece, making it an example of Burt's "painted mat inlay." It is an esoteric subdivision for which Rookwood's chemist inventories only seven examples dating from 1900 to 1905.[118] Of these seven, six are ascribed to decorators: one to Albert Valentien, one to Sara Alice Toohey, one to Amelia Browne Sprague, and three to Harriet E. Wilcox. Wilcox seems to have been more inclined than others to utilize the Painted Mat Inlay technique. Cincinnati's specimen is also by Wilcox from 1906. Combining the technical processes of Painted Mat with those of Conventional Mat must have been complex, and it is not fully understood today. Probably the most time consuming of all mat techniques, Painted Mat Inlay, ran its course in some six years of very limited production.

One final question raised by Burt's inventory is what is meant by a "Decorated Matt"? Burt always transcribes this type as a proper noun though it does not seem to have been published as a distinct category by the pottery. Once again, H. F. Bopp offers us the only definition for Decorated Mat (nos. 57–59).[119] With this technique the ground color was airbrushed onto the biscuit piece and dried, and then it seems (for the definition becomes more oblique) a decoration in mat glazes was then applied over the ground and all was fired.

One clue to help pinpoint this type is the fact that a number of the examples listed in Burt's inventory are by Charles Todd.[120] Anyone familiar with Todd's work can call to mind endless examples of mingled glaze colors hopelessly crawling over molded or thrown forms. (In all

fairness to Todd, examples by him do exist that are not flawed [no. 57].) As he worked almost exclusively in this same technique, it is assumed that it is indeed Burt's "Decorated Matt." There are two additional clues. Visually, the type of work employed by Todd does not have the same look as the Painted Mats. The compositional precision does not appear. Decorated Mats tend to be nothing more than highlights of color that emphasize a relief decoration either carved or molded on the body. It is obviously not an inlay technique as the glaze colors run into each other's boundaries. Decorated Mats are often reserved for cast pieces such as soapboxes, fern dishes, mugs, candlesticks, and bowls. Indeed, this is generally the type of object listed by Burt as Decorated Mat examples, and in his inventory they range in date from 1905 to 1915.[121] There may be some that date later, but probably not later than the mid-1920s.

The final mat that Rookwood touted is called Ombroso, an Italian word meaning cloudy, a strange choice of name. Ombroso is a transmutation mat that made its official debut in 1910, even though Burt lists the first pieces in 1909.[122] Its formal introduction marked Rookwood's thirtieth anniversary year. Decorations, if any, are in relief or incised. Burt mentions Decorated Mats in the Ombroso category, (no. 59).[123] Colors range from pinks, reds, yellows, and greens to blues, grays, blacks, and browns.[124] Most objects in this subdivision are vases, either cast or thrown. Traditionally, this has been a difficult type to spot since there are no color illustrations to offer examples, and written descriptions tend to be vague. For example, Bopp describes it as:

> A crystalline mat in quiet tones of gray and brown with occasional accents of other colors. . . . Often crystals large enough to be easily seen would separate out and being of different chemical composition than the remaining glaze would be a different color, giving the impression that two or more glazes of different colors were used.[125]

The problem with the identification of Ombroso is its wide range of colors. The best way to identify a piece is to look for two things. First, decide if the glaze is a plain or transmutation mat. A plain mat offers a flat, solid color. A transmutation mat, however, will have a mottled effect and will probably exhibit more than one mottled color. Second, determine if the date is 1909 or later. If an object is a transmutation mat and is dated 1909 or later, it is almost certainly an example of Ombroso. Like the other mats, it is difficult to determine the longevity of Ombroso. It probably continued into the 1920s.

Rookwood's mat glaze line, which includes plain, transmutation, Incised, Modeled, Conventional, Painted,

Painted Mat Inlay, Decorated, and Ombroso types, had its greatest artistic flowering during the first fifteen years of the twentieth century. No other pottery in the world offered a wider variety of mat glazed products. It is an area of Rookwood not fully appreciated today because, unlike Rookwood's other glaze lines, serious competition for the mats came mostly from American potteries. Consequently, Rookwood's product was, and is today, viewed in the home country more as one among many rather than uniquely exemplary. In spite of this, Rookwood's mat glaze line ranks among the best and its technical quality and aesthetic beauty should not be overlooked.

VELLUM

Rookwood's official publications of 1904 and after always include Vellum as part of the mat glaze line. While it is a valid assessment, Vellum is so radical a departure from the other mats that in order to understand it it is necessary to approach it as a separate category. The distinction is that, unlike the other mats, Vellum is translucent. The creation of something so seemingly oxymoronic as a translucent mat led to one of Rookwood's greatest triumphs.

The first trials for the Vellum glaze line were in 1900.[126] Initial examples were "too clouded," "too opaque," and "too thin." By 1903 progress was noticeable. One of Burt's notations for the year states, "very fine glaze no crz [crazing]."[127] The new glaze line was called Vellum because "it partakes both to the touch and to the eye of the qualities of old parchment."[128] The glaze was devoid of lustre, yet without dryness, and it was basically translucent with a slight haze. Its inventor was none other than Stanley Gano Burt.[129] Objects in this category can be thrown or cast. Rookwood chose to debut the Vellum glaze line at the 1904 Louisiana Purchase Exposition in St. Louis.[130] One reviewer of the Exposition thought Rookwood's Vellum was so technically fine that "mat glaze on pottery could develop no further."[131]

The Vellum glaze line utilized a fine white body, not the grainy faience body of the other mats. Also, adornment for this glaze line was slip-painted decoration under the glaze. Unlike the other glazes in the mat glaze line, the Vellum glaze itself was not the decoration, but rather the glass skin enveloping it. Moreover, the design painted under the glaze was applied to a wet clay body, not a biscuit-fired body.[132]

With the exception that the glass was generally non-refractive, the Vellum glaze line shared both technique and decoration with the high-gloss wares. In fact, early trails for the glaze were taken from the Standard and the Iris lines. For example, Burt's inventory offers seven vases that were decorated for the Standard yellow glaze and one decorated for the Iris glaze that were dipped in Vellum.[133]

It is not surprising that the first pieces presented to the public in St. Louis exhibited decorations in the manner of the Standard, Sea Green, and Iris lines. Virtually all the decorations were floral, with some marine depictions. Of the twenty-four examples of the Vellum glaze line illustrated in the 1904 mail-order catalogue, nineteen are floral, three are marine, one depicts a dragonfly, and one a grapevine.[134]

Not until 1905, when a new type of composition was applied to Vellum products, did the Vellum glaze line take on an identity of its own. It was then that Albert Valentien painted the first landscape under the Vellum glaze.[135] Because of the soft haziness of the glass, the landscape took on a quiet, misty quality. Tonalism, a mainstream art movement at the turn of the century that was distinguished by veiled, atmospheric landscapes, was an aesthetic familiar to many of Rookwood's artists.[136] Rookwood decorator Edward Timothy Hurley, for example, was also a painter and etcher who worked in the Tonalist mode.[137] It soon became apparent that the Vellum glaze line was a perfect vehicle for the Tonalist expression. The combination of Rookwood and Tonalism proved exceedingly popular, therefore floral Vellums soon fell from grace. Today floral Vellums (nos. 60–62) are considered relatively rare. Included in this Tonalist mode are scenes of Venice, the most frequently depicted city in the Western world at the turn of the century.[138] Venetian scenes were portrayed in the Iris glaze line by 1904, if not earlier. It is not surprising that they were soon to appear in the Vellum line. Decorator Carl Schmidt became particularly noted for such scenes. After he left Rookwood in 1927, scenes of Venice no longer appear.[139] In today's market those objects with landscapes are referred to as Scenic Vellums (nos. 66–73), and those with Venice are referred to as Venetian Vellums (nos. 64–65). The popularity of both was unending. Scenic Vellums were produced until 1948 when E. T. Hurley painted his last landscape at the end of his fifty-two–year tenure.[140]

As soon as artists began painting specifically for the Vellum glaze, they started incising a "V" on the bottom of their objects to signal the glazer to use the Vellum glaze. The first vase so marked was by Sara Sax in 1905.[141] As with the brilliant glazes, crazing was the biggest technical problem with this glaze line. And similarly, objects without crazing were, and are, considered more artistically pleasing to the buying public. By 1922, if not earlier, the clay body used for the Vellum line was a soft porcelain on which crazing rarely occurs.

Finally, there are two additional types in the Vellum glaze line that should be mentioned. One is Green Vellum

5. The showroom in 1887 at Rookwood's first location on Eastern Avenue.

(nos. 74–76), the other is Yellow Vellum. The Green Vellum has a green tint added to the glaze, while the Yellow Vellum has a yellow tint added to the glaze. Both began in 1904.[142] Incised "GV" and "YV" notations can be seen on the bottom of these. Their decorations are generally floral, with some landscapes and peacock feathers. They are particularly rare, with the latest ones dating into the 1920s.

Most Vellum examples are vases, but many are plaques. The painterly expression of the Tonalist compositions lent itself to the two-dimensional format. The decorator's signature was displayed on the front of the plaque, and Rookwood had them framed before they were sold. They were even given titles which were typed and then glued to the back of the frames. It appears that vases were never given titles for their scenes, and the artist's signatures are on the bottom, hidden from view.

The Vellum glaze line lasted a total of forty-four years, from 1904 until 1948. Its auspicious beginning was marked by two Grand Prizes at the 1904 St. Louis Exposition.[143] During its long life Vellum enjoyed its place as one of Rookwood's finest achievements, despite the fact that the Depression interrupted production and eventually caused the company bankruptcy. It was the last Rookwood glaze line to be recognized internationally and the last to be singled out for its contribution to ceramic history. Seemingly unique in its creation, and sensational in its quality, the Vellum glaze line, with its floral, Scenic, Venetian, and Green and Yellow categories, had no rivals at home or abroad.

NOTES

ROOKWOOD POTTERY: THE GLORIOUS GAMBLE

1. For more information about the Japanese influence upon Rookwood, see Kenneth R. Trapp, "Rookwood and the Japanese Mania in Cincinnati," *Cincinnati Historical Society Bulletin*, vol. 39, no. 1 (Spring 1981), pp. 51–75.

2. "Art Pottery," *Cincinnati Daily Gazette*, October 7, 1880, p. 8.

3. Taylor declared that ". . . I was in charge at the pottery [Rookwood] at least as early as the middle of June, 1883." in Transcript of Record. Laura A. Fry vs. The Rookwood Pottery Company and William W. Taylor. United States Circuit Court of Appeals for the Sixth Circuit. Appeal from the United States Circuit Court for the Western Division of the Southern District of Ohio (hereafter, Transcript of Record, LAF vs. RPC and WWT), vol. 1, 1893, p. 292.

4. The earliest sales of Rookwood's wares as entered in the Shape Record Book are often recorded by initials only. Unfortunately such an expedient practice now frustrates research into Rookwood's marketing of its wares.

5. This assertion appears often in Rookwood's promotional literature.

6. At Rookwood the adoption of the mouth atomizer, later to become a compressed airbrush, occurred over a period of time. Fry recalled that an atomizer technique had been in use at Rookwood at least a year and a half before she filed her patent application for a "new and useful Improvement in the Arts of Decorating Pottery-Ware" on March 16, 1886, which was issued on March 5, 1889. See, Transcript of Record, LAF vs. RPC and WWT, vol. 1, 1893, p. 52. If her memory was accurate, Fry instituted the mouth atomizer at Rookwood by mid-September 1884. Using Rookwood's letterpress books to inform his deposition, Taylor noted that Fry "was engaged at the pottery [Rookwood] from early in June 1884 to about October 1, 1885, and again from early in June 1886 to about August 1, 1887." Transcript of Record, LAF vs. RPC and WWT, vol. 1, 1893, p. 292. It must be remembered that depositions in the Fry vs. Rookwood Pottery and Taylor court case were taken nine years after Rookwood first began to use the atomizer to apply softly-blended colors to pottery.

7. United States patent issued to Laura A. Fry for Art of Decorating Pottery-Ware, Letters Patent No. 339, 029, March 5, 1889.

8. Herbert Peck, *The Book of Rookwood Pottery* (New York: Crown Publishers, Inc., 1968), pp. 143 and 145, writes that Daly and McDonald were hired by Rookwood in 1882. Both men had decorated pottery at the Matt Morgan Art Pottery prior to their joining Rookwood in 1884. Daly joined Rookwood on October 8, 1884, and McDonald entered the pottery soon after he left the Matt Morgan Art Pottery in September 1884. Transcript of Record, LAF vs. RPC and WWT, 1893, vol. 1, pp. 248 and 255–256.

9. I thank Susan Montgomery for bringing this information to my attention. In the Preface to *A Muramasa Blade: A Story of Feudalism in Old Japan*, Louis Wertheimber writes that Nakamura Munehiro executed five engravings on copper from original drawings for the book, while "the other pictures were drawn by Shirayama Dani, a young

porcelain painter in the employ of Fujiyama, of this city [Boston]." (Louis Wertheimber, *A Muramasa Blade: A Story of Feudalism in Old Japan*, Boston: Ticknor and Company, 1877, pp. [xi]–xii.) I am grateful to Michelle and Randy Sandler for bringing Wertheimber's book to my attention. Wertheimber owned and operated Fujiyama, an import shop of Orientalia.

Despite the fact that Shirayamadani lived in Cincinnati for some half a century, he remains an enigma. Indeed, even the spelling of his name is disputed. Kataro, Kitaro, and Ketaro are variations upon the spelling of what would be his first, or given, name in English. In a letter of July 18, 1891 to Edwin Atlee Barber, Taylor actually referred to Shirayamadani as "Kataro Shiriyamadani [sic]." Letterpress Book, 1891–1892, p. 14, Rookwood Pottery Collection, Mitchell Memorial Library, Mississippi State University (hereafter, RPC, MML/MSU). Taylor almost always referred to Shirayamadani as "Shiriyama."

Native Japanese and American scholars fluent in Japanese have told me that "Kitaro" is a traditional name in Japan, whereas "Kataro" is not. However Shirayamadani spelled his name is, in the end, a moot point. We know to whom any variation of the spellings of his names refers.

10. Trapp, "Rookwood and the Japanese Mania in Cincinnati," pp. 64–68.

11. William Watts Taylor, letter to W. H. Smyth, Atlanta, Georgia, October 4, 1887. Letterpress Book, 1886–1887, p. 480. RPC, MML/MSU. Taylor writes that "Those marked x are decorated by our native Japanese artist—K. Shirayamadani [sic]."

12. Peck, *The Book of Rookwood Pottery*, p. 102, writes that "Kataro Shirayamadani left Rookwood about this time [1915] to return to Japan, where he is thought to have taken a position working for the Japanese Government." In Herbert Peck, *The Second Book of Rookwood Pottery* (Tucson, AZ: by the author, 1985), p. 2, he corrects himself, writing that Shirayamadani ". . . returned to Rookwood, having been absent for approximately ten years, from 1911 to 1921." Peck does not document the source for either assertion. Why Shirayamadani left Rookwood remains unexplained.

The time has come to shift the research into Shirayamadani's life from his arrival and stay in the United States to the circumstances that led him to depart from Japan in the 1880s and to his return to his native land from 1911–1921.

13. Maria Longworth Storer, *History of the Cincinnati Musical Festivals and of the Rookwood Pottery* (Paris: by the author, 1919), [p. 8]. Mrs. Storer wrote this brief sketch in 1895.

14. William Watts Taylor, letter to Howell & James, Ltd., London, May 12, 1887. Letterpress Book, 1886–1887, p. 193. RPC, MML/MSU; William Watts Taylor, letter to Reed, Bennis & Co., Bloomington, Illinois, March 25, 1889. Letterpress Book, 1889, p. 209. Rookwood Pottery Collection, Cincinnati Historical Society Library (hereafter, RPC, CHSL).

15. See Rookwood Shape Record Book, p. 93, entry for shape 293. RPC, CHSL. The entry for shape 293, a pitcher, reads, "Monogram [reversed-R connected to a P] put in mold of this shape and first used on this shape on June 23rd 1886."

16. William Watts Taylor, letter to Johnstone, Norman & Co., London, April 30, 1889. Letterpress Book, 1889, p. 267. RPC, CHSL.

17. For information about the development of McLaughlin's underglaze slip-painting process, see Mrs. Aaron F. Perry, "Decorative Pottery of Cincinnati," *Harper's New Monthly Magazine*, LXII: CCCLXXI (May 1881), p. 835; Mary Louise McLaughlin, "Mary Louise McLaughlin," *Bulletin of the American Ceramic Society*, vol. 17, no.5 (May 1938), pp. 217–225; and Kenneth R. Trapp, "Toward a Correct Taste: Women and the Rise of the Design Reform Movement in Cincinnati 1874–1880," *Celebrate Cincinnati Art*, edited by Kenneth R. Trapp, (Cincinnati: Cincinnati Art Museum, 1982), pp. 48–70.

18. William Watts Taylor, letter to Briggs & Leibuis, Toledo, Ohio, April 25, 1889. Letterpress Book, 1889, p. 257. RPC, CHSL.

19. William Watts Taylor to Messrs. D. Collamore & Co., New York, August 3, 1889. Letterpress Book, 1889, p. 417. RPC, CHSL.

20. William Watts Taylor to C. W. Bonfils, Paris, September 11, 1889. Letterpress Book, 1889, p. 943. RPC, CHSL. Taylor writes: "Imitations without inferring that the Luneville people or others may not do better with further trials, we are not surprised that the first attempts [to imitate Rookwood's glazed dark wares] are comparative [sic] failures. The fact is our methods are outside the track of ordinary pottery and cannot be hit upon all at once."

21. P. W. [sic, William Percival] Jervis, "Women Potters of America," *Pottery, Glass & Brass Salesman*, December 13, 1917, p. 93. Jervis writes:

A little of the inside history of Rookwood is told in a letter to the writer dated December 2, 1917, from Mrs. Bellamy Storer, who states that the late W. W. Taylor never was her partner, but was manager of the pottery at a salary of $4,000 a year until she retired in 1891, when she made him a present of the entire pottery.

22. Peck, *The Book of Rookwood Pottery*, p. 46. Interestingly, Taylor met a Mr. Holbrook of Gorham Manufacturing Company when he was in New York in 1889. William Watts Taylor, letter to Johnstone, Norman & Co, April 20, 1889. Letterpress Book, 1889, p. 237. RPC, CHSL. It is unknown whether Taylor met Edward or John Holbrook. Taylor might have had in mind the application of silver designs to Rookwood pieces at that time.

23. Edwin Atlee Barber, *The Pottery and Porcelain of the United States: An Historical Review of American Ceramic Art from the Earliest Times to the Present Day* (New York: G. P. Putman's Sons, 1893), pp. 284–285.

24. Among the photographers whose images of Native Americans were used by Rookwood's decorators are Edward S. Curtis, John K. Hillers, James Mooney, Adolph F. Muhr, Frank A. Rinehart, and William S. Soule. See Paula Richardson Fleming and Judith Luskey, *The North American Indians in Early Photographs* (New York: Harper & Row, Publishers, 1986). A complete list of photographers whose images of Native Americans were used at Rookwood remains to be compiled. I cannot recall a Native-American portrait piece of Rookwood that was not inscribed on the bottom with the name of the subject and his or her "tribe," for example "Powder Face/Comanche."

It is unknown where and how Rookwood obtained photographs of Native Americans. Doubtless the Trans-Mississippian International Exposition in Omaha, Nebraska, in 1898 was one source. Muhr and Rinehart were official photographers at the Omaha exposition.

As Rookwood prepared to move from Cincinnati to Starkville, Mississippi, in 1960, the company sold as much of its vast library as possible. Among the items sold were portrait photographs of Plains Indians inscribed "April 1899." Several of these photographs are in a private collection.

The use of Native Americans as portrait subjects and as sources for decorative designs and subject matter in the history of American decorative arts offers rich and little explored possibilities for scholarly investigation.

25. I am grateful to Susan L. Meyn, Curator of Ethnology at the Cincinnati Museum of Natural History, for kindly sending me this fascinating information. In several conversations, Joan Hurley O'Brien, daughter of the Rookwood decorator Edward Timothy Hurley, told me that a group of Indians had gone to Rookwood to have their portraits painted. What sounded like a romantic embellishment in the oral tradition now appears entirely plausible.

Most of the Native-American portrait pieces that I have studied cluster in a brief period between 1896 and 1900. The visitations of the Cree and the Sicangu Sioux ethnological villages at the Cincinnati Zoological Gardens and the Trans-Mississippian Exposition help to explain the "sudden" appearance of Indian portraits at Rookwood.

26. Peck, *The Book of Rookwood Pottery*, p. 51. Peck does not identify the source of this quotation, which probably came from the company's corporate minutes.

27. *The Rookwood Book: Rookwood, An American Art* (Cincinnati: The Rookwood Pottery, 1904), [p.12].

28. See Kenneth R. Trapp, *Ode to Nature: Flowers and Landscapes of the Rookwood Pottery 1880–1940*, (New York: Jordan-Volpe Gallery, 1980).

29. This information comes from Nancy Danahy of Cincinnati, who remembers that her aunt, Margaret Helen McDonald, reported that Rookwood required its decorators to continue floral studies from nature.

30. Peck, *The Book of Rookwood Pottery*, p. 50.

31. For a detailed study of Maria Longworth Storer's metalwork, see Kenneth R. Trapp, "Maria Longworth Storer: A Study of Her Bronze Objects d'Art in the Cincinnati Art Museum," Master's thesis, Tulane University, 1972.

32. Clara Erskine Clement, *Women in the Fine Arts: From the Seventh Century B.C. to the Twentieth Century A.D.* (Boston and New York: Houghton, Mifflin and Company, 1904), pp. 328–329.

33. Peck, *The The Book of Rookwood Pottery*, pp. 50 and 52.

34. *Ibid.*, p. 54.

35. For an example of Bailey's trial experiments to replicate the *sang de boeuf*, see Kenneth R. Trapp, intro., and Vance A. Koehler, *American Art Pottery* (New York: Cooper-Hewitt Museum, 1987), p. 45, catalogue entry 14.

36. This point was raised by Martin Eidelberg at a conference at the American Craft Museum, New York, 17 November 1990.

37. Peck, *The Book of Rookwood Pottery*, p. 156.

38. *Ibid.*, p. 58.

39. Following his trip to the United States, Bing wrote *La Culture artistique en Amérique*, in which he praised "American painting, sculpture, architecture, and the industrial arts, partly to counteract the contempt most Frenchmen held for American creativity." (Gabriel P. Weisberg, *Art Nouveau Bing: Paris Style 1900*, New York: Harry N. Abrams, Inc., Publishers, and SITES, 1986, p. 48.) Despite inability to document that Bing actually visited Rookwood in Cincinnati, we are certain that he knew Rookwood through the 1889 Paris International Exposition and the 1893 Columbian Exposition in Chicago.

Bing may well have met and known several Cincinnatians, for there was a sizable expatriate community from the Queen City who lived in Paris in the last quarter of the nineteenth century. Maria Longworth Storer traveled frequently to the Continent following her second marriage in 1886. In the 1890s the Storers lived in Brussels, Madrid, and Vienna, cities where Bellamy Storer was posted as

American minister and ambassador. His wife was fluent in German and French. She died in Paris in 1932.

Cultivated Cincinnatians were cosmopolitan like their counterparts in Boston, New York, Philadelphia, and Chicago. Furthermore, business drew Cincinnatians to Paris. For example, Gordon Shillito, son of John Shillito, who founded Cincinnati's largest department store in 1878, was sent to Paris in 1885 as the principal buyer for his father's emporium. Robert Harvey Galbreath, president of the silver and jewelry firm of Duhme and Company, Rookwood's principal agent in Cincinnati, made frequent buying trips to Paris.

40. Oscar Lovell Triggs, *Chapters in the History of the Arts and Crafts Movement*, Vol. 5, *Rookwood: An Ideal Workshop* (Chicago: The Bohemia Guild of the Industrial Art League, Chicago, 1902; UMI facsimile 1978), pp. 159–161.

41. Storer, *History of the Cincinnati Musical Festivals and of the Rookwood Pottery*, [p. 13].

42. *Rookwood Pottery* (Cincinnati: The Procter & Collier Co., [1902]), p. 6. A promotional pamphlet.

43. Stanley Gano Burt's Record Book of Ware at the Art Museum. 2,292 Pieces of Early Rookwood Pottery in the Cincinnati Art Museum in 1916, Cincinnati Historical Society, 1978, p. 134, entries 15, 20, 21, and 55. An 1899 Rookwood bottle vase, shape 743A, decorated by Harriet E. Wilcox, which is now in a private collection, is an example of Rookwood's revival of its earlier Mahogany in which a red clay is used for the body.

44. Peck, *The Book of Rookwood Pottery*, p. 143.

45. Ibid., p. 67.

46. *Rookwood Pottery*, [1902], p. 32.

47. Ibid., p. 35.

48. *The Rookwood Book*, 1904, p. 18. A mail-order catalogue.

49. Ibid., p. 12.

50. Ibid., p. 00.

51. *Rookwood Mat Glaze* [sic] (Cincinnati: The Rookwood Pottery Company, 1905), [p. 9]. The cover reads *Rookwood Mat Glazes*, whereas the title page is printed *Rookwood Mat Glaze*. A promotional, mail-order pamphlet.

52. William P. McDonald Scrapbooks, vol. 2 of 4 vols., n.p., William P. McDonald, Jr., Family Archive. I wish to thank Ruth McDonald (Mrs. William Purcell McDonald, Jr.), Andrea McDonald, Mary Sue McDonald Zech, and Nancy Danahy for their help. Andrea McDonald brought to my attention the McDonald scrapbooks and Ruth McDonald generously permitted me to study them.

53. *The Rookwood Book*, 1904, p. 14. A mail-order catalogue.

54. The prevalence of green in the Arts and Crafts movement is given thorough explication in Diana Stradling, "Teco Pottery and the Green Phenomenon," *Tiller*, vol. 1, no. 4. (March–April 1983), pp. 8–36.

55. See Margaretta M. Lovell, *Venice: The American View 1860–1920* (San Francisco: The Fine Arts Museums of San Francisco, 1984).

56. *Rookwood Pottery: Rookwood Ombroso*, (Cincinnati: by the Rookwood Pottery Company, 1910), [pp. 1-2]. Promotional brochure.

57. *Rookwood Pottery: Rookwood Ombroso*, (Cincinnati: Ebbert & Richardson, 1910), [p.1]. Promotional brochure.

58. Peck, *The Book of Rookwood Pottery*, p. 101.

59. *Soft Porcelain* (Cincinnati: by the Rookwood Pottery Company, 1915), n.p. Unless noted otherwise, all quotations that pertain directly to the characteristics of the Soft Porcelain are taken from this promotional leaflet.

60. The connection between Rookwood's search for new glazes, shapes, colors, and artistic treatments, and the Chinese ceramics that Charles P. Taft collected, which are now in the permanent collection of the Taft Museum in Cincinnati, merits exploration that is beyond the scope of this study. Between 1902 and 1915 Taft purchased 109 Chinese porcelains. On one trip to New York in 1905, Taft purchased forty-nine Chinese monochrome porcelains from Thomas B. Clarke. Taft collected Chinese ceramics to serve as models for artists in Cincinnati. The Taft collection was well known and publicized with full-color advertisements in the *Ladies' Home Journal*.

From 1914 to 1927 Charles P. Taft was president of the Cincinnati Museum Association (Cincinnati Art Museum). He and Joseph Henry Gest, director of the Cincinnati Art Museum and the second president of The Rookwood Pottery Company, were friends and business associates intimately involved in the cultural life of the Queen City.

I wish to thank David Torbet Johnson, assistant director of the Taft Museum, for this information.

61. I am most grateful to Riley Humler for giving me this information, which was relayed to him in an interview with Patti Conant.

62. For a discussion of Rookwood's artistic wares from the 1920s to the 1940s, see Kenneth R. Trapp, *Toward the Modern Style. Rookwood Pottery, The Later Years: 1915–1950* (New York: Jordan-Volpe Gallery, 1983).

63. Peck, *The Book of Rookwood Pottery*, pp. 142, 143, and 145.

64. *Clay Decoration at Rookwood*, [Cincinnati: by the Rookwood Pottery Company, ca. 1910], n.p. Promotional brochure.

65. Whereas Rookwood carefully promoted its earlier wares by name and as glaze lines with unique properties, by the 1920s the company had abandoned the practice. Not only was the practice unnecessary, but it seems to have become undesirable. The earlier glaze lines took years to develop and were more costly. Further, some glaze lines were "dominated" by a few decorators, as the prevalence of their ciphers attests.

Ironically, Rookwood abandoned its practice of naming glaze lines at the very time when aggressive marketing and advertising became a marked feature of American business practice. Perhaps the answer to why Rookwood abandoned its earlier marketing practice is not so unexplainable as it might seem. By the 1920s Rookwood was an established corporate name in art pottery and architectural faience. The company had amassed a technically advanced "library" of glazes, experiments, and knowledge that could produce most desired effects. No longer were years required to develop a new glaze or effect. Indeed, marketing created trends, and trends demanded instant gratification. It was unwise for an art business to become too closely identified with a particular aesthetic.

The names applied to Rookwood's artistic wares during in the 1920s through the 1950s have been largely established by dealers, collectors, newspaper reviewers, and other writers. Names bestowed by recent writers have been assigned to identify wares by artistic or technical attributes.

66. Chester Davis, "The Later Years of Rookwood Pottery 1920–1967," *Spinning Wheel* 25 (October 1969), p. 10. For descriptions of these glazes see also Ralph and Terry Kovel, *The Kovels' Collectors Guide to American Pottery* (New York: Crown Publishers, Inc. 1974), pp. 224–28.

67. Mary L. Alexander, *Cincinnati Enquirer*, May 21, 1933. Cincinnati Historical Society Library, Rookwood Pottery Newspaper Clipping File.

68. Trapp, *Toward the Modern Style*, p. 25.

69. Edwin J. Kircher and Barbara and Joseph Agranoff, *Rookwood: Its Golden Era of Art Pottery 1880–1929* (Cincinnati, by the authors, 1969), plate 14, middle row.

70. S. Bing, *Artistic Japan (1888–1891)*; René Grandjean, intro., *Céramique Orientale* (Paris: Ernst Henri, n.d.); Henri Riviere, Charles Xiguier, pref. and Albert Lévy, ed., *La Céramique dans l'art d'Extrême-Orient* (Paris: Librarie Centrale des Beaux-Arts, 1923), and *Étoffes Japonaises* (Livraison).

71. Peck, *The Book of Rookwood Pottery*, p. 103.

72. See *Rookwood Cincinnati*, (Cincinnati: The Rookwood Pottery Company, n.d.), p. 5. Rookwood Pottery trade catalogue, c. 1920–30.

73. Arthur Van Vlissingen, Jr., "Art Pays a Profit," *Factory and Industrial Management* 79 (February 1930), p. 302.

74. Bopp, p. 445.

75. *Ibid*.

76. *Ibid*.

77. The history of Rookwood is divided between the five decades before 1930 and the three after 1930. The Great Depression dealt the already-waning Arts and Crafts movement a blow from which it never recovered.

78. "Last Kiln is Best!" *Cincinnati Enquirer*, November 27, 1930. From Mary R. Schiff Library, Cincinnati Art Museum, Rookwood Pottery Box, "Rookwood Pottery Clippings 1882–1968," (hereafter, MRSL/CAM, Rookwood Pottery Box), p. 30.

79. "Rookwood Pottery Celebrates 50th Anniversary with Party," *Cincinnati Commercial Tribune*, November 27, 1930, MRSL/CAM, Rookwood Pottery Box, p. 28.

80. Vlissingen, Jr., "Art Pays a Profit," p. 303.

81. Mary L. Alexander, *Cincinnati Enquirer*, May 21, 1933. Cincinnati Historical Society Library, Rookwood Pottery Newspaper Clipping File.

82. Bertha Joseph, "The Rookwood Pottery Adds Prestige to City," March 11, 1935. MRSL/CAM Rookwood Pottery Box, p. 36.

83. *Ibid*.

84. Unidentified newspaper clipping, October 1938. MRSL/CAM Rookwood Pottery Box, p. 37.

85. *Ibid*.

86. "Rookwood Features Three New Colors at Opening of Art in Industry Exhibit," *Cincinnati Post*, January 24, 1942. Cincinnati Historical Society Library, Rookwood Pottery Newspaper Clipping File.

87. *New York Times*, March 22, 1942, p. 21.

88. Mary L. Alexander, "New Crystal Glaze Described in Rookwood Masterpiece," *Cincinnati Enquirer*, Cincinnati Historical Society Library, Rookwood Pottery Newspaper Clipping File.

89. Peck, *The Book of Rookwood Pottery*, p. 125.

90. *Ibid*.

EIGHT GLAZE LINES: THE HEART OF ROOKWOOD POTTERY

1. From 1880 until 1890 the title of the firm was simply: Rookwood Pottery. When the business became incorporated in 1890, the official title became The Rookwood Pottery Company. This is noted in a letter sent March 6, 1891, from William Watts Taylor to Edwin Atlee Barber, West Chester, Pennsylvania, in The Rookwood Pottery Collection, Mitchell Memorial Library, Mississippi State University (hereafter RPC, MML/MSU), Letterpress Book, 1890–91, p. 253. This is also confirmed in The Book of Corporate Minutes (hereafter Corporate Minutes), p. 1, in the collection of Dr. Art and Rita Townley.

2. Harold F. Bopp, "Art and Science in the Development of Rookwood Pottery," *Bulletin of the American Ceramic Society*, vol. 15, Nov. 12, 1936: p. 445. Bopp was a ceramic engineer at the University of Cincinnati and was a member of the American Ceramic Society along with Stanley Gano Burt, Rookwood's ceramic engineer. They were both founding members of the Society. Harold F. Bopp was the superintendent at Rookwood from 1929 until about 1941.

3. For a more detailed and scientific definition of a glaze see Charlotte F. Speight, *Hands In Clay*, 2nd ed. (1989), p. 456; John Colbeck, *Pottery Material* (1988), p. 53; or Charles F. Binns, *The Potter's Craft* (1910), pp. 112–137. Any technical questions that may arise for the reader can be resolved in these books. It should be noted that the terms glaze and glass will be used interchangeably throughout the essay.

4. Edwin Atlee Barber, *The Pottery and Porcelain of the United States* (New York, 1893), p. 290. Barber was the country's leading authority on pottery and porcelain. In 1901, he became curator at the Philadelphia Museum of Art, and was its director from 1907 until his death in 1916. He wrote fifteen books in all on ceramics.

5. William Watts Taylor, letter to Edwin Atlee Barber, West Chester, Pennsylvania, November 10, 1891. RPC, MML/MSU, Letterpress Book, 1891-92, p. 204.

6. William Watts Taylor, "The Rookwood Pottery," *The Forensic Quarterly*, September, 1910, p. 204.

7. William Watts Taylor, letter to Mr. Alfred Cox, Detroit, Michigan, October 8, 1887. RPC, MML/MSU, Letterpress Book, 1886–87, p. 492.

8. William Watts Taylor, letter to Miss Ida M. Tarbell, Meadville, Pennsylvania, November 8, 1887. RPC, MML/MSU, Letterpress Book, 1887–88, p. 48.

9. William Watts Taylor, letter to Mrs. Sheldon, no destination given, perhaps Cincinnati, October 24, 1887. RPC, MML/MSU, Letterpress Book, 1887–88, p. 26.

10. William Watts Taylor, letter to Ms. Sheldon, no destination given, perhaps Cincinnati, December 3, 1887. RPC, MML/MSU Letterpress Book, 1887–88, p. 103. Whenever Taylor referred to Ivory ware he never capitalized the "i" in ivory, whereas he always capitalized the "C" in Cameo ware.

11. William Watts Taylor, letter to Russell Sturgis, Esq., New York, New York, February 22, 1990. RPC, MML/MSU, Letterpress Book, 1889–90, p. 179. Sturgis was an art critic in New York.

12. William Watts Taylor, letter to The Century Company, New York, New York, December 22, 1887, RPC, MML/MSU, Letterpress Book, 1887–88, p. 133. The following information is also from this source.

13. William Watts Taylor, letter to Mr. A. B. Russell, St. Augustine, Florida, February 25, 1888. RPC, MML/MSU, Letterpress Book, 1887–88, p. 289.

14. William Watts Taylor, letter to Messrs. Coulter & Brown Co., Duluth, Minnesota, October 31, 1888. RPC, MML/MSU, Letterpress Book, 1888–89, p. 306.

15. *Rookwood Pottery*, Cincinnati, 1895 (prob.), p. 23. The following information is also from this source.

16. That it was not entered in the London exhibit of 1887 can be seen in a letter sent February 28, 1887, from William Watts Taylor to Messrs. Howell & James, Ltd., London, England. RPC, MML/MSU,

Letterpress Book, 1886–87, pp. 95-98. That Cameo ware was not in the Philadelphia competition of 1888 can be seen in a letter sent October 30, 1888, from William Watts Taylor to Mr. J. E. Beebe, Denver, Colorado. RPC, MML/MSU, Letterpress Book, 1888–89, p. 309. The fact that the 1889 Philadelphia award was "for Faience" eliminates Cameo ware because of its porcelain-like body. Also, it was not sent to Paris in 1889 precisely because of this body. In a letter sent March 2, 1889, from William Watts Taylor to Messrs. Davis Collamore & Co. (Collamore handled Rookwood's representation in Paris), New York, New York, Taylor writes, "we think it [Cameo ware] might cause some trouble . . . with the Jury. It is an approach at least to porcelain and would put us into competition in a different class if rigidly considered." The Rookwood Pottery Collection, The Cincinnati Historical Society Library (hereafter RPC, CHSL), Letterpress Book, 1889, p. 134.

17. William Watts Taylor, letter to Messrs. George C. Shreve & Co., San Francisco, California, May 7, 1889. RPC, CHSL, Letterpress Book, 1889, pp. 272–273.

18. William Watts Taylor, letter to Russell Sturgis, Esq., New York, New York, February 22, 1890. RPC, MML/MSU, Letterpress Book 1890–91, p. 179.

19. T. C. Van Houten, letter to Messrs. Davis Collamore & Co., New York, New York, February 7, 1891. RPC, MML/MSU, Letterpress Book, 1890–91, p. 191.

20. T. C. Van Houten, letter to Messrs. Davis Collamore & Co., New York, New York, May 22, 1891. RPC, MML/MSU, Letterpress Book, 1890–91, p. 393.

21. Stanley Gano Burt, *Rookwood Pottery in the Cincinnati Art Museum in 1916*, (Cincinnati: Cincinnati Historical Society, 1978). Regarding the life of the Cameo line, on page 39, entry #101 of 1884, Burt writes, "suggests later cameo ware." Later on page 44, entry #8 of 1885, he writes, "This is typical 'cameo'. . . ." And, on page 100, entry #30–31 of 1892 he states, "probably last of the cameo." Stanley Gano Burt was the ceramic engineer (at the time referred to as a chemist) at Rookwood who, in 1916, made this annotated inventory of the Pottery's collection on loan to the Cincinnati Art Museum. In 1941, Rookwood was forced to sell its collection when it declared bankruptcy. While the collection has been dispersed, Burt's inventory remains an invaluable source of information.

22. William Watts Taylor, letter to Mr. Halsey C. Ives, Director, Museum of Fine Arts, St. Louis, Missouri, January 17, 1889. RPC, CHSL, Letterpress Book, 1889, p. 29.

23. William Watts Taylor, letter to Mr. Dalton Dorr, Philadelphia, Pennsylvania, October 26, 1888. RPC, MML/MSU, Letterpress Book, 1888–89, p. 286.

24. William Watts Taylor, letter to Messrs. George C. Shreve & Co., San Francisco, California, April 16, 1887. RPC, MML/MSU, Letterpress Book, 1886–87, reverse of p. 159.

25. William Watts Taylor, letter to Messrs. A. D. Vorce & Co., Hartford, October 15, 1887. RPC, MML/MSU, Letterpress Book, 1887–88, p. 9.

26. William Watts Taylor, letter to R. M. Reynolds, M. D., Fargue Falls, Minnesota, May 29, 1889. RPC, CHSL, Letterpress Book, 1889, p. 320.

27. William Watts Taylor, letter to Messrs. Howell & James, Ltd., London, England, February 28, 1887. RPC, MML/MSU, Letterpress Book, 1886–87, reverse of p. 96.

28. William Watts Taylor, letter to Mr. Arthur Kaye, Louisville, Kentucky, April 24, 1889. RPC, CHSL, Letterpress Book, 1889, p. 250.

29. William Watts Taylor, letter to Mr. John Turner, Paris, France, August 8, 1889. RPC, CHSL, Letterpress Book, 1889, p. 426.

30. William Watts Taylor, letter to Messrs. Freeman & Crankshaw, Atlanta, Georgia, September 17, 1890. RPC, MML/MSU, Letterpress Book, 1889–90, p. 421.

31. William Watts Taylor, letter to Messrs. Davis Collamore & Co., New York, New York, June 3, 1891. RPC, MML/MSU, Letterpress Book, 1890–91, p. 418.

32. Corporate Minutes, p. 217.

33. For the use of "rich glazed ware" see, for example, a letter sent May 12, 1887, from William Watts Taylor to Messrs. Howell & James, Ltd., London, England. RPC, MML/MSU, Letterpress Book 1886–87, p. 193. For the use of "dark glazed ware," see, for example, a letter sent March 25, 1889, from William Watts Taylor to Messrs. Reed, Bennis & Co., Bloomington, Illinois. RPC, CHSL, Letterpress Book, 1889, p. 209. Taylor uses the two terms liberally throughout the approximately 6,500 letters in the seven extant Letterpress books which date from 1886 to 1891.

34. Receipt Book: A Record of the Materials and Formula in Use at the Rookwood Pottery (hereafter Receipt Book), p. 103. RPC, CHSL.

35. Corporate Minutes, p. 171.

36. Corporate Minutes, p. 217.

37. *Rookwood Pottery*, 1900 (prob.), p. 3. RPC, CHSL. Pamphlet.

38. W. P. McDonald, "Rookwood at the Pan-American," *Keramic Studio*, November, 1901, p. 146.

39. *Rookwood Pottery*, 1902, p. 27.

40. Corporate Minutes, for the year ending January 31, 1900, notes the new metal mounting department on pp. 204–205. The department is last noted on p. 221, for the year ending January 31, 1903. Metal-mounted pieces should date between these years. It is possible that an 1898 piece was mounted in 1899. Also, since the record only includes the first month of 1903, pieces may not date to that year. The electro-deposited metal mounts created at the pottery should not be confused with the open work of Gorham Manufacturing Company's silver overlay.

41. Taylor, "The Rookwood Pottery", p. 207.

42. Burt, pp. 39–40, #107. It was a large vase decorated by Laura A. Fry.

43. William Watts Taylor, letter to Messrs. Sloane & Mudge, Los Angeles, California, October 17, 1887. RPC, MML/MSU, Letterpress Book, 1887–88, between pp. 14–15.

44. Burt, p. 33, #31–34.

45. Bopp, p. 445.

46. William Watts Taylor, letter to Messrs. Williams & Everett, Boston, Massachusetts, December 3, 1887. RPC, MML/MSU, Letterpress Book, 1887–88, p. 106.

47. William Watts Taylor, letter to Mr. C. D. Alexander, Philadelphia, Pennsylvania, November 13, 1888. RPC, MML/MSU, Letterpress Book, 1888–89, p. 348.

48. William Watts Taylor, letter to Mr. George W. Bram, Norwalk, Connecticut, February 10, 1891. RPC, MML/MSU, Letterpress Book, 1890–91, p. 194.

49. William Watts Taylor, letter to Messrs. Richard Briggs & Co., Boston, Massachusetts, May 6, 1891. RPC, MML/MSU, Letterpress Book, 1886–87, p. 346.

50. William Watts Taylor, letter to Messrs. George C. Shreve & Co., San Francisco, California, April 16, 1887. RPC, MML/MSU, Letterpress Book, 1886–87, p. 158.

51. Burt, p. 81, #32; p. 88, #51; p. 93, #33.

52. According to Herbert Peck, Rookwood revived this glaze in 1920 to celebrate the pottery's fortieth anniversary. Herbert Peck, *The Book of Rookwood Pottery* (New York: Crown Publishers, Inc., 1968), pp. 104–105.

53. Taylor, "The Rookwood Pottery," p. 208.

54. Burt, p. 167, #27.

55. Corporate Minutes, p. 171.

56. Burt, p. 108, #18.

57. *Rookwood Pottery*, 1895 (prob.), p. 21.

58. John Valentine, "Rookwood Pottery," *The House Beautiful*, September, 1898, p. 125.

59. McDonald, p. 146.

60. William Watts Taylor, letter to Mr. C. R. Feddersen, Copenhagen Denmark, December 5, 1890. RPC, MML/MSU, Letterpress Book, 1890–91, p. 63.

61. William Watts Taylor, letter to Messrs. Davis Collamore & Co., New York, New York, April 9, 1892. RPC, MML/MSU, Letterpress Book, 1891–92, p. 426.

62. William Watts Taylor, letter to Edwin Atlee Barber, West Chester, Pennsylvania, April 25, 1892. RPC, MML/MSU, Letterpress Book, 1891–92, p. 446.

63. Writer's underscore. Corporate Minutes, p. 171.

64. Receipt Book, p. 63.

65. Burt, p. 105, #60.

66. Burt, p. 112, #119.

67. *Rookwood Pottery*, 1895 (prob.), p. 22.

68. Valentine, p. 126. Also, Burt, p. 116, #68.

69. Burt, p. 70, #11; p. 66, #92.

70. William Watts Taylor, letter to Messrs. Coulter & Brown Co., Duluth, Minnesota, October 31, 1888. RPC, MML/MSU, Letterpress Book, 1888–89, p. 306; William Watts Taylor, letter to Messrs. W. D. M. Vitty & Co., Newark, Ohio, December 12, 1889. RPC, MML/MSU, Letterpress Book, 1889–90, p. 20.

71. William Watts Taylor, letter to Messrs. Sloan & Mudge, Los Angeles, California, February 28, 1888. RPC, MML/MSU, Letterpress Book, 1887–88, p. 300.

72. William Watts Taylor, letter to Mr. C. D. Alexander, Philadelphia, Pennsylvania, November 13, 1888. RPC, MML/MSU, Letterpress Book, 1888–89, p. 347.

73. Corporate Minutes, p. 189.

74. Burt, p. 156, #4. This is the last Sea Green noted.

75. Burt, p. 86, #31.

76. Burt, p. 92, #36.

77. Burt, p. 103, #2, #10; p. 104, #34, #41; p. 105, #68, #79.

78. Corporate Minutes, p. 171.

79. Kenneth R. Trapp, *Ode to Nature: Flowers and Landscapes of the Rookwood Pottery, 1880–1940*, 1980, p. 30.

80. Burt, p. 154, #18. Also, *Rookwood Pottery*, 1902, p. 31. It was referred to as white probably because that was its color in the unfired state.

81. McDonald, p. 146.

82. Corporate Minutes, p. 210.

83. Corporate Minutes, p. 210. The following information regarding awards is also from this source.

84. Corporate Minutes, p. 211.

85. For example, see Trapp, plate #5, p. 63.

86. McDonald, p. 147.

87. McDonald, p. 146.

88. Burt, p. 117, #78.

89. Burt, p. 139, #22, #30. #32; p. 142, #98, #102, #106; p. 144, #144, #146; p. 145, #169; p. 157, #16; p. 160, #5; p. 162, #9; p. 166, #13; p. 172, #8, #9.

90. Burt, p. 139, #22.

91. Meissen examples can be seen in Johnannes Just, *Meissen Porcelain of the Art Nouveau Period* (1983), p. 31, illus. 16. And Rorstrand examples can be seen in Antoinette Fay-Halle and Barbara Mundt, *Porcelain of the Nineteenth Century* (1983), p. 250, illus. 446.

92. William Watts Taylor to Russell Sturgis, Esq., New York, New York, February 22, 1890. RPC, MML/MSU, Letterpress Book, 1889–90, reverse of p. 180.

93. "Le dé cor se fond sous la glaçure en des finesses d'agate polie . . . le lustre devient aussi trop brillant." Alexandre Sandier, "La Céramique à l'Exposition," *Art et Décoration*, December 1900, p. 196. It should be noted that Sandier was the artistic director at Sèvres, and so one can question his objectivity.

94. "Leur matière est trop brillante et présente un aspect désagreablement vernissé." M. P. Verneuil, "L'Exposition d'Art Dé coratif Moderne à Turin," *Art et Décoration*, September, 1902, p. 106.

95. Burt, p. 173, #34.

96. "Pottery Without Lead," *The Jewellers' Journal*, 1912, p. 17. This article is in the Rookwood Collection at the Cincinnati Historical Society Library. The following information is also from this source.

97. Corporate Minutes, p. 212. H. F. Bopp, p. 445, says that mat glaze experiments began in the 1880s, but this cannot be confirmed.

98. *The Rookwood Book*, 1904, n. p. This book was a mail-order sales catalogue. Vellum will be discussed later as a category separate from the Mat glaze line.

99. Burt's book is replete with all of these terms, but specific examples of each can be found accordingly: "Incised Matt," p. 141, #76; "painted matt," p. 138, #3; "Modeled matt," p. 151, #21; "Vellum," p. 139, #42.

100. Burt, "inlaid matt," p. 141, #72; "colored matt inlay," p. 143, #127; "inlay matt painted," p. 145, #181; "painted matt inlay," p. 146, #15; "Decorated Matt," p. 170, #P7; "Plain matt," p. 146, #13 "transmutation matt," p. 146, #14.

101. Corporate Minutes, p. 212.

102. Corporate Minutes, p. 208. Unless noted, the following information is also from this source.

103. Burt, p. 146, #14.

104. Corporate Minutes, p. 212. The previous superintendent, Joseph Bailey, died in 1898, at which time Burt assumed the position.

105. Peck, pp. 68–69, for the full discussion on Van Briggle.

106. Burt, p. 118, #4–5.

107. Burt, p. 145, #172–173, for example.

108. Taylor, "The Rookwood Pottery," p. 211.

109. Burt, p. 131, #149, #151; p. 132, #152, #158.

110. *The Rookwood Book*, 1904, n.p.

111. Burt, cited numerously between pages 118–181 for the mat entries.

112. *The Rookwood Book*, 1904, n.p.

113. Burt, p. 138, #9, and p. 180, #18–20.

114. *The Rookwood Book*, 1904, n.p.

115. Burt, p. 138, #3. The following quotation is also from this source.

116. Bopp, p. 445.

117. Taylor, "The Rookwood Pottery," p. 211.

118. Burt, p. 140, #45; p. 145, #181; p. 146, #15, #22; p. 147, #28;

p. 149, #73; p. 158, #1.

119. Bopp, p. 445.

120. Burt, p. 172, #7; p. 174, #5, #7; p. 176, #6, #8.

121. Burt, p. 158, #P6; p. 162, #P8; p. 168, #P4, #P6; p. 178, #4.

122. *Rookwood Pottery: 1880–1910*, (1910), n.p. Burt, p. 166, #P4; p. 167, #P18. Pamphlet.

123. Burt, p. 170, #P9; p. 178, #P4, #P6.

124. Burt, p. 166, #P4; p. 168, #P5, #P8; p. 169 #P12, #P15; p. 170, #P6, #P7; p. 174, #P2.

125. Bopp, p. 445.

126. Burt, p. 139, #42-44; p. 140, #64; p. 141, #81; p. 142, #105; p. 144, #143, #158; p. 145, #183. The following information is also taken from this source.

127. Burt, p. 154, #15.

128. *The Rookwood Book*, 1904, n.p.

129. Taylor, "The Rookwood Pottery," p. 212.

130. *The Rookwood Book*, 1904, n.p.

131. "Louisiana Purchase Exposition Ceramics," *Keramic Studio*, January 1905, p. 193.

132. This is confirmed by William Watts Taylor in "The Rookwood Pottery," p. 212, and H. F. Bopp, p. 445. The reviewer for the Louisiana Purchase Exposition, in *Keramic Studio*, January, 1905, p. 193, states that decoration is painted on the biscuit, but this is incorrect.

133. Burt, p. 154, #8–15, for the Standard decoration, and #18, for the Iris decoration.

134. *The Rookwood Book*, 1904 n.p.

135. Burt, p. 158, #8.

136. For a detailed discussion of the Tonalist Movement see Wanda M. Corn, *The Color of Mood: American Tonalism 1880–1910*, (1972). For a detailed discussion of "American Tonalism and Rookwood Pottery," see Anita J. Ellis, in the published papers for the conference "The Substance of Style: New Perspectives on the American Arts and Crafts Movement," The Henry Francis du Pont Winterthur Museum, publication forthcoming.

137. For a detailed discussion of his Tonalist work, see Virginia K. Griffin and Jennifer Stegman Ward, *The Life and Works of E. T. Hurle*, (1985).

138. For a detailed discussion of the city of Venice as depicted in art at the turn of the century see Margaret M. Lovell, *Venice: The American View 1860–1920*, (1984).

139. Peck, p. 146.

140. Peck, pp. 144–145.

141. Burt, p. 158, #8.

142. Burt, p. 156, #P2; p. 157, #P11.

143. Corporate Minutes, p. 88.

PLATES

1

GINGER JAR
1883
Albert Robert Valentien,
possible decorator
William Auckland,
shape designer
Thrown
H. 10″ Diam. 6 ¾″
Ginger body
Dull Finish and brown tinted,
translucent gloss glazes

Marks: impressed a) kiln b) "Rook-
wood"/"1883" c) "47 E"; incised "G"

Cincinnati Art Museum, Gift of
Mrs. Lucien Wulsin (1966.498)

According to *The Rookwood Shape*
Book 1883–1900 (p. 47), the first
ginger jar of this shape was made
in October 1883 and decorated
by Albert Robert Valentien. The
decoration included a metal finish
at the base. This jar includes a
gold-metal finish applied throughout the body and lid. It is readily
visible within the gloss glaze dripping around the shoulder. The
metal effect is in the glaze, not on
top of it, which is most unusual
(see no. 2). Unusual, too, is the
combination and application of
the two glazes, which was probably inspired by the Japanese, and
can also be seen in no. 4.

2
VASE
1883
**Albert Robert Valentien,
decorator**
Thrown
H. 10″ Diam. 4 ⅛″
Ginger body
Unidentified glaze

*Marks: impressed a) kiln b) "Rook-
wood"/"1883"; incised a) "A.R.V."
b) "G"; paper label printed for the
Women's Art Museum Association,
with "83/173" inscribed in black*

Cincinnati Art Museum, Gift of
the Women's Art Museum
Association (1883.900)

This vase is published in Kenneth
R. Trapp's *Ode to Nature: Flowers
and Landscapes of the Rookwood Pottery 1880–1940*, 1980, p. 74, no. 6.
Most remarkable is the gold
metallic effect in the glaze. Other
pieces of the same period (e.g., no.
1) can also be found with the same
effect. The Cincinnati Art Museum's *Book of Donations 1881–1913* (p.
16) refers to the decoration as
"copper gilt." Woodrow Carpen-
ter, a ceramic engineer and an em-
ployee of the Rookwood Pottery
in its later years, was interviewed
about this vase by Trapp on January 14, 1984. According to Car-
penter, the metallic sheen was the
result of the glaze being loaded
with iron oxide and then fired in a
reduction kiln. The shinier leaves
of the palm fronds and other areas
that are raised had a second glaze
application, applied with a brush.
Whatever the cause, the effect is
quite beautiful, and it is curious
that more of these pieces have not
surfaced. Perhaps the metallic effect could not be controlled and,
therefore, not many such objects
were made. According to *Donations 1881–1913* (p. 16), the Wom-
en's Art Museum Association paid
eight dollars for the vase in 1883.
The paper label inscribed with
"83/178" indicates that the vase
was listed in S. G. Burt's inventory
of Rookwood Pottery in the
Cincinnati Art Museum in 1916
(see no. 14). In this case, however, it does not accord with the inventory.

3
TEAPOT
1884
Laura A. Fry, decorator
Maria Longworth Nichols,
shape designer
Thrown
H. 6 ½″ W. (handle to spout) 8″ D. 5″
Red body
Dull Finish glaze line

Marks: impressed a) kiln b) "Rookwood"/
"1884" c) "69"; incised LAF cipher

Collection of Calvin and Karen Long

According to *The Rookwood Shape Book 1883–1900* (p. 69), the first teapot of this shape was made in February 1884 after a Japanese design furnished by Maria Longworth Nichols, the founder of the Rookwood Pottery. Between February and April of that year ten such examples were made and consigned to various distributors, including Tiffany & Company of New York.

4

VASE
1 8 8 7
Albert Robert Valentien,
decorator
Shape design adapted by
William Watts Taylor from
William Auckland
Thrown
H. 16″ Diam. 7 ¾″
Sage green body
Yellow Standard and Dull Finish
glazes

Marks: impressed a) Rookwood logo
surmounted by one flame/"378" b) "S";
incised "A.R.V."/"L"

Collection of Fer-Duc, Inc.

The technique of one glaze flowing over another in this piece can also be seen in no. 1, where a brown-tinted, translucent, gloss glaze was poured over the Dull Finish glaze. In this piece a Yellow Standard glaze is dripping over the Dull Finish glaze. The yellow tint of the Standard glaze is readily visible as it flows over the white flower heads. The incised "L" on the bottom of the vase was a signal from the decorator to the glazer to use the light Standard glaze as opposed to the dark Standard glaze, which was deeper amber in color. The technique of flowing one glaze over another was probably inspired by the Japanese. Such examples as this and no. 1 probably do not represent Rookwood's Flowing glaze line because the earliest examples of this line date from 1897, as mentioned by S. G. Burt in his inventory of Rookwood Pottery in the Cincinnati Art Museum in 1916 (p. 122).

5
VASE
1885
Albert Robert Valentien,
decorator
Maria Longworth Nichols,
shape designer
Thrown
H. 20 ¼" Diam. 12"
Yellow body
Dull Finish glaze line

Marks: impressed "162"/"Rook-
wood"/"1885"/"Y"; incised "A.R.V."

Cincinnati Art Museum, Estate of
Charlotte Johnson and miscella-
neous funds (1982.66)

Rookwood decorators had access
to Katsushika Hokusai's *Manga*, a
multivolume set of random drawings by this Japanese artist. The
fish on the front of this vase and
the one on the back were inspired
by fishes in the *Manga* (fig. 1) and
appear frequently in Albert
Robert Valentien's decorations of
about 1885. The banded relief
decoration at the neck and base
was created by scoring a nailhead
and impressing it into the clay.
After the glaze firing, the gilt was
then applied over the glaze. Banded gilt decoration was often used
with the Dull Finish glaze, especially when the decoration was
inspired by the Japanese. It was
probably meant to resemble Japanese brocade. Like most Dull
Finish pieces, the interior of this
vase was lined with a high-gloss
glaze to insure vitrification of the
form.

1. Detail of a page from
Katsushika Hokusai's *Manga*.

6
VASE
1890
Anna Marie Valentien,
decorator
Kataro Shirayamadani, shape
designer
Thrown
H. 8 ½" Diam. 3 ½"
White body
Dull Finish glaze line

Marks: impressed Rookwood logo sur-
mounted by four flames/"589E"/"W";
incised "A.M.V./L̲"

Collection of Mr. and Mrs.
Ronald F. Walker

The incised, underlined "L" marked on the bottom indicates that the decorator intended the vase to be covered in the light Standard glaze. Indeed, all of the colors used in the decoration were common to the Standard glaze line. But instead the vase received a Dull Finish or smear glaze. This could have been by design or mistake. Perhaps it was purposely chosen for the Dull Finish in order to meet market demands, or perhaps the glazer accidentally used the Dull Finish. Kilns at Rookwood could hold from 1,500 to 4,500 pieces each. It was a pro-duction line process dealing with large quantities. To misglaze an object would have been easy. Another reason to glaze the vase with the Dull Finish instead of the Standard is suggested by the delicacy of the decoration. The Dull Finish allowed for an incredibly sharp definition in even the most delicate parts of the decoration, as exemplified here in the pistils of the flowers. Recognizing this, the glazer could have decided to use the smear glaze for the best aesthetic result. For a similar delicacy of detail see nos. 8 and 9.

7

VASE
1888
Albert Robert Valentien,
decorator
Thrown
H. 6 ½" Diam. 7 ¾"
White body
Dull Finish glaze line

Marks: impressed Rookwood logo sur-
mounted by two flames/"846B"/"W";
incised "A.R.V./S"

Collection of Edwin J. Kircher III

That this vase was intended for the Dull Finish or smear glaze is obvious. Decorations in the Dull Finish glaze line are often in pinks or, as in this vase, blues. The lighter colors responded to the part of the market that did not prefer the darker Standard wares. The "S" incised on the bottom by the decorator told the glazer to use the smear glaze. Common to this glaze line is the use of gold over the glaze. Here it outlines and highlights the wild roses.

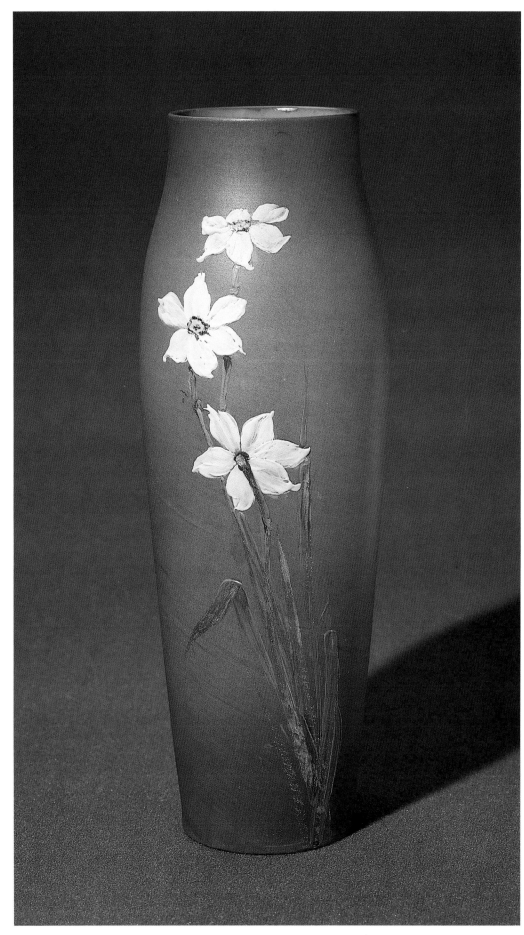

8

VASE
1886
Laura A. Fry, decorator
Alfred Brennan,
shape designer
Thrown
H. 11 ¾" Diam. 4 ¼"
Ginger body
Dull Finish glaze line

Marks: impressed Rookwood
logo/"30B"/"G"; incised LAF cipher

Collection of Margaret Pogue Fisk

Dull Finish pieces have often been mistakenly thought to be unglazed. They are, in fact, covered with a smear glaze that fills the pores of the exterior surface but is not deposited in a glassy form. William Watts Taylor was always quick to point out that this finish was as solid, durable, and washable as the gloss glazes. He often recommended that these pieces receive an occasional hard-brush scrubbing in soap and water to restore their true colors. While the precise, floral decorations make them appear delicate, they are indeed as durable as objects in other glaze lines.

9
VASE
1898
Harriet E. Wilcox, decorator
Kataro Shirayamadani,
shape designer
Thrown
H. 8 ¾" Diam. 3 ½"
White body
Dull Finish glaze line

Marks: impressed Rookwood logo sur-
mounted by twelve flames/"589E"; in-
cised "H.E.W."

Collection of Margaret Pogue Fisk

The use of the Dull Finish glaze in
1898 was somewhat anachronistic
because the glaze line was phased
out as a major profit source in the
early 1890s. The coloring of the
decoration on this vase, especially
the dark-to-light gradation of the
ground color, is more likely to be
seen in the Iris glaze line than the
Dull Finish. Nevertheless, the detailed, poetic quality of the grass-
es could not have been achieved
with any other glaze. This vase
and others (e.g., nos. 6–8) demonstrate that the Dull Finish line
offers some of the finest natural
decorations ever achieved at
Rookwood.

10
VASE
1899
Harriet E. Wilcox, decorator
Thrown and carved
H. 15″ Diam. 6 ½″
White body
Dull Finish glaze

Marks: impressed Rookwood logo surmounted by thirteen flames/"879B"; incised a) "H.E.W." b) "Garden of ?", the last word was lost when a hole was drilled into the bottom of the vase; painted in red "90?.??" The numbers in question have been rubbed off.

Collection of The Charles Hosmer Morse Museum of American Art

Rarely do Rookwood vases have a title incised on the bottom. In this case, while part of the title is missing, an educated guess would be "Garden of Eden." A watercolor of the same figure seen from a different angle was illustrated by Rookwood decorator Harriette Strafer on page 111 of the October 1904 edition of *Keramic Studio.* Strafer called the figure "Dawn." This title makes more sense as the vase pictures a female figure awakening in a field of poppies. A gold mount applied to the lip of the vase represents clouds and the rising sun.

It seems more probable that the "Garden of Eden" was simply an allusion to Eden Park, the location of the Rookwood Pottery in Cincinnati. Almost certainly, the depiction is of Dawn awakening, not Eve. The decorator used the same depiction on a smaller Black Iris vase of 1900, which can be seen illustrated in *From Our Native Clay* (1987, p. 58, no. 87). The decoration of both vases is probably applied-clay that is then carved and picked out in slip. If it were molded, the vase would have been cast instead of thrown, and it would have been noted in *The Rookwood Shape Book 1883–1900* or on Rookwood's shape cards. It is not. In fact, both sources refer to the shape as thrown. This Dull Finish vase is listed by S. G. Burt in his inventory of Rookwood Pottery in the Cincinnati Art Museum in 1916 (p. 136, #59) as "no glaze outside." This appears to be incorrect. We know that Rookwood was still using the smear glaze in the late 1890s (e.g., no. 9), at least sporadically. Also, the piece has retained its whiteness, which it could not have done for almost 100 years with no glaze. The numbers painted in red on the bottom are the Cincinnati Art Museum's loan numbers (see no. 13).

11
VASE
1899
Sara Alice Toohey, decorator
Kataro Shirayamadani,
shape designer
Thrown and carved
H. 11 ⅞" Diam. 3 ½"
White body
Standard glaze line with slight
Tiger Eye

Marks: impressed Rookwood logo sur-
mounted by thirteen flames/"589D";
incised ST cipher

Cincinnati Art Museum, Gift of
Dr. and Mrs. Herman J. Nimitz
(1986.929)

Toward the turn of the century, art pottery carved in high relief became the fashion. In this piece the decorator carved around the vase an iris, one of the most popular flowers used for decoration at Rookwood. In direct sunlight this vase evokes the famous Tiger Eye glaze as a soft sheen of gold appears just below the surface. Because of the white body one would not readily expect to see the Tiger Eye effect, which is more common to the red body Standard ware called Mahogany. Another example of a vase carved in relief by Sara Alice Toohey can be seen in no. 56.

12
PLAQUE: INDIAN CORN
1895
Albert Robert Valentien, decorator
Press molded
H. 9 ⅞" W. 8 ¼"
White body
Standard glaze line

Marks: impressed on left edge Rookwood logo surmounted by nine flames; painted in black on front, lower left "A.R.V."

Cincinnati Art Museum, Gloria W. Thomson Fund for Decorative Arts (1983.48)

Indian corn is indigenous only to the Americas. As such, this plaque shows that Rookwood was proudly proclaiming that its wares were first and foremost American. They were produced from native clays and materials, decorated by American-born and American-trained artists and celebrated subjects drawn from American life. Originally this plaque was set into a fireplace along with twenty-three others, but they were removed from their original setting in 1977. No doubt the fireplace had been a commission. Its scheme suggests a celebration of the seasons and the abundance of nature. This and the twenty-three others are rare examples of Standard plaques. Most Rookwood plaques are in the Vellum glaze line, which was not introduced until 1901.

13

VASE
1897
Kataro Shirayamadani,
decorator
Thrown
H. 11″ Diam. 4 ½″
Ginger body
Standard glaze line

Marks: impressed a) Rookwood logo
surmounted by eleven flames/"792C"
b) a trial mark in the form of a V-
shaped arrowhead; incised Kataro Shi-
rayamadani in Japanese characters;
painted in red a) "303.06" b) "35 00";
paper label inscribed."1897"

Collection of Roz and Peter
Thayer

The trial mark on the bottom indicates that this vase was experimental in decoration, glaze, or
both, but the exact nature of the
experiment is not clear. The Dog-
wood and swirling cloud decoration reflects the Japanese origin of
the decorator. This vase was in
Rookwood's corporate collection
that was on loan to the Cincinnati
Art Museum, and it is listed in
S. G. Burt's inventory of Rookwood Pottery in the Cincinnati
Art Museum in 1916 (p. 125,
#95). The "35 00" painted in red
on the bottom suggests an original price of thirty-five dollars.
Rookwood obviously valued this
vase highly since most pieces at
the time ranged in price from five
to fifteen dollars. The "303.06"
painted in red on the bottom is
the Cincinnati Art Museum's loan
number indicating that the vase
was the three-hundred-and-third
loan of 1906.

14
VASE
1898
**Kataro Shirayamadani,
decorator
William Auckland,
shape designer**
Thrown
H. 12 ¼" Diam. 5 ⅛"
White body
Standard glaze line

Marks: impressed Rookwood logo with twelve flames/"216"; incised Kataro Shirayamadani in Japanese characters; painted in red "364.02"; paper label, covered by second label inscribed "98/81"

Cincinnati Art Museum, Gift of Walter E. Schott, Margaret C. Schott, Charles M. Williams, Lawrence H. Kyte (1952.298)

The numbers painted in red on the bottom indicate that the vase was in Rookwood's corporate collection on loan to the Cincinnati Art Museum (see no. 13). The vase is listed in S. G. Burt's inventory of Rookwood Pottery in the Cincinnati Art Museum in 1916 (p. 129, #81). The paper label inscribed "98/81" gives us Burt's listing; it is his eighty-first entry for the year 1898. Sometimes, for an unknown reason, the paper labels inscribed in this manner do not correspond to Burt's inventory (see no. 2), but that is not the case here. It is interesting that the decorator consciously made this white-bodied vase appear to have a red body by painting the visible portion of the interior lip a rusty brown. One can only guess that he did this for aesthetic reasons. The black ground color is not a thickly applied cobalt blue as in Black Iris examples. Here it is simply a reaction of the brown ground and Standard glaze to the firing process.

15

**PLAQUE: GOVERNOR
AHFITCHE
1893
Artus Van Briggle, decorator**
Press molded
Diam. 15 ½"
Faience body
Standard glaze line

*Marks: on the back a) stenciled on the
clay body, Rookwood logo surmounted
by seven flames b) paper label inscribed
with "50," "Standard"/"1883"
[sic]/"A. Van Briggle" c) paper strip
typed with "not for sale"; incised on the
front, underglaze, lower right "A.V.B."*

Collection of Marge Schott

Rookwood decorators often used photographs as a source for their compositions. Here a photograph (fig. 1) by John K. Hillers, staff photographer for the Bureau of American Ethnology, which was administered by the Smithsonian Institution, was used. We know from *The North American Indians in Early Photographs* by Paula Richardson Fleming and Judith Luskey (1988, p. 139), that the subject is Governor Ahfitche, called José Quivera, of the San Felipe Pueblo, New Mexico, demonstrating the pump and drill method of making holes in turquoise and shells. Hillers took the photograph in the winter of 1880. Rookwood probably acquired a copy from the Smithsonian Institution to add to its photographic archives for use by decorators. According to S. G. Burt in his inventory of Rookwood Pottery in the Cincinnati Art Museum in 1916 (p. 105, #45) this plaque and a similar one (cat. no. 16) were exhibited at the World's Columbian Exposition in Chicago in 1893. He also states that the plaques were made of "sagger clay." A sagger is a protective case of fire clay for baking finer ceramics in the kiln. It consists of a coarse, gritty body made with grog to prevent shrinkage and warping (see no. 48). Rookwood later adapted this body, which it called architectural faience, for its architectural department. If these plaques are not the first, they are certainly one of the earliest instances of its use.

1. Governor Ahfitche

16

PLAQUE: HOPI MAN SPINNING WOOL
1893
Artus Van Briggle, decorator
Press molded
Diam. 19″
Faience body
Standard glaze line

Marks: impressed on the back Rookwood logo surmounted by seven flames, impressed five times; incised on the front, underglaze, lower right "A.V.B."/"93"

Collection of Marge Schott

Rookwood Pottery often acquired photographs, especially of Native Americans, for use by their artists as a source of decorations. According to records in the Smithsonian Institution, this plaque depicts a Hopi man spinning wool. The subject is drawn from a photograph (fig. 1) taken by John K. Hillers at the Pueblo of Walpi, Arizona, in 1879. Hillers shot many documentary photographs of Native Americans for government survey teams, which were administered by the Smithsonian Institution where the original photograph is held. According to

1. Hopi man spinning wool

S. G. Burt's inventory of Rookwood Pottery in the Cincinnati Art Museum in 1916 (p. 105, #62), this plaque and the one depicting Governor Ahfitche (cat. no. 15) were exhibited at the World's Columbian Exposition in Chicago in 1893. Native-Americans were fitting depictions at a world's fair celebrating our continent. The architectural faience body used for the plaque is very unusual for 1893 (see no. 15).

17

VASE: "LONE ELK"
1899
Matthew Andrew Daly,
decorator

Thrown
H. 13 ¼" W. (incl. handles) 10 ½"
D. 9 ½"
White body
Standard glaze line

Marks: impressed Rookwood logo sur-mounted by thirteen flames/"581C"; in-cised a) "MA Daly" b) "Lone Elk—Sioux"

Collection of Mr. and Mrs. W.
Roger Fry

Even though outside sources were sought for the many Native-American portrait photographs that Rookwood used as a basis for decoration, the company could also supply its own photographic needs. Rookwood's *Book of Corporate Minutes* (p. 200) shows that photography supplies had become a separate line item in its budget by 1898. Research by Susan Labry Meyn, Curator of Ethnology at the Cincinnati Museum of Natural History, demonstrates that Rookwood could have had access to Native Americans within the city. A group of Sicangu Sioux encamped for three months during the summer of 1896 on the grounds of the Cincinnati Zoo. The encampment was a living village for Cincinnati to see. It seems inconceivable that the pottery, which had already been using Native-American portrait photographs (e.g., nos. 15, 16), would not have taken advantage of the situation. Because of the green ground, this vase is an example of Green Standard ware, which is very rare for a Native-American portrait. Most are of the Yellow Standard (e.g., nos. 15, 16) or Brown Standard (e.g., no. 18) varieties. The shape was taken from a vase made by the Royal Copenhagen Porcelain factory of Denmark (see no. 18).

18

**VASE: "RICHARD TAIL—
OGALLALA SIOUX"**
1900
Grace Young, decorator
Thrown
H. 13 ¼" W. (incl. handles) 10 ½"
D. 9 ½"
White body
Standard glaze line

*Marks: impressed Rookwood logo sur-
mounted by fourteen flames/"581C";
incised a) GY cipher b) "Richard
Tail—Ogallala Sioux"*

Private Collection in memory of
Mr. and Mrs. E. N. Woistmann

As with many of Rookwood's Native-American portraits, this one
is wonderfully detailed in costume
with Richard Tail holding a club
in his right hand. The portrait was
almost certainly taken from a photograph in Rookwood's photographic library (e.g., nos. 15 and
16). Decorator Grace Young was
especially noted for her depictions of Native Americans. According to *The Rookwood Shape Book
1883–1900* (p. 181), the shape of
this vase was taken from an example by Royal Copenhagen Porcelain of Denmark, who in turn bor-
rowed it from a Greek example.
Rookwood and Royal Copenhagen were considered the two finest
art potteries in the world at the
turn of the century, and, as competitors, they were very aware of
each other's products.

19

VASE
1898
Kataro Shirayamadani,
decorator
John Menzel, shape designer
Thrown and carved
H. 9 ½" Diam. 6 ⅝"
White body
Standard glaze line with copper
electrodeposit

Marks: impressed Rookwood logo sur-
mounted by twelve flames/"604C", in-
cised Kataro Shirayamadani in
Japanese characters

Cincinnati Art Museum, Gift of
the Rookwood Pottery Company
(1900.380)

In Rookwood's *Book of Corporate Minutes* (pp. 204–205), William Watts Taylor states for the year ending January 31, 1900:

During the year a new department has been equipped for applying metal mountings by electrodeposit—the credit of applying this method and working out the most important details being due to Mr. Shirayamadani [sic]. The results recently obtained after much patient experiment give promise of a decided success and the specimens are to be shown first at the Paris Exposition.

This vase is an example of the electrodeposit method of metal mounting. The 1898 date of the vase is not problematic: the technique was developed during the year of 1899, and it would have been easy for Shirayamadani to use a vase thrown in 1898 for mounting in 1899. After the vase was thrown, the decorator incised the swirling clouds in the green clay and fashioned a clay dragon around the lip and shoulder. We know from S. G. Burt's inventory of Rookwood Pottery in the Cincinnati Art Museum in 1916 (p. 129, #98), that the area to be electroplated was left dry and unglazed for the metal mount. When the final firing was complete, the reptile was coated with a metal, in this case copper, by an electrodeposit technique. It is important to note that the dragon is made of clay covered with an electrodeposit; it is not a solid metal mount. Because this is such a fine example made immediately before the debut of the technique in 1900 at Exposition Universelle in Paris, it probably was exhibited there. Rookwood thought enough of the vase to donate it to the Cincinnati Art Museum in 1900, perhaps after it returned from Paris.

20

VASE
1900
Kataro Shirayamadani, decorator

Thrown and carved
H. 10 ½" Diam. 4 ¾"
White body
Standard glaze line with copper electrodeposit

Marks: impressed Rookwood logo surmounted by fourteen flames/"732B"; incised a) Kataro Shirayamadani in Japanese characters

Collection of Mr. and Mrs. Randy Sandler

Rookwood liked the electrodeposit technique (see no. 19) because, according to a 1902 promotional brochure entitled *Rookwood Pottery* (p. 36), "this method gives the piece a variety and richness of texture and color, while retaining the unity of design usually lost in metal mounting." The dragon on this vase is completely unified with the composition as it tangles with the swirling decoration. This is in marked contrast to Rookwood's earlier metal overlays by the Gorham Manufacturing Company, where the metal and ceramic create two separate, conflicting compositions. The vase was probably exhibited at the 1900 Exposition Universelle in Paris where the electrodeposit technique was first offered to the public. A notation in *The Rookwood Shape Book 1883–1900* (p. 132) states that the shape was taken from a vase by Hugh Robertson in Rookwood's corporate collection.

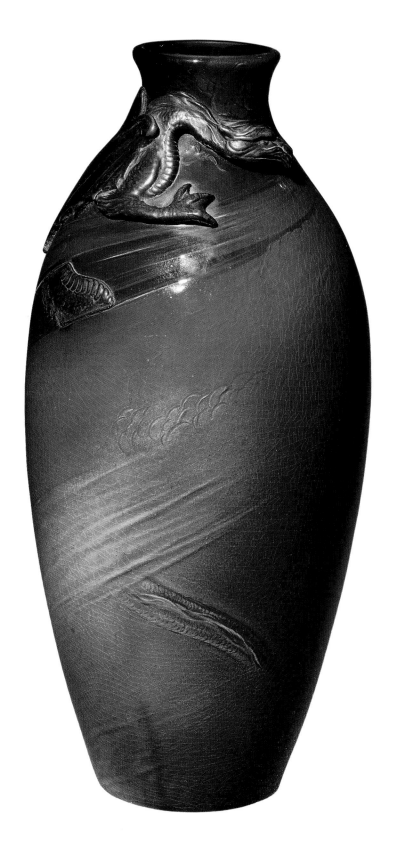

21
VASE
1900
**Matthew Andrew Daly,
decorator
Henry Yelland,
shape designer**
Thrown and carved
H. 12 ½" Diam. 5 ¼"
White body
Standard glaze line with silver
electrodeposit

*Marks: impressed Rookwood logo sur-
mounted by fourteen flames/"538C";
incised "MA Daly"/"G". The "G,"
which is incised in script, might be an
"L"; wheel ground "X"*

Collection of Mr. and Mrs. Randy
Sandler

The two types of electrodeposited metals that Rookwood used
were copper (e.g., nos. 19, 20)
and silver. Here silver is deposited over the relief of two moths,
possibly luna moths. If luna
moths, they represent the moon
or night as they flit about poppies representing sleep or death.
These very symbolic motifs were
typical for the turn of the century. The vase is quite sophisticated
in design and technique, and it
was probably exhibited at the
1900 Exposition Universelle in
Paris where Rookwood first displayed its electrodeposited wares.
The wheel-ground "X" on the
bottom of the vase means that it
was kept from the sales room. At
Rookwood pieces could be kept
from sales for several reasons.
Objects referred to as "seconds"
because of technical flaws were
marked in this manner. Sometimes an experiment with a glaze,
a body, or a decoration produced
such fine results that the piece was
held back by the decorator or the
pottery for future reference. As it
is obviously not a "second," this
particular vase could have been
kept from sales so that it could be
sent to the Paris exposition.

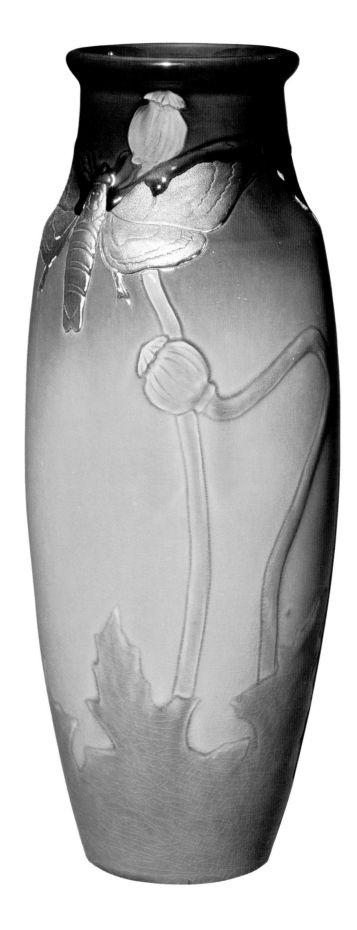

22

VASE
1894
John Hamilton Delaney
Wareham, decorator
Thrown
H. 6" Diam. 5"
Red body
Mahogany and Goldstone
glaze lines

*Marks: impressed Rookwood logo
surmounted by eight
flames/"763C"/"R"; incised "JDW";
painted in red "93.'02"*

Collection of Charles E. Deye

A red body covered with Standard glaze is the formula for the Mahogany glaze line. In this example, the Goldstone effect of sparkles within the glaze is also visible, especially around the lip. The dripping red (seen again in no. 23) was intentional. The Goldstone, however, was often a fortuitous result and could not be controlled. Goldstone (see also no. 23) and Tiger Eye (cat. nos. 24, 25) effects were unexpected aberrations in the Mahogany glaze line. They first occurred in a firing of October 1884, much to the delight of the pottery.

23
VASE
1898
Artus Van Briggle, decorator
William Watts Taylor, shape
designer
Thrown
H. 8″ Diam. 4 ½″
Red body
Goldstone glaze line with some
Tiger Eye

Marks: impressed Rookwood logo sur-
mounted by twelve flames/"745B"; in-
cised "A.V.B."

Collection of Esta and Jim Brett

This is an excellent example of
the Goldstone glaze line. Goldstone, named after the stone it resembles, gives the effect of millions of little flecks of gold within
the glaze. It is often confused with
Tiger Eye (see nos. 24, 25), which
offers a golden sheen under the
glaze. Most decoration, if any, in
the Goldstone line was incised, as
were the fish on this vase. Goldstone could not be produced at
will and had a high loss-ratio.
Consequently, the vases were usually created small to keep the loss-
es to a minimum. Goldstone was
unique to Rookwood and brought
the pottery much international
acclaim.

24
VASE
1898
Kataro Shirayamadani,
possible decorator
Thrown and carved
H. 8 ½" Diam. 3 ½"
Red body
Tiger Eye glaze line with copper
electrodeposit

Marks: impressed Rookwood logo surmounted by twelve flames/"S1363"

Collection of Fer-Duc, Inc.

This is a fine and rare example of the Tiger Eye glaze (see no. 25) combined with an even rarer electrodeposited copper mount (see nos. 19, 20). Glaze on the bottom of this vase obscures the marks, and an X ray reveals only the logo with flames and the shape number. Because Kataro Shirayamadani was perfecting the electrodeposit technique at this time and seems to be the only one at Rookwood using it with three-dimensional mounts, he is the likely decorator. The rarity and quality of the vase suggests that it was sent to the 1900 Exposition Universelle in Paris where Rookwood first introduced the electrodeposit technique.

VASE
1900
Matthew Andrew Daly,
decorator
Thrown
H. 17″ Diam. 11″
Red body
Tiger Eye glaze line

Marks: impressed Rookwood logo surmounted by fourteen flames/"787A"; incised "MA Daly"; paper label Exposition Universelle, Paris, 1900

Collection of Mrs. George
Newman III

This is perhaps the finest Tiger Eye example ever made. Like Goldstone (cat. no. 23), the Tiger Eye glaze line was a fortunate, accidental by-product of the Mahogany glaze line (e.g., no. 22). It displayed a radiant shimmer, as if a sheet of gold foil were deep within the glaze. When it first appeared in 1884, William Watts Taylor named it Tiger Eye after the stone it resembled. Rookwood constantly tried to repeat the effect at will but without success. Because of the high loss-ratio in production attempts, most pieces were made in smaller sizes of five to eight inches in order to lessen the cost of failure. This example is remarkable for its size as well as its quality. Successful Tiger Eye specimens varied widely in quality from barely visible effects (e.g., no. 11) to a radiant shimmer, as seen in this example. The finest effects occurred perhaps once every four years at most. The Tiger Eye quality of this vase is perhaps unique since it is even finer than the famous Uranus vase sent to the 1889 Exposition Universelle in Paris. Usually decoration was limited to incised compositions, but this one displays two cranes on the shoulder in underglaze slip. Like Goldstone, the Tiger Eye glaze was unique to Rookwood. Rookwood was highly successful at the Paris 1900 Exposition Universelle, receiving many awards including the Grand Prix. Without question, this vase contributed to that success. The shape can also be seen in no. 43. According to *The Rookwood Shape Book 1883–1900* (p. 187), the shape was taken from a Japanese vase.

26

VASE
1897
William Purcell McDonald,
decorator
Thrown
H. 14 ½" Diam. 12"
White body
Sea Green glaze line

Marks: impressed Rookwood logo
surmounted by seven flames/"S";
incised "W.P.McD."

Collection of
Ms. Nancy Daly

The Sea Green Glaze line made its debut in 1894. The glaze offered a rich, green-tinted, translucent, high-gloss effect. The actual color of the green tint can be seen on this vase in the depicted coral, which was painted with white slip under the glaze. Marine life was most often depicted because of its compatibility with the green tint. Blue and white were generally the only compositional colors used. Here the blue ground color, which looks blue-green under the glaze, highlights the sea life painted in white.

27

VASE
1898
Sara Sax, decorator
William Purcell McDonald,
shape designer
Thrown
H. 6″ Diam. 5″
White Body
Sea Green glaze line

Marks: impressed Rookwood logo surmounted by twelve flames/"S1393"; incised a) "S.S." b) "o" c) "G" d) "G"

Collection of Jonathan Alk

Marine life was the subject matter most chosen by Rookwood decorators for the Sea Green glaze line (see no. 26). The "G" incised on the bottom of this vase is an indication from Sara Sax to the glazer to use the Sea Green glaze. It is incised twice suggesting that the decorator wanted to make certain that the glazer got the message. Indeed, one cannot imagine the composition under any other glaze. Shape numbers preceded by an "S," such as "S1393," were given to new shapes being tried on the market. Once a shape had proven its salability, it was added to the shape book and given a regular number. According to *The Rookwood Shape Book 1883–1900* (p. 80), "S1393" was sufficiently successful to be given the regular number "880," and the first piece using this number was thrown in May 1899. The meaning of the "o" incised on the bottom is undetermined. A similar circle can be seen on the bottom of no. 33, a vase of the same year.

28
VASE
1898
Sara Sax, decorator
Thrown and carved
H. 5 ⅞" Diam. 3 ½"
White body
Sea Green glaze line

*Marks: impressed Rookwood logo sur-
mounted by twelve flames/"860"; incised a) SAX cipher b) "G"*

Cincinnati Art Museum, Gift of
Walter E. Schott, Margaret C.
Schott, Charles M. Williams,
Lawrence H. Kyte (1952.300)

This vase was part of Rookwood's
corporate collection on loan to the
Cincinnati Art Museum. It is listed
in S. G. Burt's inventory of Rookwood Pottery in the Cincinnati
Art Museum in 1916 (p. 132,
#174), as "gr [green] modeled."
The floral decoration is carved
into the clay and picked out with
slip. The yellow ground color,
more common to the Standard
glaze line, is unusual for Sea
Green. According to the *The Rookwood Shape Book 1883–1900* (p. 60),
the shape number was originally
"S1188" and changed to "860" in
September 1898 (see no. 27). Floral, as well as carved compositions,
are uncommon in the Sea Green
glaze line, which normally displays underglaze slip decorations
of marine life (e.g., nos. 26, 27).

VASE
1901
Frederick Sturgis Lawrence,
decorator
Thrown
H. 15″ Diam. 7 ½″
White body
Sea Green glaze line

Marks: impressed Rookwood logo
surmounted by fourteen
flames/"I"/"192AZ"; incised a) "SL"
b) "G"; wheel ground "X"

Collection of Carole and Ray Kolb

The wheel-ground "X" on the bottom indicates that the vase was held from sales for some reason (see no. 21). This vase is so fine it could have been retained for display at the 1904 Louisiana Purchase Exposition in St. Louis. The year 1901 is not too early for Rookwood to be holding pieces for an international exposition three years away. It might also have been withheld for the unusual style of the composition. The stems and leaves of the flowers are outlined in black (actually a heavy application of cobalt blue that appears black). Compositions outlined in black were the result of the Arts and Crafts movement taking hold at about this time. The technique was not common to the Sea Green glaze line nor, indeed, to any of the high-gloss glaze lines, which were shaped by earlier aesthetic beliefs. It was a technique used almost exclusively for Arts and Crafts mat glazes. Curiously, the impressed shape number on the bottom ends with a "Z", which indicates that the vase was made for a mat glaze finish. This is an early example of the Arts and Crafts influence at Rookwood.

30
PLAQUE: SNOW SCENE WITH CROWS
1895
**Matthew Andrew Daly,
decorator**
Press molded
H. 11″ W. 7⅞″
White body
Aerial Blue glaze line

*Marks: impressed on the back Rook-
wood logo surmounted by nine flames,
impressed four times; incised on the
back "MAD"; painted in white on
front, lower left "MA DALY"/"95"*

Collection of Mr. and Mrs.
Harold K. Omer

In *The Rookwood Shape Book* 1883–
1900 (p. 188), shape #188 illustrates a circular plaque with a similar decoration, if not a duplicate
of the composition seen here. It
notes that the circular plaque was
decorated in monochrome and
that the shape was "not salable."
The low shape number of 188
suggests that the composition was
first used in the early 1880s. The
glaze, or glaze line, used on the
circular plaque is unknown, but
since Aerial Blue was not developed for the market until 1894, it
would not have been this glaze or
glaze line. Decorator Matthew
Andrew Daly used the same photographic or illustrated source as
the plaque in the *Shape Book*, probably retained in Rookwood's library. No doubt the source was a
monochromatic depiction that
lent itself to the monochromatic
decorations that were a trademark
of the Aerial Blue glaze line. This
particular plaque is an exceptional
example of that line. Using a difficult technique, the decoration is
partially suspended between layers of glaze, adding unusual depth
and quality.

31
VASE
1907
Carl Schmidt, decorator
Joseph Bailey, shape designer
Thrown
H. 14 ½″ Diam. 8″
White body
Iris glaze line

*Marks: impressed a) Rookwood logo
surmounted by fourteen
flames/"614B"/"VII" b) CS cipher in a
circular cartouche; incised "W"*

Private Collection

The Iris glaze line, as exemplified
in this vase, offered background
colors that were generally graded
from light to dark, or dark to
light, in combination with lyrical
floral decorations. The use of
black in the ground colors was
common in 1907 (see no. 38).
The shape of this vase can also be
seen in nos. 36, 42, 61, 62, 75, and
93. Carl Schmidt's cipher is impressed, not incised. He is one of
the few decorators who had a
stamp made, or made one himself,
to impress his touchmark on his
work (see also no. 37).

32
VASE
1903
Carl Schmidt, decorator
Thrown
H. 14″ Diam. 6″
White body
Iris glaze line

Marks: impressed a) Rookwood logo surmounted by fourteen flames/"III"/"907C" b) CS cipher in a circular cartouche; incised "W"

Collection of Roz and Peter Thayer

The decoration on this vase is slightly unusual in that the ground color does not gradate from light to dark as strongly as most Iris glaze line examples (e.g., nos. 31, 37, 39). The painting is very sensitive, with exceptional delicacy given to the milkweed seeds floating in the air. As usual, decorator Carl Schmidt's cipher on the bottom of the vase is impressed, not incised (see no. 31). A larger version of this shape can be seen in no. 64. The vase was exhibited at the Milwaukee Art Museum in "Rookwood Pottery and the Arts and Crafts Movement 1880–1915" in 1987.

33

VASE
1898
Lenore Asbury, decorator
Thrown
H. 6″ Diam. 7″
White body
Iris glaze line

Marks: impressed Rookwood logo surmounted by twelve flames/"762C"; incised a) "L.A." b) "0"

Collection of Roz and Peter Thayer

A vase almost identical to this one exists in a private collection in Cincinnati. The two were perhaps originally made as a pair, although Rookwood did not intentionally make pairs (e.g, nos. 89, 93, 96) until the 1920s. More likely, the same source was used for both decorations, giving a very similar appearance to the vases. Rookwood always insisted that no two artist-signed pieces were alike. The three pink whiplash curves divided evenly around the vase reflect the influence of Art Nouveau at the turn of the century. The meaning of the incised circle on the bottom of the vase is unknown. It is also seen in another vase of the same year (see no. 27). This piece was displayed at the Milwaukee Art Museum in the exhibition "Rookwood Pottery and the Arts and Crafts Movement 1880–1915" in 1987.

34
VASE
1902
Albert Robert Valentien,
decorator
Thrown
H. 14 ¾" Diam. 8 ¼"
White body
Iris glaze line

*Marks: impressed Rookwood logo
surmounted by fourteen
flames/"II"/"905B"; incised
"A.R.VALENTIEN"*

Collection of Jay and Emma Lewis

Rookwood thought very highly of this vase when it was made. In a 1902 advertising brochure of 47 pages, simply titled *Rookwood Pottery* (p. 29), the company featured the vase as an example of the Iris glaze line. Later, in a 1904 sales catalogue called *The Rookwood Book* (no. 37), the vase was again depicted by Rookwood. The fact that decorator Albert Robert Valentien spelled out his last name on the bottom instead of incising his regular "A.R.V." signature, indicates that he, too, was proud of the piece. Full signatures were usually reserved only for the finest work.

35
VASE
1898
John Hamilton Delaney
Wareham, decorator
Thrown
H. 12 ½" Diam. 5 ¾"
White body
Iris glaze line

Marks: impressed a) Rookwood logo
surmounted by twelve flames/"846B"
b) a trial mark in the form of a V-
shaped arrowhead with tip pointing up,
superimposed on the same mark with tip
pointing down, all between two dots;
incised "JDW"; wheel ground "X"

Cincinnati Art Museum, Gift of
Mrs. Joyce Clancy in memory of
her husband, Jesse K. Clancy
(1977.8)

The trial mark impressed on the bottom of this vase tells us that Rookwood was experimenting with the glaze or decoration. According to S. G. Burt in his inventory of Rookwood Pottery in the Cincinnati Art Museum in 1916 (p. 117, #78), the pottery first began experimenting with the use of black under the Iris glaze in 1895. The black color was in fact a cobalt blue oxide applied so thickly as to appear black. In this vase the blue is visible along the edges of the iris flowers where the cobalt has bled or become thin.

An oxide color of true black, called Jet Black, was not developed for use under glaze until 1916 (see Burt, p. 180, #P3). This vase probably represents an experiment to develop a black color. That the experiment was successful can ultimately be determined by the wheel-ground "X" on the bottom. Objects so marked were held from sales for various reasons. It could be speculated that

Rookwood thought the trial failed, and marked the vase with an "X" in order to designate it as a "second" that would not be sold. More likely, it was withheld precisely because the experiment was successful, and the vase would therefore be needed for future reference. This theory is confirmed by the fact that in September 1898, Rookwood featured the vase in an article titled "Rook-

wood Pottery," by John Valentine for *House Beautiful* (p. 127). It was obviously a very successful early trial of the use of underglaze black in the Iris line. Within a year Rookwood would build upon this experiment to create the Black Iris glaze line (e.g., nos. 40–45), which produced some of the finest specimens in the history of art pottery.

36

VASE
1906
Kataro Shirayamadani,
decorator
Joseph Bailey, shape designer
Thrown
H. 12 ¼" Diam. 7 ½"
White body
Iris glaze line

Marks: impressed Rookwood logo
surmounted by fourteen
flames/"VI"/"614C"; incised Kataro
Shirayamadani in Japanese characters

Collection of
Ms. Nancy Daly

It seems that when Rookwood artists decorated with poppies there was often a conscious symbolic intent (e.g., nos. 10, 21, 45). Here the ground color is sharply divided between black at the shoulder and a light yellow below, which could easily be read as night and day. The poppies that reach into the black, or night, have closed flower heads; those that remain in the yellow area, or day, have open flower heads. The two contrasting ground colors, in combination with the poppies, symbolize day and night, to be awake and to be asleep, and life and death. The same vase shape can also be seen in nos. 31, 42, 61, 62, 75, and 93.

37
VASE
1907
Carl Schmidt, decorator
Thrown
H. 10″ Diam. 5 ½″
White body
Iris glaze line

*Marks: impressed a) Rookwood logo
surmounted by fourteen
flames/"VII"/"917B" b) CS cipher in a
circular cartouche; incised "W"*

Collection of Mrs. and Mrs.
Ronald F. Walker

Generally, the impressed marks
on the bottom of a vase are by the
potters and the incised marks are
by the decorators. Carl Schmidt's
signature is an exception because
he had a stamp made which he
used to impress, instead of incise,
his cipher (see also no. 31). The
incised "W" was an instruction
from the artist to the glazer to use
the Iris glaze. At Rookwood the
Iris glaze was referred to as the
"white" glaze, thus the "W." It was
probably called "white" because
that was its color before it was
fired. Carl Schmidt often used this
type of mushroom in his decorations. Another such example can
be seen illustrated in *From Our Native Clay* (1987), page 30, no. 40.

38
VASE
1907
Kataro Shirayamadani,
decorator
Thrown
H. 8 ½" Diam. 6 ¼"
White body
Iris glaze line

Marks: impressed Rookwood logo surmounted by fourteen flames/"VII"/"942B"; incised Kataro Shirayamadani in Japanese characters

Private Collection

Many Iris glaze line examples dating from 1907 exhibit grounds that grade from black to a lighter color (e.g., nos. 31, 37, 39). Rookwood began experimenting with black in 1895 and was producing successful compositions with it no later than 1898 (see no. 35). By the turn of the century, a solid black ground was used (e.g., nos. 40–45), and later the ground was graded from black to a lighter color as in this example. The fact that so many of these examples date from 1907 suggests that Rookwood touted this style at the 1907 Jamestown Tercentennial Exposition, where the pottery won a gold medal.

39
VASE
1907
Carl Schmidt, decorator
Thrown
H. 14 ½" Diam. 6"
White body
Iris glaze line

*Marks: impressed a) Rookwood logo
surmounted by fourteen
flames/"VII"/"950A" b) CS cipher in
a circular cartouche; incised "W"*

Cincinnati Art Museum, Barney
Hugger Memorial (1975. 344)

Wisteria was a very common floral motif at Rookwood (see also
no. 62). It was one of the three
most popular flowers used, along
with the iris and the tulip. Here it
is shown against a background
fading from black to white. This
was typical for 1907 (see no. 38).
Carl Schmidt's signature on the
bottom is impressed, not incised
(see no. 37), and the incised "W"
was an indication from the decorator to the glazer to use the Iris
glaze (see no. 37).

VASE
1903
Carl Schmidt, decorator
Thrown
H. 13 ⅓" Diam. 6"
White body
Black Iris glaze line

Marks: impressed a) Rookwood logo surmounted by fourteen flames/"III"/"904B" b) CS cipher in a circular cartouche; incised "W"

Collection of The Charles Hosmer Morse Museum of American Art

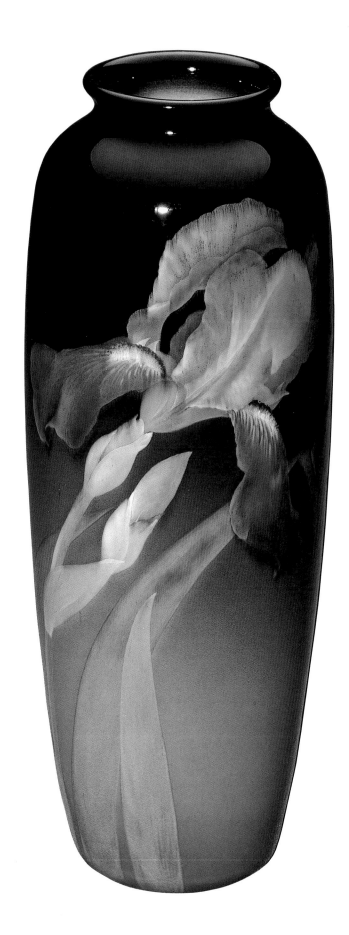

In a November 1901 article for *Keramic Studio* titled "Rookwood at the Pan-American" (p. 146), decorator William Purcell McDonald stated that there was a subdivision of the Iris glaze line into a glaze called Dark Iris, "the Dark Iris is similar in general treatment [to the regular Iris] but the colors are much darker, the ground sometimes being a rich luminous black." Later, in an inventory of Rookwood Pottery in the Cincinnati Art Museum in 1916 (p. 139, #22), S. G. Burt titles Iris glazes with the black ground "Black Iris." It can be argued that this vase is a Dark Iris piece because of the dark blue color towards the bottom. The overall effect of the black ground, however, places it in the more commonly recognized category of Black Iris. The black color was the result of long experimentation at Rookwood (see no. 35) that culminated in Black Iris ware being sent to the 1900 Exposition Universelle in Paris. This is probably an early transitional piece between the solid–ground Black Iris examples from 1900 (e.g., nos. 41–45) and the later Iris examples from 1907 (e.g., nos. 31, 37–39), where the black ground fades to a lighter color. It is not unusual for Carl Schmidt's signature to be impressed, or for an incised "W" to be found on an Iris glazed vase (see no. 37).

41
VASE
1900
Kataro Shirayamadani, decorator
Thrown and carved
H. 14 ½" Diam. 9"
White body
Black Iris glaze line with copper
and silver electrodeposit

Marks: impressed Rookwood logo surmounted by fourteen flames/"S1523"; incised Kataro Shirayamadani in Japanese characters

Collection of Truett M. Lawson

This is a Black Iris example with a copper and silver electrodeposit applied to a carved decoration. The Black Iris category was the result of Rookwood's achievement of a black underglaze color (see no. 35). The pottery sent many such specimens to the 1900 Exposition Universelle in Paris, where they were received with great acclaim. The electrodeposit technique was developed in 1899, and it was also featured at the 1900 Paris exposition (see nos. 19–21). The two metals generally used in the technique were copper and silver. Unusually both metals appear in this vase. For the carving the decorator added clay to the vase and then carved the water lilies in relief (see also no. 44). The extremely rare combination of Black Iris and electrodeposit strongly suggests that the vase was sent to Paris for display in 1900. It can be seen in an old photograph, perhaps taken at the Paris exposition, used by Herbert Peck in his article, "Some Early Collections of Rookwood Pottery," in Parke–Bernet Galleries' magazine *Auction* (September 1969, page 21).

42
VASE
1900
Kataro Shirayamadani,
possible decorator
Joseph Bailey, shape designer
Thrown
H. 14" Diam. 7 ½", stand: H. 7 ¾"
White body
Black Iris glaze line

Marks: impressed Rookwood logo
surmounted by fourteen flames/"614B"

Collection of Gloria Shapiro

This Black Iris vase is in the original stand that Rookwood ordered from the Orient. Because this is the only example known to survive, it is difficult to make generalizations, but it is safe to assume that only vases with Oriental decorations were thought appropriate for display in this manner. Depicting birds flying through bamboo trees, this Black Iris specimen is supported physically as well as aesthetically by the stand. The quality and date of the vase are persuasive indications that it was exhibited at the 1900 Exposition Universelle in Paris. It was there that Black Iris examples (see nos. 40, 41, 43–45) were first displayed for the international market. There is no artist's mark on this vase. It was probably lost when Rookwood fitted the bottom to the stand. The quality and Oriental character suggest that it was made by decorator Kataro Shirayamadani. The vase shape can also be seen in nos. 31, 36, 61, 62, 75, and 93.

43

VASE
1899
Kataro Shirayamadani,
decorator
Thrown
H. 17 ⅜" Diam. 11 ½"
White body
Black Iris glaze line

Marks: impressed Rookwood logo
surmounted by thirteen flames/"787A";
incised Kataro Shirayamadani in
Japanese characters; paper labels
a) Exposition Universelle, Paris, 1900
b) inscribed with "1500f"

Philadelphia Museum of Art, Gift
of John T. Morris

One paper label on the bottom of
this Black Iris vase certifies that it
was on display at the 1900 Exposition Universelle in Paris. The other paper label inscribed with
"1500f" probably indicates that
the price of the vase at the exposition was 1500 francs. The raised,
salmon-colored rose decoration is
painted in relief with underglaze
slip. A painted decoration could
be flush with the surface of a vase
or it could be in relief depending
on how thickly the slip was applied. Sometimes the appearance

of relief could be the result of the
decoration being carved in the
clay. That is not the case here,
however, where it is the result of
built-up slip that is possibly then
carved back. The black ground
color developed from much experimentation at Rookwood (see
no. 35), and it made its international debut at the 1900 Paris exposition with great success (see
also nos. 40–42, 44, 45). The

shape of this vase can also be seen
in no. 25. According to *The Rookwood Shape Book 1883–1900* (p.
187), the shape was taken from a
Japanese example. This vase was
exhibited at the Delaware Art
Museum in "The Pre-Raphaelite
Era" in 1976; and at the Everson
Museum of Art in "A Century of
Ceramics in the United States:
1878–1978" in 1979.

44
VASE
1900
Matthew Andrew Daly,
decorator
Thrown and carved
H. 10 ¾" Diam. 7 ½"
White body
Black Iris glaze line

Marks: impressed Rookwood logo sur-
mounted by fourteen flames/"886C";
incised "MA Daly"/"W"

Cincinnati Art Museum, Gift of
Dr. and Mrs. Herman J. Nimitz
(1986.928)

This is an unusual Black Iris example because it is carved. The decorator added clay to the vase and
then carved the pineapple plants
in relief. The type of carved relief
decoration where clay is applied
to the vase is more often seen covered with electrodeposited silver
or copper (e.g., nos. 19, 20, 24,
41). In this example it is simply
slip painted under the glaze. The
pineapple is an atypical motif, and
the reason for its use is unknown.
Because of the fine quality of the
vase, it was probably sent to the
1900 Exposition Universelle in
Paris. Perhaps Rookwood displayed the pineapples as a symbol
of hospitality to the international
market. The Black Iris glaze line
was first introduced in Paris at the
Exposition after several years of
development (see no. 35). The
"W" incised by the artist on the
bottom of the vase was a signal to
the glazer to use the Iris glaze (see
no. 37). Decorator Daly spelled
out his surname in his signature
on this vase. Normally just his initials would suffice. Rookwood
artists reserved full signatures for
their finest work (see also no. 34).

45

VASE
1900
Edward George Diers,
decorator
William Watts Taylor,
shape designer
Cast
H. 9 ⅛" Diam. 3 ¼"
White body
Black Iris glaze line

Marks: impressed Rookwood logo sur-
mounted by fourteen flames/"742E";
a) incised ED cipher b) "W"

Cincinnati Art Museum, Gift of
Walter E. Schott, Margaret C.
Schott, Charles M. Williams,
Lawrence H. Kyte (1952.322)

Poppies on a black ground seem to
symbolize sleep or death. The
poppy was a popular motif at the
turn of the century, and Rookwood used it often (see nos. 10,
21). In this vase the evocative
flowers stand out in slight relief
because of the thickly applied underglaze slip. *The Rookwood Shape
Book 1883–1900* (p. 142) displays
two types of lips for the vase, one
straight and one slightly flared.
This one is slightly flared. The
Black Iris glaze line was extremely
popular when it was introduced at
the 1900 Exposition Universelle
in Paris (see no. 40). It was the culmination of years of experimentation with a black underglaze color
(see no. 35). The "W" incised by
the decorator on the bottom of
the vase was an indication to the
glazer to use the Iris glaze (see no.
37).

46

VASE

1904

Olga Geneva Reed, decorator

Thrown

H. 6 ½" Diam. 4"

Faience body

Incised Mat glaze line

Marks: impressed Rookwood logo surmounted by fourteen flames/"IV"/"39EZ"; incised "O.G.R."

Collection of George Edward Breen

It is unusual for an Incised Mat glaze line example to have a decorator's signature. According to Rookwood's *Book of Corporate Minutes* (p. 208), for the year ending March 2, 1901, incised decorations were done by the clay workers under the supervision of decorator William Purcell McDonald. Such vases did not pass through the decorating room. Obviously this one is an exception. The impressed "Z" following the shape number and size letter on the bottom of the vase indicates that the shape was meant for the Mat glaze line, and it can be found on virtually all Mat examples from 1900 until 1904 when it was discontinued.

LAMP
1902
Sara Alice Toohey and
William Purcell McDonald,
decorators
Cast
H. (incl. metalwork) 20 ¾"
Diam. 7 ¼" H. (lamp base) 10 ¾"
Faience body
Conventional Mat glaze line

Marks: impressed Rookwood logo
surmounted by fourteen
flames/"II"/"326AZ"; incised
"WMcD"; painted in black ST cipher,
painted over the incised mark

Collection of Don F. Mahan

Conventional Mat decorations are composed of solid colors outlined in black (see also no. 48). While serving an aesthetic function, the slip-trailed black outline also serves a practical function by keeping the glaze colors separate. There are two artists' signatures on the bottom of the lamp. Decorator William Purcell McDonald's cipher is incised, whereas Sara Alice Toohey's is painted. The incised mark was made before the biscuit firing when the clay was leather hard; the painted mark was made after the lamp was biscuit fired, before the glaze firing. After an object is fired the clay cannot be incised, thus at that point all marks must be painted on. All of this tells us that decorator McDonald composed the hyacinth decoration with a slip-trailed black line before the first firing, and that decorator Toohey applied the colored mat glaze, something that would have been done after the first firing. The feet of the lamp are glazed black. The metalwork (i.e., the plate that caps the lamp base, the stem, and two electrical sockets), were purchased and applied by Rookwood. The missing lamp shade, which was probably a leaded-glass or copper dome, was also purchased and applied by Rookwood. The impressed "Z" on the bottom is a Mat glaze line designation (see no. 46).

48
PLAQUE: WOMAN SMELLING LILIES
1902
Albert Robert Valentien, decorator
Press molded
H. 21" W. 15"
Faience body
Conventional Mat glaze line

Marks: impressed on the back Rookwood logo surmounted by fourteen flames/"II"; painted in brown on front, lower left "A.R.V."

Collection of Jerome and Patricia Shaw

The architectural faience body was made of clay with a high proportion of grog (fired and crushed clay) added to prevent shrinkage and warping. Most large plaques were made with architectural faience (see also nos. 15, 16) to eliminate these problems. This plaque was not meant to be a part of a larger architectural mural because the decoration is complete within the rectangle and it was signed at the lower left corner. An outline of the composition was slip trailed in black on the green clay form, which was then biscuit fired. Afterwards, colored mat glazes were painted between the lines and the plaque was fired a final time (see also no. 47). The motif of a woman, or women, in a field of lilies was very common at the turn of the century. There might be a religious connotation in this example because the sun could be read as a nimbus.

VASE
1901
Albert Robert Valentien,
decorator
Thrown
H. 14 ½" Diam. 8 ½"
Faience body
Painted Mat glaze line, possibly

Marks: impressed Rookwood logo
surmounted by fourteen
flames/"I"/"299AZ"; painted in cobalt,
a) "A.R.Valentien" b) "X"; paper label,
inscribed with "451"/"6500"/"Ea"

Collection of
Dr. and Mrs. Herman J. Nimitz

This is a very curious Painted Mat glaze line example because the decoration was not inlaid (see nos. 50–52). Instead the large iris flower heads were painted over the mat glaze. It is the only known example to display this variation in the Painted Mat technique. The fact that Valentien's signature is painted, not incised, indicates that he began the decoration after the vase was fired. This is not unusual, however, since decoration in the Mat glaze line is applied after the first or biscuit firing. The "X" on the bottom was painted, not wheel-ground like others (see, nos. 21, 35). It is not known what this means. Like the wheel ground "X," it may indicate that the artist was experimenting with the technique and wanted the vase to be withheld for future reference. Decorator Valentien obviously thought that the vase was special because he included the full spelling of his surname in his signature on the bottom (see no. 34). The paper label notes a price of sixty-five dollars each, suggesting that the vase might have been one of a pair. This would have been unusual in 1901 as Rookwood did not begin marketing pairs seriously until the 1920s. The meaning of the "451" on the paper label is undetermined. The impressed "Z" was reserved for mat glazed shapes (see no. 46). A hole has been drilled (not by Rookwood) into the bottom of the vase to transform it into a lamp. The discoloration around the lip has been caused by a metal cap that was part of the lamp fitting.

50
VASE
1902
Harriet Elizabeth Wilcox, decorator
Thrown
H. 10 ¼″ Diam. 5 ½″
Faience body
Painted Mat glaze line

Marks: impressed Rookwood logo surmounted by fourteen flames/"II"/ "192CZ"; painted in black "HEW"

Collection of R. A. Ellison

The Painted Mat technique was very difficult and time consuming. Ground colors were atomized from dark to light on a biscuit-fired vase. Sometimes just one color was applied throughout. Once the ground was dry, the design was outlined, cut through to the clay, and removed. Then glazes of different colors that constituted the decoration were inlaid into the spaces. Generally, where an inlaid color met the ground color, a slight ridge or shoreline can be seen. This is the result of a wet glaze meeting a dry glaze. Shorelines, if any, are barely visible on this vase, which is very unusual. Decorator Harriet Elizabeth Wilcox was a master at the extremely difficult inlay technique (see also nos. 51–53). Her signature was painted, not incised, which is typical in the Mat glaze lines (see no. 47). The impressed "Z" on the bottom was given to Mat Glazed shapes (see no. 46). Red poppies on a dark ground could be symbolic of sleep or death (see nos. 10, 21, 45). This vase is illustrated in *From Our Native Clay* (1987), page 32, no. 44.

51
VASE
1901
Harriet Elizabeth Wilcox,
decorator
Thrown
H. 10 ½" Diam. 5 ½"
Faience body
Painted Mat glaze line

Marks: impressed Rookwood logo surmounted by fourteen flames/"I"/ "201Z"; painted in black "HEW"

Collection of R. A. Ellison

This is an early example of the difficult Painted Mat technique (see no. 50). S. G. Burt in his inventory of Rookwood Pottery in the Cincinnati Art Museum in 1916 (p. 138, #3), records the first example, which was by Albert Robert Valentien, in 1900. Harriet Elizabeth Wilcox was one of the few Rookwood decorators to become proficient in this style of decoration (see also nos. 50, 52, 53). Typically, her signature is painted, not incised, on the bottom (see no. 47), and an impressed "Z" follows the shape number (see no. 46). This vase is illustrated in *From Our Native Clay* (1987), page 32, no. 46.

VASE
1906
Harriet Elizabeth Wilcox,
decorator
Thrown
H. 12 ½" Diam. 5 ¾"
Faience body
Painted Mat glaze line

Marks: impressed Rookwood logo sur-
mounted by fourteen flames/"VI"/
"951B"; painted in black "HEW"

Collection of William A. Stout

Painted Mat examples are so rare
that, to date, fewer than ten are
known. Almost all are by Harriet
Elizabeth Wilcox (see nos. 50, 51,
53), with others by Albert Robert
Valentien (e.g., *From Our Native
Clay*, 1987, p. 32, no. 45). The
technique was difficult to master,
requiring much skill and patience.
It was not uncommon for a Rookwood artist to specialize exclusively in one technique. Decorators
were encouraged to work at the
technique or techniques in which
they were best suited. By 1906, the
date of this vase, Wilcox had been
working in the Painted Mat style
for six years. She helped Rookwood bring it to perfection. No
other pottery in the world could
match it. Her signature on the
bottom is not incised, but painted,
which is expected in the Mat glaze
lines (see no. 47). The same vase
shape can be seen in no. 60.

53
VASE
1906
Harriet Elizabeth Wilcox, decorator
Thrown
H. 13 ¾" Diam. 5 ½"
Faience body
Painted Mat Inlay glaze line

Marks: impressed Rookwood logo surmounted by fourteen flames/"VI"/"907C"; painted in black "HEW"

Cincinnati Art Museum, Gift of the Louis Haffner family (1975.6)

This is perhaps the rarest of all of Rookwood's glaze lines. The decoration is a cross between the Painted Mat (see no. 50) and the Conventional Mat (see no. 47) glaze lines. The ground colors were atomized on the biscuit-fired vase and left to dry. An outline of the decoration was then cut away and black slip was trailed along the edges of the unglazed area. When this was completed, the colors of the floral composition were inlaid with a brush. The black lines ensured the separation of the glaze colors and helped visually to clarify the composition. Harriet Elizabeth Wilcox worked in the difficult Painted Mat technique for at least six years (see nos. 50, 51, 52), and was quite capable of taking it one step further by adding a slip-trailed black outline to produce a Painted Mat Inlay decoration.

54
PUNCH BOWL
1900
Anna Marie Bookprinter
Valentien, decorator
Thrown and carved
H. 11" W. 17" D. 14 ½"
Faience body
Modeled Mat glaze line

Marks: impressed Rookwood logo surmounted by fourteen flames/ "S1686"; painted in black "A.M.V."

Collection of Mr. and Mrs. Randy
Sandler

The "Art Academy Students" file in the Mary R. Schiff Library at the Cincinnati Art Museum reveals that Anna Marie Bookprinter Valentien studied sculpture at the Art Academy of Cincinnati for eight years, from 1888 until 1897 with the exception of the 1891–92 school year. Her sculpting abilities are apparent in this punch bowl with cabbage leaves and three nudes gracing the lip. According to S. G. Burt's inventory of Rookwood in the Cincinnati Art Museum in 1916 (p. 131, #149, #151; p. 132, #152, #158), the first Modeled Mat glaze line examples were created in 1898 by Artus Van Briggle. These developed flaws in firing. By 1900, however, many of the technical problems had been resolved, and Anna Valentien was able to apply her training in sculpture to her work as a decorator at Rookwood. Indeed, many of the Modeled Mat pieces known today are by her. A Modeled Mat example of this caliber would almost certainly have been sent to the 1901 Pan-American Exposition in Buffalo, New York, where Rookwood's mat glazes were new to almost everyone.

55
VASE
1900
John Hamilton Delaney
Wareham, decorator
Thrown and carved
H. 19 ½" W. 6" D. 6"
Faience body
Modeled Mat glaze line

*Marks: impressed Rookwood logo
surmounted by fourteen
flames/"S1668"; incised "JD
Wareham"; paper label inscribed with
"Property of JDW"*

Collection of Mr. and Mrs.
Randy Sandler

The subject matter for this piece is undetermined. It is suggestive of a woman rising from a plant form. While the mat glaze is a result of the emerging Arts and Crafts Movement at the beginning of the twentieth century, the long hair and flowing tendrils reflect the earlier Art Nouveau influence that was strong at the end of the nineteenth century. Decorator John Hamilton Delaney Wareham thought the piece was so significant that he included the full spelling of his surname in his signature on the bottom (see no. 34). Moreover, according to the paper label, he kept the vase for his own collection. Because of the high technical and aesthetic quality of this Modeled Mat example, it was probably included in the display at the 1901 Pan-American Exposition in Buffalo, New York, where the public first recognized Rookwood's Mat Glaze.

56
VASE
1908
Sara Alice Toohey, decorator
Thrown and carved
H. 12 ¾" Diam. 6 ½"
Faience body
Modeled Mat glaze line

*Marks: impressed Rookwood logo
surmounted by fourteen flames/"VIII";
incised ST cipher*

Cincinnati Art Museum, Gift of
Mr. and Mrs. James J. Gardner

According to Herbert Peck in *The
Book of Rookwood Pottery* (1968, p.
147), decorator Sara Alice Toohey
was placed in charge of glazing for
Rookwood's architectural faience
department around 1908, the date
of this vase. Since architectural elements were usually finished with
mat glazes, it is not surprising to
see Toohey working with a mat
glaze at this time. Indeed, her sensitivity to its nature was rarely surpassed by any of the other decorators. In this example she applied
clay to the unfired vase and
sculpted in relief a lyrical array of
cattails. Toohey was quite accomplished at the carved relief technique (see also no. 11). After the
vase was biscuit fired, she chose a
soft brown mat glaze to enhance
the marsh plants, especially their
brown, fuzzy, cylindrical flower
spikes. Toohey knew that the flow
of the glaze during the firing
would cause the mat finish to get
thinner at high points or ridges in
the relief, thus highlighting the
composition in a subtle but masterful way.

57

VASE
1912
Charles Stewart Todd,
decorator
William Watts Taylor,
shape designer
Thrown and carved
H. 22" Diam. 10"
Faience body
Decorated Mat glaze line

Marks: impressed Rookwood logo
surmounted by fourteen
flames/"XII"/"303"; incised on the side
at the base "CST"

Collection of William A. Stout

The Decorated Mat technique exhibits highlights of color that
loosely pick out a carved or relief
decoration. In this case the decoration was carved by Charles
Stewart Todd. Once the relief-
carved vase was biscuit fired,
Todd applied the ground colors
with an atomizer and then picked
out the decoration with blue
glaze, which he applied over the
ground. Charles Stewart Todd
worked almost exclusively in this
technique even though it was
fraught with the problem of
crawling. When glazes crawled in
the firing, their downward flow
distorted the composition and
caused colors to run together.
This example, however, was not
affected by that problem. The
peacock and its feathers were very
popular motifs early in the century (see nos. 63, 74, 76, 83). It was
very unusual for a decorator to
sign his or her name on the side of
a vase instead of its bottom. This
practice was reserved for pieces
thought by the artist to be especially fine (see no. 34).

58
LAMP VASE
1905
Kataro Shirayamadani,
decorator
Thrown and carved
H. 10 ⅓" Diam. 5 ½"
Faience body
Decorated Mat glaze line

Marks: impressed a) Rookwood logo
surmounted by fourteen
flames/"V"/"935C" b) two separate
trial marks in the form of V-shaped ar-
rowheads; incised Kataro Shiraya-
madani in Japanese characters

Private Collection

The trial marks on the bottom of the lamp vase suggest that the vase was used for an experiment of some kind. According to S. G. Burt in his inventory of Rookwood Pottery in the Cincinnati Art Museum in 1916 (p. 158, #P5, #P6), the first examples of the Decorated Mat glaze line were recorded in 1905. Because of its 1905 date, perhaps this lamp vase was an experiment in the Decorated Mat technique (see no. 57). The shape, recorded in *The Rookwood Shape Book 1883–1900* (p. 135), shows that the feet have been added by the artist as part of the decoration. They also serve to allow room for an electrical cord. A hole has been drilled by Rookwood into the bottom of the vase to accommodate lamp fittings. Holes drilled by the pottery are neat, without chips missing at the edges, and all the exposed ceramic is covered with glaze. Holes drilled later by other sources do not exhibit these traits.

59

VASE
1915
William E. Hentschel,
decorator
Cast and incised
H. 8 ¾″ Diam. 4 ¾″
Faience body
Decorated Mat glaze line with
Ombroso glaze

Marks: impressed Rookwood logo
surmounted by fourteen flames/"XV"/
".900C"; incised WEH cipher

Collection of Don F. Mahan

The Ombroso glaze line made its official debut in 1910, marking Rookwood's thirtieth anniversary. Ombroso is a transmutation mat, generally appearing as a mottled gray or, as in this case, brown, with occasional accents of other colors. The artist incised the decoration in the unfired clay. After the biscuit firing, he applied the Ombroso glaze and then picked out the decoration with additional colors of green, red, and violet. Using the Decorated Mat technique (see no. 57) with the Om-broso glaze is noted as early as 1911 by S. G. Burt in his inventory of Rookwood Pottery in the Cincinnati Art Museum in 1916 (p. 170, #P9). Incised decorations in mat glazed examples are common, and the incised decoration alone constitutes a separate glaze line (see no. 46).

VASE
1908
Sara Sax, decorator
Thrown and carved
H. 9″ Diam. 4″
White body
Floral Vellum glaze line

Marks: impressed a) Rookwood logo
surmounted by fourteen
flames/"VIII"/"951D" b) a trial mark
in the form of a V-shaped arrowhead;
incised a) SAX cipher b) "V"

Collection of Edwin J. Kircher III

The Vellum glaze line was introduced to the public in 1904 at the Louisiana Purchase Exposition in St. Louis. Vellum differed from all other mat glaze lines because it was translucent, allowing slip decorations to be seen under the glaze. With this example, decorator Sara Sax added clay to the vase and carved two hollyhocks in relief, one on either side. This technique was common at Rookwood (see no. 44), but it is almost never seen in the Vellum glaze line, which is perhaps the reason for the trial mark on the bottom of the vase. Such marks indicate that Rookwood was experimenting with the glaze, the decoration, or possibly the body. The incised "V" on the bottom of the vase was a signal from the decorator to the glazer to use the Vellum glaze. According to S. G. Burt in his inventory of Rookwood Pottery in the Cincinnati Art Museum in 1916 (p. 158, #5), Sara Sax was the first to use this mark. The vase shape can also be seen in no. 52.

61

VASE
1927
Lenore Asbury, decorator
Joseph Bailey, shape designer
Thrown
H. 13″ Diam. 7″
Soft Porcelain/Jewel Porcelain body
Floral Vellum glaze line

Marks: impressed Rookwood logo
surmounted by fourteen
flames/"XXVII"/".614C"; incised "LA"

Collection of Mr. and Mrs. Randy
Sandler

When the Vellum glaze line was introduced in 1904 (see no. 60), most decorations were floral. After the first Scenic Vellums made their debut in 1905 (see no. 66), they soon became so popular that Floral Vellums began to decline in number. Later, in the 1920s they began to appear again. This vase differs from the earlier Floral Vellums because the ground color on the interior is in contrast to the ground color on the exterior and corresponds to a color used in the floral composition. Rookwood did not begin using interior colors in this manner until the second decade of the century (see also nos. 66, 77, 81–83, 88). The poppies do not seem to offer the symbolism of sleep or death as they did earlier in the century (e.g., nos. 10, 21, 36, 45). There is no impressed or incised "V" on the bottom to indicate the Vellum glaze (see no. 60), suggesting that the decision was left to the glazer. The biggest difference between this Vellum vase and earlier examples is the clay body. In 1915 Rookwood introduced its Soft Porcelain body (see no. 77) for use with high-gloss vases. By about 1920 Rookwood had developed a Vellum glaze compatible with this body. While the earlier Vellum clay was a high-fired, white body, it was not porcelaneous. The difference is readily visible. There is virtually no crazing on Vellum examples made with the Soft Porcelain body. The bottom of this vase does not display an impressed "P" to designate the body (see no. 77). By 1920 Rookwood was rarely, if ever, using that symbol (see no. 79). By about 1921, or slightly later, all of Rookwood's Vellum examples utilized the new body. The first indication of the porcelaneous body is the absence of crazing. The second, and more exact method is the translucency of the body. If a strong light directed at the bottom of a vase is visible on the interior and appears slightly red, the body is Soft Porcelain. No other clay body will transmit light. This vase shape can also be seen in nos. 31, 36, 42, 62, 75, and 93.

62
VASE
1927
Edward Timothy Hurley,
decorator
Joseph Bailey, shape designer
Thrown
H. 13 ⅛" Diam. 7"
Soft Porcelain/Jewel Porcelain body
Floral Vellum glaze line

Marks: impressed Rookwood logo
surmounted by fourteen
flames/"XXVII"/"614C"; incised
a) ETH cipher b) "V"

Collection of Milton Mazo, M.D.

The 1927 date of this vase makes it a later example of a Floral Vellum (see no. 61). Still, it is very much in keeping with the early Floral Vellums where interior ground colors accord with exterior ground colors. Also, the use of the wisteria is a legacy of Rookwood's past (e.g., no. 39). The decorator obviously had no qualms about creating a traditional piece. The incised "V" on the bottom means that Edward Timothy Hurley intended the Vellum glaze for the vase (see no. 60). Even though it is not so marked, the vase is made of Rookwood's Soft Porcelain body (see no. 61). Its popular shape can also be seen in nos. 31, 36, 42, 61, 75, and 93.

63
VASE
1907
Sara Sax, decorator
Thrown
H. 10 ⅝″ Diam. 5 ½″
White body
Vellum glaze line

*Marks: impressed Rookwood logo
surmounted by fourteen
flames/"VII"/"1655D"/"V"; incised
a) SAX cipher b) "V"*

Collection of William A. Stout

Sara Sax liked working with pink
(e.g., nos. 68, 81, 82, 83), which
was generally difficult to achieve.
Here she uses it as a lush ground
color. The peacock and the peacock feather were common motifs
during the Art Nouveau period at
the turn of the century, and Sara
Sax used them often (e.g., nos. 74,
76, 83). In this vase she incorpo-
rates a masterful stylization of
three peacock feathers in a very
Art Nouveau style. On the bottom of the vase a "V" is impressed
by the potter and then later incised by the decorator to indicate
the Vellum glaze. Sara Sax wanted to make certain that the potter's mark was not overlooked.

64
VASE
1920
Carl Schmidt, decorator
Thrown
H. 21 ½" Diam. 8 ½"
Soft Porcelain/Jewel Porcelain body
Venetian Vellum glaze line

*Marks: impressed a) Rookwood logo
surmounted by fourteen
flames/"XX"/"907A"/"V" b) CS cipher
in a circular cartouche*

Collection of Helen Kohnen
Lynch

According to a Rookwood sales
catalogue of 1904 simply titled
The Rookwood Book (no. 98), the
pottery was producing "Marine"
Vellums the year the glaze line
was introduced (see no. 60). It is
impossible to tell from the illustration if Venice was the site of the
sailing vessel, especially since the
vessel itself is unlike those later
depicted in Venetian settings. But,
it can be assumed that what have
come to be known as Venetian
Vellums, or scenes of Venice with
Venetian boats, fishing pots, etc.,
all covered in the Vellum glaze,
were made soon after 1904, if not
during that year. Decorator Carl
Schmidt was the master of the
Venetian decoration at Rookwood. Because of the quiet mood
and the soft sheen created by the
glaze, such examples are considered Tonalist expressions (see no.
66). Even though it is not so
marked, the vase is made of Rookwood's Soft Porcelain body (see
no. 61). Carl Schmidt was one of
the few decorators to use an impressed, rather than an incised,
touchmark (see no. 31). The same
vase shape can be seen in no. 32.

65
PLAQUE: LOBSTER POTS
1912
Carl Schmidt, decorator
Press molded
H. 8 ¼" W. 10 ½"
White body
Venetian Vellum glaze line

Marks: impressed Rookwood logo sur-
mounted by fourteen flames/"XII"; in-
cised on back "V"; painted in red on
the back "3.1984"; painted in black on
front, lower right C. SCHMIDT

Collection of Jay and Emma
Lewis

The lobster pots are placed in front of Venetian fishing vessels and the Venetian coast line. The scene is calm and poetic with a soft diffusion of light enhanced by the Vellum glaze. These qualities mark it as part of the Tonalist movement in America that was prevalent at the time (see no. 66). Carl Schmidt was the finest Rookwood decorator to work in the Venetian Vellum glaze line (see no. 64). He thought so highly of this plaque that he used his full surname instead of just initials for his signature (see no. 34). The decorator incised the "V" on the back to signal the glazer to use the Vellum glaze. It is obvious that Schmidt wanted the Vellum glaze to compliment the mood of the composition. The numbers painted in red on the back are a loan number from the Cincinnati Art Museum: the plaque was the third loan that the Museum received in 1984.

66
VASE
1913
Sara Sax, decorator
Thrown
H. 9 ¾" Diam. 4 ½"
White body
Scenic Vellum glaze line

*Marks: impressed Rookwood logo
surmounted by fourteen
flames/"XIII"/"2032"/"D"; incised
a) SAX cipher b) "V"*

Collection of Judge and Mrs.
Norman A. Murdock

In his inventory of Rookwood Pottery in the Cincinnati Art Museum in 1916 (p. 158, #8), S. G. Burt tells us that Albert Robert Valentien painted the first landscape under the Vellum glaze in 1905. Because of the soft haziness of the glaze, the landscape took on a quiet, misty appearance. At the time, Tonalism was a mainstream American art movement in painting characterized by quiet, atmospheric landscapes. Rookwood's Scenic Vellum glaze line epitomized the Tonalist expression in art pottery. Accordingly, this vase displays a foggy, serene landscape that promotes a mood of peaceful reverie. The incised "V" on the bottom was a notation by Sara Sax to instruct the glazer to use the Vellum glaze that so integrally compliments the mood of the composition. The interior ground color is in contrast to the exterior ground color, and it is also used in elements of the painted landscape. Rookwood's artists began using this decoration technique at about this time. It can also be seen in nos. 61, 77, 81, 82, 83, 88, 95, and 97.

67

VASE
1920
Carl Schmidt, decorator
Thrown
H. 13 ¼" Diam. 6"
White body
Scenic Vellum glaze line

*Marks: impressed a) Rookwood logo
surmounted by fourteen
flames/"XX"/"925B"/"V" b) CS cipher
in a circular cartouche*

Collection of Blumie Sway

Even though he is better known
for his Venetian Vellums (e.g.,
nos. 64, 65), Carl Schmidt was
also a master in the Scenic Vellum
glaze line. In this example, a sunrise offers a quiet Tonalist landscape (see no. 66). Typically, Carl
Schmidt's signature is impressed,
not incised (see no. 31). The
shape of the vase can also be seen
in no. 74.

68
PLAQUE: FROZEN STREAM
1915
Sara Sax, decorator
Press molded
H. 10 ¾" W. 8"
White body
Scenic Vellum glaze line

Marks: impressed a) Rookwood logo
surmounted by fourteen
flames/"XV"/"V"; inscribed in pencil
"FROZEN STREAM"/"BY"/"SARA
SAX"; typed on paper on the back of
the frame "Frozen Stream"/"by"/"Sara
Sax"/"1915"; painted in black on
front, lower right "SAX"

Private Collection

A quiet stream or pond bordered by trees was a typical motif of the American Tonalist movement (see no. 66). Rookwood's Tonalist artists used this motif often (see nos. 67, 72, 73). Seen less commonly was the same scene shrouded in snow (see nos. 70, 71). In "Frozen Stream," Sara Sax uses a sunrise, or perhaps a sunset, to offer a pink glow on the horizon and the reflecting ice. Pink was a difficult color to achieve successfully, and Sax could use it at will. Titles were typed on paper and then glued to the backs of frames that Rookwood supplied with the plaques. This plaque still retains its original frame complete with title. Sometimes a title is also written on the back of the plaque, as it is here, but that is unusual.

69
VASE
1908
Edward Timothy Hurley,
decorator
Thrown
H. 9" Diam. 5 ¼"
White body
Scenic Vellum glaze line

*Marks: impressed a) Rookwood logo
surmounted by fourteen
flames/"VIII"/"1126C" b) a trial mark
in the form of a V-shaped arrowhead;
incised a) ETH cipher b) "V"; wheel
ground "X"*

Collection of Dr. and Mrs.
William E. Heil

The trial mark on the bottom of
this vase probably indicates that
the artist was experimenting with
the composition. Unlike most
Scenic Vellum compositions (e.g.,
cat nos. 67, 68, 70–73), it does
not contain the typical stream or
pond in summer or winter. Instead
it depicts a forest in autumn with
falling leaves and a fallen tree.
Perhaps, too, there was a new col-
or. The "V" on the bottom of the
vase was incised by the decorator,
not impressed by the potter,
which means that Hurley determined the glaze (see no. 60). The
wheel-ground "X" (see no. 21) indicates that the vase was withheld
from sales. Since there are no flaws
in this piece and the decoration
is so unusual, the "X" probably
means that the experiment was
thought to be very successful, and
the vase was held for future reference. In another vase (cat. no. 35),
a trial mark and a wheel-ground
"X" suggest the same situation.

70

**PLAQUE: WINTER
LANDSCAPE
1919
Sara Elizabeth Coyne,
decorator**
Press molded
H. 11″ W. 8 ¾″
White body
Scenic Vellum glaze line

*Marks: impressed Rookwood logo sur-
mounted by fourteen flames/"XIX"; inscribed in blue a) "2199–2 1/2–330"
b) "50"; painted in black on front,
lower right SEC cipher*

Private Collection in memory of
Mr. and Mrs. E. N. Woistmann

A quiet landscape shrouded in a hazy atmosphere was a featured image in American Tonalist paintings (see no. 66). It was also the featured image in Rookwood's Scenic Vellum plaques. Such landscapes covered in snow, however, were generally uncommon at the pottery. Their compositions, exemplified by this plaque (see also nos. 68, 71), tend to follow a formula. A stream bordered by trees flows from the background to the foreground of the composition beckoning the viewer psychologically to enter the landscape. The meaning of the numbers inscribed in blue on the back of the plaque is unknown.

71

VASE
1912
Frederick Daniel Henry
Rothenbusch, decorator
Thrown
H. 12 ¾" Diam. 6 ½"
White body
Scenic Vellum glaze line

*Marks: impressed Rookwood logo
surmounted by fourteen
flames/"XII"/"1664C"/"V"; incised
a) FR cipher b) "V"*

Collection of Elizabeth and
George Meredith

With the influence of the Arts and Crafts Movement beginning in the first decade of the century, there was a change in Rookwood's decorating philosophy. Previously the entire surface of a vase was viewed as one integral unit of space for decoration (e.g., nos. 66, 67, 69). Sometime early in the century, however, Rookwood began dividing the surface of a vase into sections that were treated differently. In this example the upper and lower parts of the vase were painted black to distinguish them from the landscape. Black is an unusual color to use in the Scenic Vellum palette. Here the black of the top and bottom bands is echoed in the stark trees and frozen water of the winter landscape. While winter landscapes were unusual at Rookwood (e.g., nos. 68, 70), black winter landscapes seem to be nonexistent except for this vase. Perhaps the use of black was simply a compositional device to unify the three sections of the vessel. Or it is possible that the black bands framing the landscape with dead trees are symbolically mourning the loss of nature to urbanization and industrial pollution. The "V" on the bottom of the vase, which signaled the glazer to use the Vellum glaze, was impressed by the potter and then incised by Rothenbusch. Generally there is only one mark or the other, but sometimes both are present (e.g., no. 63) suggesting that the decorator wanted to reinforce the potter's signal to use the Vellum glaze.

72
PLAQUE: MOUNTAIN LANDSCAPE
1929
Lenore Asbury, decorator
Press molded
H. 16" W. 14"
Soft Porcelain/Jewel Porcelain body
Scenic Vellum glaze line

Marks: impressed Rookwood logo surmounted by fourteen flames/"XXIX"; painted in blue on front, lower right "LA"

Private Collection

This plaque is unusually large. Because of the technical problems of shrinkage and warping, plaques made from the traditional white body used for Vellums were rarely larger than eleven inches high and eight inches wide. This plaque is made of Rookwood's Soft Porcelain body, however, and it is not only large, but free of crazing (see no. 61). It is often difficult, if not impossible, to use the light test (see no. 61) on plaques. The light must be strong enough to penetrate the thickness of the body, and the room must be sufficiently dark to see it. The plaque's late date of 1929, however, allows us to safely assume that it was made of Soft Porcelain.

73
VASE
1920
Edward Timothy Hurley,
decorator
John J. Menzel, shape designer
Thrown
H. 11 ¼" Diam. 6 ¼"
White body
Scenic Vellum glaze line

*Marks: impressed Rookwood logo
surmounted by fourteen
flames/"XX"/"892B"/"V"; incised
ETH cipher*

Collection of Edwin J. Kircher III

Rookwood's Scenic Vellum landscapes were a product of American Tonalism (see no. 66). According to Wanda M. Corn in *The
Color of Mood: American Tonalism
1880–1910* (1972, p. 1), moonlit
landscapes were desirable because
their evocative half-lights created
a quiet, personal experience with
nature. Edward Timothy Hurley
was one of the finest Tonalist
artists working at Rookwood, and
his Scenic Vellum compositions,
such as this moonlit landscape
(see also no. 69), epitomize the
meditative, evocative mood of the
movement.

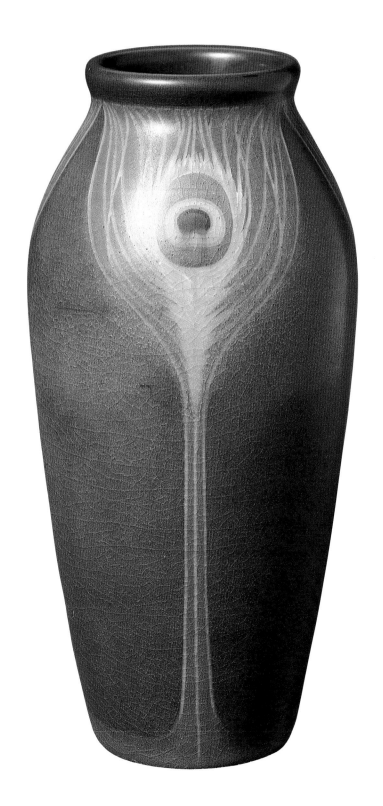

74
VASE
1909
Sara Sax, decorator
Thrown
H. 8 ¼" Diam. 4"
White body
Green Vellum glaze line

Marks: impressed a) Rookwood logo surmounted by fourteen flames/"IX"/"925D" b) a trial mark in the form of a V-shaped arrowhead; incised a) SAX cipher b) "GV"

Collection of Constance A. Hudson

The trial mark on the bottom of this vase suggests that Sara Sax was experimenting with the glaze and/or decoration. She was probably testing the colors in combination with the Green Vellum glaze. The blue, white, and amber colors were also used under the earlier, similarly tinted Sea Green glaze (see e.g., nos. 28, 29). Peacocks and peacock feathers were common motifs (see nos. 57, 63, 83). Sara Sax liked the stylized peacock feather (see e.g., no. 63), and did not hesitate to use it under the Green Vellum glaze (see e.g., no. 76). The incised "GV," for Green Vellum, on the bottom of the vase tells us that she, not the potter, determined the green-tinted, mat finish. The same vase shape can also be seen in no. 67.

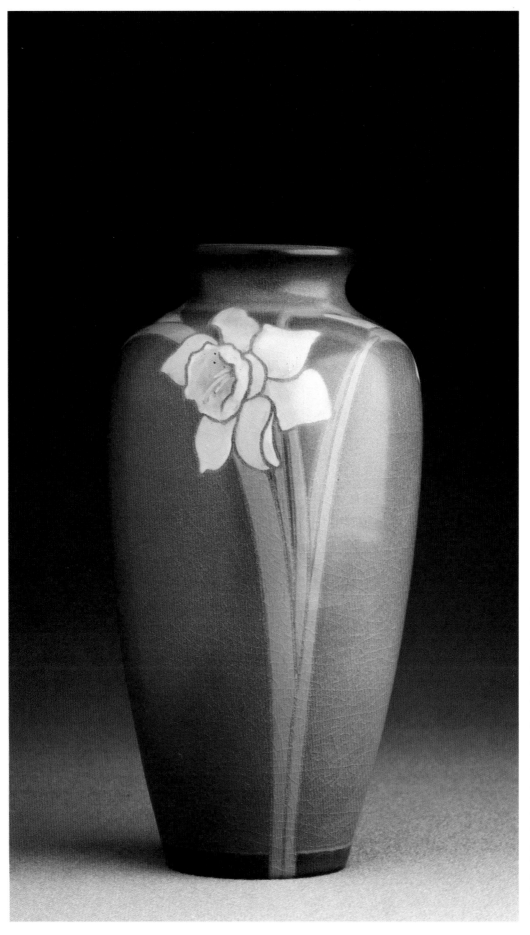

75
VASE
1909
Sara Sax, decorator
Joseph Bailey, shape designer
Thrown
H. 8 ¼" Diam. 4 ⅛"
White body
Green Vellum glaze line

Marks: impressed a) Rookwood logo surmounted by fourteen flames/"IX"/"614E" b) "V"; incised a) SAX cipher b) "GV"

Collection of Isak Lindenauer

Sara Sax mastered every glaze line she worked in, and the Green Vellum glaze line is no exception (see also nos. 74, 76). Here three stylized daffodils outlined in black cling harmoniously to the shape of the vase. The influence of the Arts and Crafts Movement can be seen in a number of ways in this vase. The glaze itself, because of its mat appearance, is a product of the Movement. As for the decoration, the black outline (see no. 29) and the division of the foot from the rest of the vase (see no. 71) are the results of Arts and Crafts design principles. The army-green ground color (see also no. 76) is common in the Green Vellum glaze line. The same vase shape can also be seen in nos. 31, 36, 42, 61, 62, and 93.

76
VASE
1911
Sara Sax, decorator
Cast
H. 8″ Diam. 3 ¾″
White body
Green Vellum glaze line

Marks: impressed a) Rookwood logo surmounted by fourteen flames/"XI"/"939D" b) "V"; incised a) SAX cipher b) "GV"

Collection of The Newark Museum, Purchase 1914

Here the stylized peacock feather calls to mind similar depictions used by the Arts and Crafts Movement in Great Britain, especially those of Charles Rennie Mackintosh and the Glasgow School. It is in marked contrast to the decorator's slightly earlier stylized peacock feather (cat. no. 74), where the flowing curves of the Art Nouveau Movement are still apparent. The "V" impressed on the bottom of the vase by the potter is a signal for the Vellum glaze. The "GV" incised by Sara Sax is an instruction to the glazer to use the Green Vellum glaze. The vase is also published by Ulysses Dietz in *The Newark Museum Collection of American Art Pottery* (1984, p. 104, no. 213); and *The Arts and Crafts Movement in America 1876–1916,* (1972, p. 153, no. 222).

77
VASE
1917
Arthur P. Conant, decorator
John Hamilton Delaney
Wareham, shape designer
Thrown
H. 5 ¾" Diam. 9"
Soft Porcelain/Jewel Porcelain body
Blue tinted, translucent, gloss glaze

Marks: impressed a) Rookwood logo
surmounted by fourteen flames/"XVII"/
"2259C" b) "P"; incised C within a
rectangle;inscribed in black "477"

Cincinnati Art Museum, Bequest
of Kathryn Rogers Gates
(1980.157)

According to the decorator's wife, Patti Conant, as told to Riley Humler, Arthur Conant once worked as a designer for Herter Looms, a carpet manufactory in New York. As such he often made sketches from Far and Near Eastern carpets on display at the Metropolitan Museum of Art and used them as design sources in his work. With this in mind, it is much easier to understand many of his decorations at Rookwood, which were unlike those by other artists. Here the colors were perhaps inspired by Near Eastern tiles; the jumping stags and esoteric trees around the neck of the vase are probably also Near Eastern in source. The use of a con-

trasting interior color began at the pottery during the second decade of the century (see no. 61). The exterior of the vase does not have an underglaze ground color; the turquoise blue color of the ground is created by the tinted glaze alone as it covers the white porcelaneous body. On the bottom of the vase is an impressed "P" for Soft Porcelain. This low-fired porcelain body was introduced by Rookwood during the Easter period of 1915, marking the thirty-fifth anniversary of the pottery. In a Rookwood advertising pamphlet, probably of 1915, titled *Rookwood Pottery: Soft Porcelain*, the new ware is announced and described with great pride. A later

advertising brochure that could not date earlier than 1945, titled *The Rookwood Pottery of Cincinnati Ohio* (pp. 8–9), discusses the product introduced at Easter in 1915, but calls it "jewel porcelain." The name change was probably a marketing device. The incised signature informs us that the decoration was painted on the greenware, or unfired clay, and therefore the decorated porcelain technique of layering glazes was not used (see no. 96). The "477" inscribed in black on the bottom is over the glaze. It might be an inventory number applied later by the pottery or a collector.

78
VASE
1917
Arthur P. Conant, decorator
Thrown
H. 12 ¾" Diam. 7 ½"
Soft Porcelain/Jewel Porcelain body
Clear, translucent, gloss glaze

*Marks: impressed a) Rookwood logo
surmounted by fourteen
flames/"XVII"/"2301" b) "P"; incised
C within a rectangle*

Private Collection

The artist's wife, Patti Conant, related to Riley Humler that Arthur Conant painted two-dimensional backdrops for the stage. The composition on this vase with its use of perspective and receding landscape would also be appropriate for a stage set. It is generally unlike anything in Rookwood's scenic repertory including the Vellum glaze line. Even more unusual is the fact that it was left as a line drawing and backed with an underglaze pink ground. Arthur Conant's work at Rookwood can hardly be considered the typical product of the pottery. While Rookwood artists in general were moving away from floral decorations, Conant's use of color and composition tended to be unlike that used by other decorators. The impressed "P" on the bottom of the vase notes that this is a Soft Porcelain example, later called Jewel Porcelain (see no. 77). Conant's incised signature indicates that the vase was decorated before it was fired. It therefore does not represent the layered glaze technique of decoration often used with the porcelaneous body (see no. 96). This vase was made as one of a pair (see also no. 90). Its "mate" is in another private collection. According to Rookwood's shape card, the shape was originally designed with a domed, knopped lid. Here the lid could be missing, but the lack of wear marks around the lip (and that of its counterpart) suggests that the vase never had a lid.

VASE
1919
Arthur P. Conant, decorator
Thrown
H. 9 ½" Diam. 4"
Soft Porcelain/Jewel Porcelain body
Clear, translucent, gloss glaze

*Marks: impressed Rookwood logo
surmounted by fourteen
flames/"XIX"/"1882"; incised C within
a rectangle*

Private Collection

The introduction of Soft Porcelain in 1915 signaled a return to high-gloss glazes. Even though the impressed "P" for Soft Porcelain is missing from the bottom of this vase, it can be assumed that the body is Soft Porcelain. Rookwood used the impressed "P" only for the first few years after the introduction of the body in 1915, to distinguish it from other bodies that were still in use. Later when the other bodies had been discontinued and only the porcelaneous body was made, the "P" no longer served a purpose and was abandoned. Glazes had to be developed that were compatible with the new high-fired body. The glossy, clear, translucent glaze of this period is not the same as the earlier, lower-fired Iris glaze. This vase exemplifies the high-fired Soft Porcelain body, later called Jewel Porcelain (see no. 77), and the later high-gloss glaze that became the norm at Rookwood after 1915. True to form, Arthur Conant's decoration is somewhat unusual (see no. 78). The exotic cockatoo is gracing an equally exotic tree with flower heads in plums and pinks and gray. Conant's incised signature tells us that the vase was not fired before the decoration was applied, and therefore, the decoration is not between glaze layers, a technique often found, especially after 1924, on the porcelaneous body (see no. 96)

VASE
1920
Sara Alice Toohey and "HI"
(unidentified), decorators
John Hamilton Delaney
Wareham, shape designer
Thrown
H. 18 ⅜" Diam. 6 ⅜"
Soft Porcelain/Jewel Porcelain body
Unidentified crystalline glaze

*Marks: impressed Rookwood logo
surmounted by fourteen
flames/"XX"/"2499A"; painted in
black a) ST cipher (smeared) b) "HI"*

Collection of Max Palevsky
in the Los Angeles County
Museum of Art

According to Herbert Peck in *The Book of Rookwood Pottery* (1968, p. 147), Sara Alice "Sallie" Toohey was placed in charge of the glaze room for Rookwood's vase department sometime after 1917. This vase tells us that she was in charge by 1920. Her signature on the bottom of the vase is painted, not incised. Therefore, she decorated it after it was biscuit fired. Vases would be biscuit fired before going to the glazing department. The unidentified "HI" is probably the mark of a glazer in her department. It was rare for glazers to sign their pieces, suggesting that this vase was considered special, or made for some special reason. The idea that shape and glaze alone (i.e., no underglaze decoration) could constitute the beauty of a vase is Oriental in origin, and it reached the West in a profound manner with the Arts and Crafts Movement early in the twentieth century. Beginning in 1915 with its new porcelain body, Rookwood looked to the Chinese for inspiration, and vases emphasizing shape and glaze alone could subsequently be seen in ever increasing numbers. Even though there is no impressed "P" on the bottom of the vase, it can be assumed that the body is Soft Porcelain (see no. 79). The glazes in this example are layered without the use of a painted decoration in between, making it a variation of a Soft Porcelain decorating technique (see no. 96).

81

VASE
1921
Sara Sax, decorator
Thrown
H. 6 ¼" Diam. 3 ¼"
Soft Porcelain/Jewel Porcelain body
French Red glaze line

*Marks: impressed Rookwood logo
surmounted by fourteen flames/"XXI"/
"1926"; incised SAX cipher*

Collection of Elizabeth Dooley-
Warner

Here the French Red glaze (see no. 83), which is glossy by nature, is combined with a brown mat glaze that has been hand painted in an overall geometric pattern. This vase alone is evidence of the considerable technical advances Rookwood had achieved by 1921. Combining a mat and gloss finish in one vase was an exceptional achievement. It was a remarkable design accomplishment as well. Decorator Sara Sax was always exploiting the latest technology at Rookwood to achieve new expressions in decoration. Virtually all examples known that combine a mat and gloss glaze are by this artist. It is not unusual for Sax's work to be marked by new glazes and technology. Consequently, unlike some decorators, her name is not associated with one type of Rookwood more than another. Even though there is no impressed "P" on the bottom of the vase, it is a Soft Porcelain body (see no. 79). The incised signature indicates that the decoration was applied to the vase before it was fired, and that the glaze is not layered (see no. 96).

82

VASE
1922
Sara Sax, decorator
John Hamilton Delaney
Wareham, shape designer

Thrown and carved
H. 5 ½" Diam. 5 ¼"
Soft Porcelain/Jewel Porcelain body
French Red glaze line

*Marks: impressed Rookwood logo
surmounted by fourteen flames/"XXII"/
"2268E"; incised SAX cipher*

Private Collection

This example of the French Red glaze line (see no. 83) is remarkable for its Art Deco style. The shape, the colors, and the repeated, stylized, fan-like decoration epitomize that major style of the 1920s. It is interesting to note that the Exposition International des Arts Décoratifs et Industriels Modernes (International Exposition of Modern Decorative and Industrial Art) that gave us the term Art Deco, was held in Paris in 1925. This vase was made in 1922, three years before the name of the style that categorized it was coined. Rookwood decorators, especially Sara Sax (see no. 81), were in the vanguard of almost every major art movement throughout the history of the pottery. It can be assumed that the clay body is Soft Porcelain even though there is no impressed "P" on the bottom of the vase (see no. 79). We know that the decoration was applied to the vase in its unfired state, and that the glaze is not layered because of the fact that Sax's signature is incised (see no. 96). The use of a contrasting interior color for vases became a decorating technique at Rookwood beginning in the 1910s (see no. 61).

VASE
1921
Sara Sax, decorator
John Hamilton Delaney
Wareham, shape designer
Thrown
H. 16 ¼" Diam. 9"
Soft Porcelain/Jewel Porcelain body
French Red glaze line

Marks: impressed Rookwood logo surmounted by fourteen flames/"XXI"/ "2372"; incised SAX cipher

Collection of David and Mary Verkamp

According to Rookwood master potter Ruben Earl Menzel as told to Edwin J. Kircher III, the red glaze used in the 1920s was referred to at the pottery as French Red because the oxide was obtained in France. Accordingly, the oxide was very expensive and Rookwood did not carry it for very long. A small vase dated 1919, in the collection of Judge and Mrs. Norman A. Murdock, is an apparent trial piece for the glaze. Other known pieces (e.g., nos. 81, 82) date from the early 1920s, and the Lindbergh vase (see Herbert Peck, *The Book of Rookwood Pottery*, 1968, pp. 108–109) dates no later than 1927. All of this suggests the period of use of French Red to be from 1919 to about 1927. For an unknown reason, the glaze was used almost exclusively by decorator Sara Sax. The color itself is more of a rose, ranging from a pinkish to a purplish red. In known examples, the French Red glaze is always combined with a black decoration, either high gloss or mat. Even without the impressed "P" we can assume that this is a Soft Porcelain example (see no. 79). The incised signature tells us that the decoration was applied on the unfired clay body, an earlier Soft Porcelain technique (see no. 96).

VASE
1921
Sara Sax, decorator
Thrown
H. 11″ Diam. 8″
Soft Porcelain/Jewel Porcelain body
Later Tiger Eye glaze line

Marks: impressed Rookwood logo
surmounted by fourteen flames/"XXI"/
"2448"; incised SAX cipher

Collection of Ms. Nancy Daly

In 1920 Rookwood introduced a later version of its famous Tiger Eye glaze (see no. 85), which was considerably different from the former (see no. 25) and offered a different range of color that included yellow and green. This example is exceptional because it combines both the yellow and green later Tiger Eye in one piece. It is not surprising that Sara Sax was the decorator attempting this achievement. She was constantly working with Rookwood's latest glazes and technology to expand her range of decoration (see no. 81). Rookwood's shape card for the vase includes a molded, floral lid. On this vase the decoration near the neck is intentionally discontinued, suggesting that there might indeed have been a lid.

Even though there is no impressed "P" on the bottom of this vase, it can be assumed that it is Rookwood's porcelaneous body (see no. 79). The incised signature tells us that the vase was decorated in the unfired state and that the glaze is not layered (see no. 96).

85

VASE
1930
Unknown glazer, decorator
John Hamilton Delaney
Wareham, shape designer
Thrown
H. 7 ⅞" Diam. 7 ⅛"
Soft Porcelain/Jewel Porcelain body
Later Tiger Eye glaze line

*Marks: impressed Rookwood logo
surmounted by fourteen flames/"XXX"/
"6183C" b) six radiating notches;
printed in black kiln with "50" in center*

Cincinnati Art Museum purchase,
Gift of the family and friends of
Hannah Rauh in honor of her
100th birthday (1987.43)

According to an advertising brochure titled *The Rookwood Pottery of Cincinnati Ohio* (ca. 1945, pp. 9–10), the pottery celebrated its fortieth anniversary in 1920 by reissuing the famous Tiger Eye glaze (see no. 25) "in a new and more varied range of color." Although a lovely crystalline glaze, the new Tiger Eye had little in common with the old. The body and the glaze used for the namesake were substantially different from those used in the original, and the use of the old name was more a marketing tactic than a serious description. The new range of color seems to have been from yellow, to yellow-green, to green (see no. 84 for yellow and green). This vase displays the yellow-green variety. From about 1915 on, shape and glaze alone could constitute a finished vase at Rookwood (see no. 80). This vase is an example of that philosophy. It did not pass through the decorating department, but moved instead from the potter to the glazer. Consequently, there is no decorator's signature. The glaze alone served as the decoration, and glazers rarely signed pieces (see e.g., no. 80). It is interesting that the potter did not erase the ribs in the clay wall caused by throwing the vase on a wheel. The subtle horizontal ridges serve to enhance the aesthetic quality of the glaze (see also no. 94). The impressed mark of six radiating notches on the bottom is the fiftieth anniversary symbol (see no. 92). The printed kiln mark on the bottom also notes the fiftieth anniversary. Objects so marked were drawn from the the kiln on Thanksgiving Day 1930, fifty years after the first kiln was drawn. Even without the impressed "P" on the bottom, it can be assumed that it is the Soft Porcelain body (see no. 79).

86

VASE
1916
**Unknown glazer and
decorator**
Cast
H. 4 ⅞" Diam. 4 ½"
Soft Porcelain/Jewel Porcelain body
Unidentified crystalline glaze

*Marks: impressed Rookwood logo
surmounted by fourteen
flames/"2095"/"X248X"*

Private Collection

The impressed mark "X248X" on the bottom of the vase denotes a trial or experiment. The small size of the vase also suggests the same purpose. Almost certainly, the ex- periment was trying to create an artistic effect with the glaze in combination with the new porce- laneous body. In 1920 Rookwood introduced a new Tiger Eye glaze line (see no. 85). The new Tiger Eye had a crystalline effect similar to that seen here. This vase prob- ably represents one of the many trials that took place in the years leading to the 1920 introduction of the later Tiger Eye. The vase did not pass through the decorat- ing department, so there is no decorator's signature on the bot- tom. The glaze alone is the deco- ration, and glazers rarely signed their names. Even though it is not marked as such, the vase repre- sents Rookwood's Soft Porcelain body (see no. 79).

87
___
**VASE
1921
Kataro Shirayamadani,
decorator
John Hamilton Delaney
Wareham, shape designer**
Thrown
H. 8″ Diam. 10″
Soft Porcelain/Jewel Porcelain body
Brown-tinted, translucent,
gloss glaze

*Marks: impressed Rookwood logo
surmounted by fourteen
flames/"XXI"/"2466"; incised Kataro
Shirayamadani in Japanese characters; wheel-ground "X"*

Collection of
Mr. and Mrs. Ivan R. Rudy

The wheel-ground "X" on the bottom of the vase notes that it was
withheld from sales for some reason (see no. 21). A composition of

water lilies in swirling water is
veiled behind a dripping, translucent, dark brown glaze. The unusual quality about this vase is the
dripping glaze, and it was probably withheld from sales because of
it. The brown drips were probably
not considered a mistake when
the vase was made. According to
Herbert Peck in *The Second Book of
Rookwood Pottery* (1985, p. 36), the
artist Kataro Shirayamadani had
just returned from a ten-year stay

in his native Japan. He no doubt
brought the dripping technique
with him on his return. Today, as
then, the drips are considered an
aspect of beauty.

This is Rookwood's Soft
Porcelain body even though there
is no impressed "P" on the bottom
of the vase (see no. 79). Shirayamadani's incised signature denotes
that the decoration was applied
on the unfired clay and that the
glaze is not layered (see no. 96).

88
VASE
1923
Lorinda Epply, decorator
John Hamilton Delaney
Wareham, shape designer
Cast
H. 8 ½" Diam. 5 ¾"
Soft Porcelain/Jewel Porcelain body
Yellow-tinted, translucent,
gloss glaze

Marks: impressed Rookwood logo
surmounted by fourteen flames/"XXI-
II"/"2734"; incised LE cipher

Collection of James J. Gardner

This vase is strikingly simple with its Art Deco shape and delicate floral motif. Moreover, the yellow-tinted glaze makes it unusual. Yellow was a difficult color to achieve. The earlier "yellows" seen for example in Rookwood's Standard ware (e.g., nos. 12, 15, 16), tended toward amber. It was not until after 1915, when Rookwood introduced its Soft Porcelain body (see no. 77), that a true yellow could be achieved with a tinted glaze. Even then, it is rarely seen. Here it simply covers the white porcelaneous body. No ground color has been added under the glaze. The contrasting interior color was a typical design element used during the period (see no. 61). The vase is made of Soft Porcelain even though it is not noted as such with an impressed "P" on the bottom (see no. 79). The incised artist's signature tells us that the decoration was applied to the vase in its unfired state and that the glaze is not layered (see no. 96).

89
PAIR OF VASES
1924
John Hamilton Delaney
Wareham, decorator and
shape designer
Thrown
H. 16 ½" Diam. 9 ½" each
Soft Porcelain/Jewel Porcelain body
Clear, translucent, gloss glaze

Marks: impressed Rookwood logo
surmounted by fourteen
flames/"XXIV"/"2820"; painted in
black JDW within a rectangle; on the
bottom of one printed Rookwood label
inscribed in black with "2820" and
"not for sale"

Private Collection

The idea of creating a pair of vases was a marketing concept probably inspired by the use of lamps in pairs. Matching electric lamps came into fashion sometime during the first quarter of the century. Rookwood had been making oil lamps by the 1890s, and electric lamps as early as 1902 (see no. 47), so the firm was familiar with trends in the lighting business. Perhaps the first "pair" of Rookwood vases was made to be lamps. Whatever the case, the pottery began actively marketing pairs of vases around 1915. They are virtually all large and suggestive of lamps (see also nos. 78, 90, 93, 96). In fact, today some of these pairs are found with an impressed circle in the center of the bottom of each. This is where a hole was intended to be drilled after biscuit firing to accommodate the electrical cord. The fact that such impressed circles were not drilled to become holes indicates that, for some unknown reason, a decision was made not to make lamps. Since pairs, such as this one, exist without the circular impression, Rookwood also marketed vases in sets of two. The paper label on one of the vases here tells us that the pair was "not for sale." It could be that Wareham chose to keep them for his personal collection. The fact that the blue flower heads crawled and dripped in the firing was serendipitous since it added to their aesthetic appeal. Wareham's signature is painted, not incised under the glaze. This indicates that he decorated the vases in the biscuit state (see no. 96). They are made of the Soft Porcelain body even though they are not marked with an impressed "P" (see no. 79).

90
VASE
1927
Sara Sax, decorator
William Auckland,
shape designer
Thrown
H. 17 ¼" Diam. 9"
Soft Porcelain/Jewel Porcelain body
Black Opal glaze line

*Marks: impressed Rookwood logo surmounted by fourteen flames/"XXVII"/
"324"; painted in blue SAX cipher*

Collection of Joseph David Nelson

It is not certain when the Black Opal glaze line was introduced, but it was probably after Rookwood's introduction of porcelain bodies in 1915. All known examples date from the 1920s. With this glaze line, floral decorations in blues and plums are covered with a milky-gray translucent glaze. In this example, the gray quality of the glaze can be seen in the muted white of the flower head. The combination of the blue and plum colors under the milky-gray glaze offers an appearance of the black opal stone, hence the name. The fact that this vase is a Black Opal specimen is confirmed by its original Rookwood Pottery invoice dated April 21, 1937, still in the possession of the owner. This vase was almost certainly one of a pair. Its "mate" is currently in another private collection. Pairs were promoted at Rookwood beginning around 1915 (see no. 89), but Rookwood did not hesitate to split the pair for the sake of a sale. The original invoice from the pottery notes the sale of only this vase. Consequently, we know that the pair was divided by Rookwood, not a later owner. The sale date was 1937, which was during the height of the Depression. It is no wonder that Rookwood, with its growing financial problems, did not hesitate to separate the set. Because Sax's signature is painted instead of incised, she decorated it after it had been fired (see no. 96). It is without qustion a Soft Porcelain example in spite of the fact that it is not marked as such with an impressed "P" on the bottom (see no. 79).

VASE
1927
Jens Jacob Herring Krog
Jensen, decorator
John Hamilton Delaney
Wareham, shape designer
Cast
H. 9 ⅝" Diam. 5 ¼"
Soft Porcelain/Jewel Porcelain body
Clear, translucent, gloss glaze

*Marks: impressed Rookwood logo
surmounted by fourteen
flames/"XXVII"/"2782"; painted in
blue Jens Jensen cipher*

Collection of Fern Simon

Decorator Jens Jensen stands out
at Rookwood for his depictions of
impressionistic, somewhat blurred
nudes. According to Herbert Peck
in *The Book of Rookwood Pottery*
(1968, p. 108), in about 1925
Rookwood "introduced a new
type of decoration having the thin
effect of water colors with indis-
tinct floating outlines." Jensen
seems to have taken advantage of
this new decoration technique,
and he is the artist most noted for
its use. Jensen once told Edwin J.
Kircher III that the pottery always
tried to restrain his depictions of
nude figures, considering them inappropriate for the corporate image. Peck notes (p. 145) that
Jensen did not begin at the pottery until 1928. The fact that this
vase is dated 1927 does not negate
that point. A vase cast or thrown
in 1927 could easily have been
decorated in 1928, especially if it
were cast or thrown at the end of
the year. Jensen's signature on the
bottom of the vase is painted, not
incised, indicating that he decorated the vessel after it had been
fired (see no. 96). Even though
the vase is not marked with an impressed "P", it represents the Soft
Porcelain body (see no. 79).

92
VASE
1930
Lorinda Epply, decorator
Kataro Shirayamadani,
shape designer
Cast
H. 7 ¾" Diam. 7"
Soft Porcelain/Jewel Porcelain body
Clear, translucent, gloss glaze

*Marks: impressed a) Rookwood logo
surmounted by fourteen
flames/"XXX"/"6176" b) six radiating
notches; painted in brown LE cipher*

Collection of Evelyn and Stanley
Shapiro

The shape of this vase with its
geometric composition exemplifies the Art Deco style of the period. The repeated parallel lines of
the decoration reflect the modern
lines of cityscapes profiled with
skyscrapers. The mark of six radiating notches impressed on the
bottom of the vase celebrates
Rookwood's fiftieth anniversary
year, November 1930 to November 1931. All pieces made during
that period are marked in this
way. Instead of being incised, the
signature of Lorinda Epply is
painted on the bottom of the vase.
This indicates that the vase was
decorated after the first firing (see
no. 96). The vase is a Soft Porcelain example even though it is not
impressed with a "P" on the bottom (see no. 79).

93
PAIR OF VASES
1926
Edward Timothy Hurley, decorator
Joseph Bailey, shape designer
Thrown
H. 15" Diam. 8" each
Soft Porcelain/Jewel Porcelain body
Blue-tinted, translucent
high-gloss glaze

Marks: impressed Rookwood logo surmounted by fourteen flames/"XXVI"/ "614B"; painted in black ETH cipher; paper label (torn) inscribed in black "Sales Museum Collection"

Private Collection

This matched set was purposely made as a pair. The concept of pairs was first actively promoted at Rookwood beginning around 1915 (see no. 89). They are almost all large size (e.g., nos. 78, 89, 90, 96) with a general height of more than twelve inches. At Rookwood the largest pieces always exemplified the finest work of the time. They cost more to make because they used more materials, took longer to decorate, limiting the decorator's output, took up more room in the kiln, limiting the number of pieces that could be fired, and they had a higher loss-ratio in firing. To ensure the best possible results for such an investment, only senior decorators were allowed to apply their talents to the large vases. Consequently, pairs tended to be of very fine quality. Hurley's signature on the bottom of the vases is painted, indicating that they were fired before he decorated them (see no. 96). The paper labels inscribed with "Sales Museum Collection," suggest that the pair was part of Rookwood's own collection of its wares. This collection was sold as a Rookwood Company asset when the pottery went bankrupt in 1941. Even though the impressed "P" for Soft Porcelain is not seen on the pair, they are unquestionably made of the porcelaneous body (see no. 79). These two vases were exhibited in 1985 in *Maryland Collects: American Art Pottery 1882–1946,* at the Baltimore Museum of Art. The same vase shape can also be seen in nos. 31, 36, 42, 61, 62, and 75.

94
VASE
1928
**Unidentified glazer, decorator
John Hamilton Delaney
Wareham, shape designer**
Thrown
H. 15 ½" Diam. 8 ½"
Soft Porcelain/Jewel Porcelain body
Oxblood glaze line

*Marks: impressed Rookwood logo sur-
mounted by fourteen flames/"XXVI-
II"/"2983"*

Collection of Daniel J. Ransohoff

Rookwood was interested in the Oxblood glaze as early as the 1890s. In an advertising booklet published about 1895, titled *Rook-wood Pottery* (pp. 20–21), the company discusses the achievement of various solid colors including a red "of the 'Sang de Boeuf' quality." It was not until 1915, with the introduction of its Soft Porcelain body (see no. 77), that Rookwood renewed its interest in developing Oxblood. The company looked to Chinese soft porcelain to research the glazes that covered it. One of the Chinese glazes was, of course, the "Sang de Boeuf." In *The Rook-wood Pottery of Cincinnati Ohio* (p. 10), an advertising brochure of about 1945 recounting Rook-wood's history, the pottery discusses the new glazes of the 1920s: "Then came a gradual and full perfection of the 'Oxblood' and Flambé types, originated long ago by the great Chinese potters. . . ." This vase represents Rookwood's perfection in the 1920s of the Oxblood glaze. The shape is very Chinese, in keeping with the heritage of the finish. The white lip is a product of the glaze. In the Binns Papers in the American Archives of Art, there is a letter dated May 31, 1927, from Rookwood chemist Stanley Gano Burt to the noted ceramic engineer Charles Fergus Binns in which Burt notes, "An interesting case of the same thing occurs in Oxblood red vases where the glaze has run thin at the top, you have a white band." Horizontal ridges in the clay wall caused when throwing the vase were not erased, giving added interest to the glaze (see also no. 85). According to the owner, this vase was purchased in Paris at the 1937 Exposition Internationale. There is no reason to disbelieve this as the vase is certainly of International Exposition quality, and we know from a previous example (see no. 90) that Rookwood might retain a vase for ten years before selling it, especially during the Depression. Even though it is not marked as such, the vase is clearly made of Soft Porcelain (see no. 79). The same vase shape can be seen in no. 96.

VASE
1930
William E. Hentschel,
decorator
John Hamilton Delaney
Wareham, shape designer
Thrown
H. 18 ¾" Diam. 10 ⅛"
Soft Porcelain/Jewel Porcelain body
Later Mat glaze

Marks: impressed a) Rookwood logo
surmounted by fourteen
flames/"XXX"/"6079" b) six radiating
notches; incised WEH cipher

Cincinnati Art Museum, Gift of
Mr. and Mrs. Carl Vitz (1973.458)

With the development of the new
Soft Porcelain body by 1915, the
development of new mat glazes
was soon to follow. The new mats
were different from the older varieties introduced at the beginning
of the century (see nos. 46–59).
The later porcelaneous bodies
were fired at higher temperatures
than the former faience bodies.
Moreover, with the earlier mats,
painted signatures tell us that the
decoration was applied after firing
(see no. 47). The newer examples,
such as this vase (and also no. 97),
display incised signatures, indicating that the decoration was applied
before firing. The other obvious
difference is style. The later mat
creations of the 1920s exemplify
their time by displaying the Art
Deco style, whereas the earlier
wares exhibit the influence of the
Arts and Crafts Movement. Decorator William E. Hentschel is considered one of the finest Art Deco
artists at Rookwood. Here he con-
trasts new blue, purple, and gray
mat colors on the exterior with a
soft black mat on the interior. This
was a typical decorating technique
at Rookwood that began in the
1910s, and was used especially during the 1920s (see no. 61). The impressed mark of six radiating lines
notes that the vase was produced
during the fiftieth anniversary year
of the pottery (see no. 92). There is
no question that this vase exemplifies the Soft Porcelain body in spite
of the fact that it is not marked as
such with an impressed "P" on the
bottom (see no. 79).

96

PAIR OF VASES
1930
Edward Timothy Hurley,
decorator
John Hamilton Delaney
Wareham, shape designer
Thrown
H. 15 ½" Diam. 8 ½"
Soft Porcelain/Jewel Porcelain body
Pink-tinted, translucent, gloss glaze

Marks: impressed a) Rookwood logo
surmounted by fourteen
flames/"XXX"/"2983" b) six radiating
notches; painted in black ETH cipher;
painted in black on the bottom of one
"9730"; painted in black on the bottom
of the other "9731"

Collection of Joseph David Nelson

Pairs of vases were actively marketed at Rookwood after 1915 (see no. 89). They are generally very large and very fine (see no. 93). Hurley's signature on the bottom of the vases here is painted, not incised. This is true of many signatures on high-gloss vases especially from about 1924 onwards, when decorators worked on fired vessels. This is confirmed by H. F. Bopp in his 1935 article "Art and Science in the Development of Rookwood Pottery" in the *Bulletin of the American Ceramic Society* (vol. 15, no.12, p. 445). In it he states, "The decorated porcelain type is often made by painting glaze on the biscuit piece. After drying, the design is painted on, using underglaze colors, colored glazes and mixtures, and more glaze over the decoration; all are then fired together, resulting in a decoration suspended between two layers of glass and giving a depth and quality that we do not know how to get in any easier way."

It can be assumed that gloss vases dating from 1915 with painted signatures are decorated in this manner. It can also be assumed that they are made of Rookwood's Soft Porcelain body (see no. 79), later called Jewel Porcelain (see no. 77). The impressed mark of six radiating notches on the bottom of each tells us that these two vases were made during the fiftieth anniversary year of the pottery (see no. 92). The two sequential numbers painted on the bottom of the pair are under the glaze, suggesting that they were probably applied by Hurley in order to be better able to distinguish the vases for some unknown reason. The original invoice for the pair, from the Loring Andrews Company of Cincinnati, dated May 18, 1937, is still in the possession of the owner. Unfortunately, it does not specify the glaze or glaze line. The same shape can be seen in no. 94.

97
VASE
1927
**William E. Hentschel,
decorator**
Thrown
H. 17 ¾" Diam. 8"
Soft Porcelain/Jewel Porcelain body
LaterMat glaze

*Marks: impressed Rookwood logo sur-
mounted by fourteen flames/
"XXVII"/"2523"; incised WEH cipher*

Collection of Mr. and Mrs.
Thomas W. Ulrich

The new mat glazes of the 1920s were marked by greater control than the earlier mats produced between 1900–1915. The new finishes did not crawl in the firing as much as before, and, consequently, the colors generally remained separate and distinct as seen in this example. There was some crawling, however, and horizontal ridges in the lower portion of such vases (see also no. 95) were a helpful device to inhibit any flow. The porcelaneous body and relatively greater control of the glazes allowed for larger vases to be made. Even though it is not marked with an impressed "P", the vase is made of Rookwood's Soft Porcelain (see no. 79) A mat vessel the size of the vase here would have been unheard of during the first part of the century. While we know much about the techniques involved in decorating the earlier mat ware, little is known about the later mat techniques. Signatures on mat vases of the 1920s are not painted, but rather incised. This indicates that they were decorated before firing, unlike the earlier mat pieces that were decorated in the biscuit state. How the colors were applied is not known. In ceramics, where size has always been a tour de force, Rookwood's large mat vases of the 1920s are as impressive today as they must have been when they were made.

INDEX

Numbers in italic refer to plate numbers.

Aerial Blue Glaze line 20, 43, 46, 50; *30*
Abel, Louise 33, 153
Art Academy of Cincinnati 12, 18, 119
Art Deco 35, 147, 153, 157, 160
Art Nouveau 23, 25, 98, 128, 141
Arts and Crafts movement 24, 31, 33, 52, 94, 120, 140, 141, 143
Asano, E. H. 23
Asbury, Lenore 24, 98, 126, 137
Aukland, William 66, 79

Bailey, Joseph, Sr. 12, 23, 96, 101, 126, 127, 158
Barber, Edwin Atlee 19, 44
Bing & Grøndahl Porcelain Factory 27
Bing, Siegfried 23
Black Opal glaze line 35, 90
Bopp, Harold 37, 54, 55, 161
Brennan, Alfred 73
Burt, Stanley Gano 23, 25, 48, 50, 51, 52, 53, 54, 55, 56; Inventory of Rookwood Pottery in the Cincinnati Art Museum 67, 69, 75, 78, 79, 80, 81, 84, 93, 100, 116, 119, 123, 124, 125, 131
Butterfat glaze 35

Cameo Ware 16–17, 43, 44–45, 46
Cincinnati Art Museum 12, 18, 26, 32, 36, 39
competitors 26, 27
Conant, Arthur 33, 142, 143, 144
Covalenco, Catherine Pissoreff 33
Coyne, Sara Elizabeth 26, 135

Dallas, Frederick 11, 12
Daly, Matthew Andrew 14, 22, 23, 25, 26, 51, 82, 90, 95, 109
Daum Frères 27
Designed Crystal 40
Diers, Edward George 110

Dull Finish glaze line 16–17, 43, 44, 46; *3, 5–9*

Epply, Lorinda 26, 36, 38, 40, 153, 157
Exposition Universelle 1889: 16, 18, 23, 45, 48, 49; 1900: 24, 25, 51, 84, 85, 86, 89, 90, 105, 107, 108, 109; 1925: 35

Flambe glaze 35, 38
Floral decoration 17, 20–22
Flowing glaze 27
French Red glaze line 38; *81–83*
Fry, Laura Ann 14, 68, 73
Furukawa, Lois 40

Gallé, Emile 14, 27
Gest, Joseph Henry 32, 38
Goldstone glaze line 14, 48–49; *22, 23*
Gorham Manufacturing Company 18–19, 47, 85
Grueby Faience Co. 26

Hentschel, William 26, 35, 38, 124, 160, 162
Herter Looms 33, 142, 143
Hokusai, Katsushika 70
Hurley, Edward Timothy 24, 26, 30, 36, 40, 56, 127, 134, 138, 158, 161

Institutum Divi Thomae (St. Thomas Institute), Cincinnati 39
Iris glaze line 20, 26, 27; *31–45*; Black (Dark) Iris *40–45*

Japonisme 13, 14, 17, 25, 36, 66, 108
Jenson, Elizabeth Barrett 35, 40
Jenson, Jens Jacob Herring Krog 33, 39, 40, 156
Joseph, Bertha 38

Kyte, Lawrence H. 39

Lawrence, Frederick Sturgis 94
Louisiana Purchase Exposition, 1904 26, 51, 56, 57

Mahogany glaze line 16; *22*
Marketing strategies 17–18, 24, 27–29, 32, 38
Mat glaze lines 27, 38, 33, 35, 52–56; *46–59, 95, 97*; Conventional 47, 48; Decorated 57–59; Incised 46; Later (Moderne) 95, 97; Modeled 54–56; Painted 49–52; Rookwood Mat Glazes, 1905 29–30
McDonald, Margaret Helen 40
McDonald, William Purcell 14, 23, 25, 26, 30, 37, 51, 52, 53, 91, 92, 105, 112
Meissen 27
Menzel, John 84, 138

Native American influences 19–20, 30, 53; *15–18*
Newcomb Pottery 26
Nichols, Maria Longworth 11, 12, 13, 14, 18, 24, 68, 70

Ombroso glaze 32, 55, 59
Oxblood glaze line 23, 33, 38, 94

Peck, Herbert 53
Pictorial decoration 36
Plaques 28, 31, 57; *12, 15, 16, 30, 48, 65, 70, 72*

Reed, Olga Geneva 26, 111
Rhem, Wilhelmine 40
Roblin Pottery 26
Rookwood Book, The 28–29
Rookwood mark 16
Rookwood Pottery 27, 28
Rookwood Shape Book 1883–1900 14, 21, 66, 75, 83, 85, 90, 92, 93, 95, 108, 110, 123
Rörstrand Pottery and Porcelain Factory 27
Rothenbusch, Frederick Henry Daniel 26, 136

Royal Copenhagen 20, 24, 27, 50, 82, 83
Royal Worcester 46

Sax, Sara 24, 26, 56, 92, 93, 125, 128, 131, 133, 139, 140, 141, 146, 147, 148, 149, 153
Schmidt, Carl 24, 26, 32, 56, 96, 97, 104, 105, 129, 130, 132
Schott, Walter E., and Margaret 39
Sea Green glaze line 20, 22, 26, 27, 28, 29, 43, 46, 50–51; *26–29*
Sèvres 27
Shirayamadani, Kataro 15–16, 23, 24, 26, 30, 34, 38, 40, 71, 74, 76, 78, 79, 84, 85, 89, 101, 103, 106, 107, 108, 123, 152, 157
Soft porcelain (jewel porcelain) 33, 35
Sperti, Inc., Cincinnati 39, 40
Sprague, Amelia Brown 26, 55
Standard Ware 16, 20, 22, 26, 28, 29, 43, 44, 46, 47; *11–21*; Green Standard *17*
Stickely Gustav 27
Storer, Bellamy, Jr. 15, 23
Storer, Maria Longworth see Nichols
Sung Plum glaze 38–39

Taft Museum, Cincinnati 33, 36
Taylor, William Watts 14, 16, 17, 18, 20, 21, 23, 24, 25, 32, 44, 45, 46, 47, 49, 54, 69, 73, 84, 88, 90, 110, 122
Tiffany & Co 68
Tiger Eye glaze line 14, 18, 27, 47–48; *11, 23–25*; Later Tiger Eye 33; *84–86*
Todd, Charles Stewart 55, 122
Toohey, Sara Alice 26, 55, 76, 112, 121, 145
Tonalism 30–31, 56–57, 130, 131, 132, 133, 138
Triggs, Oscar Lovell 24

Valentien, Albert Robert 12–13,
    14, 22, 23, 25, 26, 51, 54,
    55, 56, 66, 67, 69, 70, 72,
    77, 99, 113, 114, 131
Valentien, Anna Marie
    Bookprinter 15, 22, 25, 26,
    71, 119
Van Briggle, Artus 23, 25, 26, 53,
    80, 81, 88
Van Vlissingen, Arthur, Jr. 37
Vellum glaze line 28, 30–32, 43,
    56–57; 60–76; Floral
    60–62; Green Yellow
    74–76; Scenic 66–73;
    Venetian 64–65

Wareham, John Hamilton
    Delaney 23, 26, 37, 38, 87,
    100, 120, 142, 145, 148,
    150, 152, 153, 154, 156,
    159, 160, 161
Wilcox, Harriet Elizabeth 22, 29,
    37, 55, 74, 75, 115, 116,
    117, 118
Williams, Charles M. 39
World's Columbian Exposition,
    1893 18, 20, 23, 49, 80, 81

Yelland, Henry 86
Young, Grace 26, 83

Zettle, Josephine 26

PHOTO CREDITS